If you have a home computer with Internet access you may:
- request an item to be placed on hold.
- renew an item that is not overdue or on hold.
- view titles and due dates checked out on your card.
- view and/or pay your outstanding fines online ($1 & over).

To view your patron record from your home computer click on Patchogue-Medford Library's homepage: www.pmlib.org

unlikely
LIBERAL

Related Titles from Potomac Books

The Obama Haters:
Behind the Right-Wing Campaign of Lies, Innuendo & Racism
—John Wright

Tortured Logic: A Verbatim Critique of the George W. Bush Presidency
—Joseph Russomanno

Personality, Character, and Leadership in the White House:
Psychologists Assess the Presidents
—Steven J. Rubenzer and Thomas R. Faschingbauer

Sarah Palin's Curious Record as Alaska's Governor

Matthew Zencey

Potomac Books
Washington, D.C.

Library of Congress Cataloging-in-Publication Data
Zencey, Matthew, 1957–
  Unlikely Liberal : Sarah Palin's curious record as Alaska governor / Matthew Zencey.
  — 1st ed.
  p. cm.
  Includes bibliographical references and index.
  ISBN 978-1-61234-185-9 (hardcover : alk. paper)
  ISBN 978-1-61234-186-6 (electronic)
  1. Palin, Sarah, 1964– 2. Alaska—Politics and government—1959– 3. Governors—
Alaska—Biography. 4. Women governors—Alaska—Biography. I. Title.
  F910.7.P35Z46 2012
  979.8'052092—dc23
  [B]
                                                                    2012018886

Printed in the United States of America on acid-free paper that meets the American National Standards Institute Z39-48 Standard.

Potomac Books
22841 Quicksilver Drive
Dulles, Virginia 20166

First Edition

10 9 8 7 6 5 4 3 2 1

To Cindy, Nathan, and Kyle

Contents

Preface

For twenty-one years, I wrote editorials about Alaska politicians and public affairs. When Sarah Palin was governor, I was the editorial page editor of the *Anchorage Daily News*, the state's largest newspaper. I followed Palin's career since she broke onto the statewide scene with her surprising second-place finish in the Republican primary for lieutenant governor in 2002. She made multiple visits to us at the *Daily News* editorial board, as a candidate for governor and after she won election.

Our paper did not endorse Palin for governor. Her experience as small-town mayor paled in comparison to the former two-term governor she ran against, and we disagreed with her socially conservative stands. But once she took office, we enthusiastically supported her three major initiatives: ethics reform, oil tax reform, and her brand-new approach to promoting a gas pipeline from Alaska's North Slope to the Lower 48. When she fired her public safety commissioner, giving reasons that didn't make sense at the time, my colleagues and I wrote critical editorials, holding her accountable in what soon erupted into the Troopergate scandal.

After John McCain picked Palin to run for vice president, I did numerous interviews about her for national and international media, including appearances on ABC, NBC, CNN, PBS, Al Jazeera, Irish Radio, and others. As the campaign progressed, our paper ran a series of editorials candidly assessing her performance as governor—both her strengths and her weaknesses. That series was co-winner of the 2009 Alaska Press Club prize for public service journalism. Judge Loretta Tofani, herself a Pulitzer Prize winner, said, "Through these editorials, I learned more about the record of Sarah Palin than I did from any of the dozens of stories I read about her in national newspapers and magazines. Compared to these editorials, everything else I read about Sarah Palin feels like fluff."[1]

That series reflects my personal philosophy as a journalist who works the opinion side of the trade: no permanent friends, no permanent enemies, only permanent principles. I try to apply these principles in a fair-minded way to public issues and public officials. I am a commentator, not a reporter, but it's not my job to mindlessly cheerlead for, or attack, any particular politician or cause. I have written critical editorials about politicians whose policies I generally supported, such as U.S. senator Mark Begich (D-AK) and Alaska's previous Democratic governor Tony Knowles. I have written editorials supporting initiatives announced by Palin's successor, Republican Sean Parnell, and welcoming his enthusiasm for serving in the office that Sarah Palin vacated.

Many of Palin's critics and supporters engage in ad hominem attacks. That was not my style. To me, the point of journalistic commentary is not to tear down the public official in question; it is to express a legitimate difference of opinion or hold the official accountable. Throughout my career, I strove to be an intellectually honest commentator, not a polemicist or propagandist.

You'll have to look elsewhere if you care about Bristol's pregnancy, the feud with Levi, Trig's birth, the state of Palin's marriage to Todd, her career in high school basketball, Piper's progress in school, and other parts of Palin's personal life. In my view, a politician's personal life is a public issue only if it reveals hypocrisy on a political question or significantly compromises his or her ability to do the job.

One surprising thing about Sarah Palin's career is how a governor who once enjoyed a 90 percent approval rating became such a polarizing figure after she vaulted onto the national stage.[2] Americans seem to either love her or hate her—their opinions of her are black or white. Her conservative supporters appear to think she can do nothing wrong and blast the media for daring to note anything critical about her. Palin's critics appear to think she can do nothing right—that she got where she is on good looks and good luck.

What I offer here is what we at the *Anchorage Daily News* offered in our prize-winning series of editorials: an intellectually honest look at Palin's performance as Alaska's governor, her strengths and weaknesses, her triumphs and her failures, and what her time as governor says about her capabilities to serve as vice president or president.

Acknowledgments

Many thanks to Potomac Books for agreeing to publish my work. Whatever one may think of Sarah Palin as a potential national leader, I hope readers will find this is a fair account of both her accomplishments and failures while serving as governor of Alaska.

My agent, Jim Schiavone, was instrumental in helping get the book published. I'm thankful he made that trip to the Alaska Writers' Conference, where we met. I appreciate Elizabeth Demers's willingness to recommend publishing my work and her guidance on the manuscript. Copy editor Deirdre Ruffino flagged several duplicative passages and spared me the grunt work of ensuring the text meets the necessary conventions of style.

Thanks also to my wife, Cindy, who was supportive even though she definitely does not share my enthusiasm for politics. My sons, Nathan and Kyle, who were born and raised in Alaska and began paying attention to politics when Palin was governor, were also a great source of encouragement.

My goal in writing the book was to create a single volume that pulls together what is known about Palin's performance as governor, including my own observations as a journalist who followed some of her major initiatives. As I mention in the Source Notes section, this account draws heavily on excellent reporting by colleagues at the *Anchorage Daily News*, as well as reports by the *Juneau Empire*, Associated Press, and many other national media outlets.

This is the first book about Palin to include material from the archive of publicly released e-mails during her term as governor. I am indebted to the media organizations that obtained the e-mails and created online, searchable archives.

State senator Hollis French and Palin aide Marty Rutherford were generous in speaking about their dealings with Palin, and doing so on the record. Others who remain unnamed also supplied useful perspective. Thanks to Pat Forgey, Bob

Tkash, and Sabra Ayres for talking about their experience as Alaska-based journalists who covered Palin. Other helpful sources include the memoir by Palin's former aide Frank Bailey, the Mudflats blog, and the blog written by Andrew Halcro. In the final chapter, I expand on an insight supplied by my longtime colleague, former *Anchorage Daily News* editorial page editor Michael Carey, with whom I enjoyed working for a dozen years.

Thanks to Bob Lohr and Celia Foley for offering a hospitable base of operations on return trips to Anchorage. A final note of thanks to my brother Eric, the published author, who prompted this project by suggesting, "Hey, why don't you write a book?"

1

Highlights and Lowlights: From Bipartisan Maverick to "Pitbull with Lipstick" to Former Governor

How much do you know about Sarah Palin? Test your knowledge with these true-or-false questions.

1. She pushed for and signed the biggest tax increase in Alaska history.[1]
2. In 2007, the first full year of Palin's term, Alaska state government spent 50 percent more, per resident, than the next highest spending state.[2]
3. She vetoed an antigay-rights bill during her first year as governor.[3]
4. She appointed a pro-choice woman to Alaska's highest court.[4]
5. Her decision to resign as governor was not the first time she left a government post before her term was up, with complaints about how state ethics laws applied to her.
6. When Palin was governor, the state spent record-breaking amounts of money on small-scale alternative energy projects and energy conservation.[5]

If you answered true to all six, so far so good.
Now try another round. True or false?

7. Every single ethics complaint against her was found to be baseless.[6]
8. She promptly fired her aide who was recorded on tape during the Troopergate scandal, telling a trooper official that Palin and her husband can't understand why the governor's abusive, law-breaking ex-brother-in-law is still a state trooper.[7]
9. The Alaska legislature's independent investigation into Palin's handling of Troopergate "vindicated" Palin.[8]
10. She vetoed a bill requiring the state to pay every Alaskan—man, woman,

and child—$1,200, regardless of need, because it was a wasteful way to spend government money.[9]

11. Thanks to her leadership, a $40 billion natural gas pipeline is now being built from Alaska's North Slope to Lower 48 markets.[10]

12. Most Democrats in the Alaska legislature staunchly opposed Palin's three biggest legislative initiatives because they knew she was a rising star in the Republican Party.

The answer to all these is false.

Welcome to the paradoxical career of Gov. Sarah Palin.

The Sarah Palin Americans saw in the 2008 vice-presidential campaign was not the Sarah Palin Alaskans knew from her first year and a half as governor. In Alaska, Palin had governed as a bipartisan maverick. Her most reliable allies in the legislature were the Democrats. Her most vocal critics were staunch Republicans and the state's business establishment.

Democrats solidly supported the three major accomplishments of Palin's first two years. They helped her pass ethics legislation (which the Republican majority had stymied in previous years). Democrats worked with her to pass the biggest tax increase in the state's history, when they reformed the state's oil production tax, which had been passed amid a bribery scandal.

Democrats also helped Palin set up innovative incentives to promote a $40 billion natural gas pipeline from Alaska's North Slope. These incentives, awarded by competitive bid to an independent pipeline company, were bitterly opposed by the state's biggest oil and gas companies, which have been sitting on Alaska's vast natural gas deposits for three decades. Three times, Palin and her Democratic allies in the legislature took on Big Oil, and three times they won. Many influential Republicans and business leaders were appalled at Palin's willingness to buck the state's powerful oil industry. Though the industry had been discredited by a bribery scandal, Palin's critics considered her a political and intellectual lightweight who was leading the state to economic ruin, even as her approval rating approached 90 percent.

Palin was so popular in part because she wasn't the man who preceded her. Gov. Frank Murkowski was seen as an arrogant bumbler. When he left the U.S. Senate to be sworn in as governor, he appointed his daughter to fill his seat. He bought an official state jet to ferry him and his wife around the state and the Lower 48. Two of his high-profile appointees eventually resigned amid ethics scandals. Compared with the young and charismatic Sarah Palin, he looked frumpy and dull. In the Republican primary for governor, Palin thrashed Murkowski, who got only 19 percent of the vote.[11]

Few people in the Lower 48 had any idea that Palin's early record as governor was so progressive.

At my thirtieth college reunion, some classmates overheard me mention that I'd been living in Alaska for almost thirty years. They let me know that they thought Palin was an incompetent Republican extremist. I tried to explain the strange-but-true part of her record as governor. They looked at me like I was trying to convince them that aliens really had landed in Roswell, New Mexico.

The Palin they knew was the darling of the nation's social conservatives, even though she hadn't done much on their issues as governor. In running for governor, she had not played up her personal opposition to abortion in all circumstances, even rape and incest. She soft-pedaled her other controversial views, such as "teaching the controversy" about intelligent design versus evolution. Instead, she portrayed herself as a reformist insurgent who would bring an end to ethics scandals and put the public interest above partisan politics.

Once in office, she left divisive social issues in the background. She even vetoed an antigay-rights measure because she noted, correctly, that it was an unconstitutional attempt to circumvent a politically unpopular state supreme court ruling. She appointed a pro-choice woman to the state's highest court. (The state's merit system for selecting judges presented her with only two nominees, and the other one was an even more liberal male.)

Palin concentrated on cleaning up after previous scandals, while an FBI corruption investigation began producing arrests. She convinced the legislature to take a dramatically new approach to promoting a possible $40 billion natural gas pipeline to the Lower 48. It was a high-stakes issue where she wasn't afraid to insist on a course that was politically unpopular.

A big majority of Alaskans wanted the state to promote an "all-Alaska" pipeline route, which would export the gas on tankers, instead of an all-land route going through Canada. When running for lieutenant governor in 2002, Palin supported a ballot initiative that endorsed the "all-Alaska" route, and the measure passed with 62 percent of the vote.

Once in office, she hired capable staff and independent experts to recommend the best way the state could promote a natural gas pipeline. Their work convinced her that the politically unpopular Canadian route was the most practical. Palin rejected her predecessor's industry-friendly approach to promoting the gas pipeline. He had offered Exxon, Conoco, and BP huge financial and legal concessions, without getting any guarantee the line would be built. She convinced the legislature to define the terms the state wanted—access rights, financing, rate structure—and offer financial incentives to be awarded by competitive bid. Eventually the state selected an independent pipeline company to pursue the project, much to the dismay of Alaska's big three oil companies, which had boycotted the bidding.

In her vice-presidential campaign, Palin made it sound like construction on this huge gas pipeline was already under way. It wasn't true—and still isn't.[12] The project is moving through preliminary stages, with the state providing partial funding, but a final go/no-go decision on construction has yet to be made.

It was not the only time on the campaign trail she'd stretch the truth about her record back in Alaska. When the legislature's investigator concluded that Palin had violated state ethics law in the Troopergate scandal, she told the nation the investigation "cleared" her. The Troopergate scandal ended inconclusively, with a fundamental question left hanging. Her public safety commissioner testified under oath that he spoke to Palin about why her ex-brother-in-law was still a state trooper. Palin, under oath, denied having any such conversations with him. One of them has given false statements under oath, but there has been no investigation of potential perjury in the case. In Alaska, the state's chief law enforcement officer and chief prosecutor are appointed by the governor, so the lack of follow-up is perhaps not surprising.

In the 2008 presidential campaign, the nation saw the Sarah Palin who decried big government and enthusiastically bashed her Democratic opponents as socialists. Those attacks were ironic, coming from the governor of the most socialist state in the union.

In Alaska, state government owns the land where most major oil fields on the North Slope were found. Those fields have yielded the state more than $100 billion (yes, billion) in revenue since the late 1970s[13]—enough to run state government without need for a state sales tax or personal income tax. That oil money, plus abundant aid from the federal government, allows Alaska's state government to spend more per capita than any other state. In 2007, Alaska spent 50 percent more per resident than the next biggest spending state, Wyoming.[14]

Alaska also has a $35 billion oil savings account, which allows the state to pay a "dividend" each year to every Alaskan.[15] The last year that Palin signed those checks, the payment each resident got from the state's "Permanent Fund" was $2,069.[16]

Palin told the nation she kept a tight rein on spending as governor, and that's half true. She cracked down on pork barrel spending—although she was more tolerant of items headed to her home region of the state. In her first two years, she vetoed more than a half-billion dollars in spending, mostly capital projects. However, she kept a loose rein on the part of the budget that pays for state government's day-to-day operations, which grew steadily on her watch.

During her term, the state set aside at least $95 million for alternative energy projects and $200 million to help Alaskans make their homes more energy-efficient. If the federal government spent as much, per person, on those programs as Palin did in Alaska, the bill would be $134 billion.

Palin also pushed through the kind of expensive government handout a big-spending Democrat might love. As oil prices spiked to $140 a barrel and money poured into the state treasury, Palin persuaded the legislature to give each Alaskan an extra $1,200 of state money as an "energy rebate." Combined with that year's "dividend" from its oil savings account, the state was sending each Alaskan a check for $3,269—at the same time she was campaigning around the nation as a skeptic of government spending. "She was a pretty good socialist governor," according to Elstun Lauesen, a liberal columnist in the *Anchorage Daily News*.[17]

While Palin portrayed herself as a foe of earmarks, her approach to them was somewhat elastic. She did scale down the state's list of requests for federal funding. But as the nation learned in the vice-presidential race, she was *for* the "Bridge to Nowhere" in Ketchikan before she was against it. During her time as governor, she declined to kill Alaska's second notorious federally funded bridge to empty land, the Knik Arm Crossing. Starting in Anchorage, this bridge would conveniently open a large, vacant swath of her home county to rapid real estate development.

Public anger over ethics scandals had helped elect Palin, and she delivered on that score in her first year with a new state ethics law. But she soon found herself in ethics trouble of her own. She billed the state for her children to come with her on some official trips—even when children had no official role in the activity. She billed the state for some travel expenses—daily meal money—when she was living at her home in Wasilla and commuting to her Anchorage office. (Doing so was widely criticized but it was legal, since under state rules she was "traveling" to the Anchorage office from her official duty station in the state capital, Juneau.)

Having set herself up as a paragon of ethical behavior, Palin made herself a target for critics eager to play "gotcha." She drew a steady stream of citizen ethics complaints, which she repeatedly said were frivolous charges to harass her. Most of them were quickly dismissed by investigators. But at least three charges had some legitimate basis. One case—questionable billings for her children's travel—was serious enough that she repaid some of the questioned expenses.

Nonetheless, her spokesman portrayed her as having a perfect record on ethics complaints at that point. Bill McAllister decried the "flurry of ethics complaints that have yet to substantiate a single infraction." Palin consistently defended her ethics record with the kind of legalistic hairsplitting that Palin the ethics reformer would have condemned.

Just before she left office, an investigator found "probable cause" that she had committed an ethics violation. This one involved a legal defense trust fund others set up to help her. Though she hadn't yet taken any money from the trust fund, the investigator found "the governor expressly authorized the creation of the trust" and that "the trust website quite openly uses the governor's position to solicit donations." An initial investigation concluded, "There is probable cause to believe that Governor Palin used, or attempted to use, her official position for personal gain in violation of Alaska statute." After a new investigator took over the case and came to the same conclusion, she returned the money.

When it came to the ethics of her staff, Palin's standards were curiously flexible. She fired an aide who had an affair with a married woman whose husband was a friend of the Palins. But Governor Palin didn't fire her aide who was caught on tape in the Troopergate scandal, trying to get Palin's ex-brother-in-law fired from the state troopers.

Palin repeatedly talked about running an "open and transparent" administration—but she had a private e-mail network set up so she and her aides could conduct state business without having it show up in official state records. Those private e-mails may have contained important evidence in the Troopergate scandal, but investigators never recovered them.[18]

After she and John McCain went down to defeat, a different Sarah Palin came back to Alaska.

With her partisan attacks, she had fractured her governing coalition. Democrats no longer had common cause with her on any big issues, and they certainly didn't want to help someone who so enthusiastically attacked their party. Pro-oil Republicans in the legislature refused to fill the void in her political support left by alienated Democrats. When Palin selected a controversial conservative to be her second attorney general, and he made remarks suggesting the governor could ignore a particular state law, the Republican-dominated legislature vented its frustration with her and voted him down. It was the first time in the state's history that a governor had a cabinet appointee rejected.[19]

To keep her national credentials as a conservative leader, Governor Palin had to bad-mouth government, while she tried to run a state whose economy is dominated by state and federal government spending. She told Sean Hannity of Fox News that high oil prices were not good for Alaska because they gave government too much money to spend.[20] She grabbed headlines by saying she would refuse roughly a third of the federal economic stimulus headed for Alaska. As it became clear that various pieces of the federal money did not carry the "strings" Palin complained about, she kept reducing the amount she planned to refuse. In the end, she insisted on vetoing $28.6 million of energy conservation funds, making exaggerated claims about the requirements that came with the money.[21] Shortly after she left office, the legislature overrode her veto.

The contradiction between her national ambitions and her responsibilities to govern the state of Alaska proved to be untenable. Having enjoyed national fame and the adulation of adoring crowds, facing huge legal bills from a steady stream of ethics complaints (most of which were trivial and easily dismissed), and with a special needs toddler at home, she resigned with a rambling and unconvincing explanation involving unspecified future plans that would "progress" Alaska.

It was not the first time she left a state government post before her term was up, with complaints about how the state's ethics law applied to her. Before running for governor, she served only eleven months on a technical regulatory panel, the Alaska Oil and Gas Conservation Commission, and then quit.[22] She discovered a fellow commissioner had been using his office for Republican Party business but she couldn't talk publicly about the case because state ethics law kept the matter confidential. She cited the gag order as her reason for quitting, even though many others suspected she didn't like the highly technical work and the long commute from her home in Wasilla.

Eventually, Alaskans and the nation learned that while still governor, Palin had obtained a $1.25 million golden parachute out of the governor's office, in the form of a book contract.[23] Freed from duties as governor, she limited her public appearances while she worked on her book. She kept up her public profile by issuing pronouncements from the disembodied media of Facebook and Twitter, which was ironic, given her powerful personal charm. Her ability to connect with people one-on-one worked well in the small pond that is Alaska, but not so well in the big ocean of national politics, with its constantly probing media scrutiny.

Sarah Palin's career beyond Alaska, including her time as a vice-presidential candidate, is a story for others to tell. I knew her work before she burst onto the national scene, before partisans and campaign spin doctors went to work, building her up or tearing her down.

In looking at her record in Alaska, partisans on either side of the great Sarah Palin divide will find a bundle of contradictions: bipartisan maverick in Alaska, partisan pitbull on the national campaign trail. Critic of big government, while running a big government back in Alaska. Political foe of Big Oil in Alaska, cheerleader chanting "Drill, baby, drill" in the Lower 48. Ethics crusader who failed to uphold the high standards she promised to Alaskans.

Like any famous political figure, Sarah Palin has strengths and weaknesses. They have combined to make her a national political figure who is strikingly different from the governor Alaskans elected.

2

The Key to Palin's Popularity as Governor:
Meet Her Predecessor

To understand Sarah Palin's success as Alaska's governor, you have to understand how unpopular her predecessor was.

Gov. Frank Murkowski was a fellow Republican who displayed a CEO's arrogance about enjoying publicly funded perks, was indifferent to ethics controversies in his ranks, and had to make difficult budget cuts when the price of oil plummeted.

Murkowski had served twenty-two years in the U.S. Senate before returning to Alaska to run for governor, a race he easily won in 2002. As senator, he had served in the shadow of legendary Sen. Ted Stevens, beloved for bringing home billions of federal dollars to Alaska. Reliably pro-business and pro-development, Murkowski had no outstanding expertise or accomplishments in the senate, but he had done nothing to alienate the state's heavily Republican voters.

All that changed shortly after he took office. As governor, he had the power to appoint his own replacement in the U.S. Senate. He made a great show of interviewing many candidates, but in the end he appointed a respected Republican from the State House of Representatives, who just happened to be his daughter, Lisa. It was a defensible choice on the merits—Lisa Murkowski has served capably since then and won election in her own right. But the obvious nepotism enraged many Alaskans. It was the kind of politically tone-deaf move Murkowski would make again and again.

Another example was his insistence on obtaining a state jet, which he used for both official duties and personal trips. Alaska is a vast state with few roads, so a governor has to fly often. As governor, Murkowski could travel on the state troopers' aircraft, but it was a relatively small and slow turboprop that lacked the kind of amenities a former bank executive and long-serving U.S. senator expected. Murkowski was determined to upgrade his ride.

First, he tried to use Homeland Security funds to buy the jet, but the federal government rejected that move. When legislators learned of his continuing efforts to buy a state jet, they refused to provide state funding for it. Murkowski went around the legislature and bought the jet anyway, using borrowed state funds. Democratic state senator Kim Elton tracked some of Governor Murkowski's trips on the new jet. He discovered that Murkowski had used the jet to take himself and his wife to Park City, Utah, where they have a condominium. Murkowski also used the jet to fly home from a vacation trip on his yacht.

While Murkowski's arrogance was alienating Alaskans, the price of oil was plunging. Alaskans rely on oil revenue to pay for almost all routine state government expenses. With that painless source of money shrinking, Murkowski had no easy options. He could pursue new taxes, slash spending, or raid the oil savings account that pays each Alaskan a yearly dividend.

Murkowski opted to make some big budget cuts. Most noticeable was killing off a monthly payment to senior citizens, known as the longevity bonus. The program, which once offered $250 a month to any Alaska resident over age 65, was gradually being phased out, but Murkowski decided to end it right away. That alienated Alaska's senior citizens, a small but influential and reliably pro-Republican voting bloc.[1]

Murkowski was steadily losing political support. To make matters worse, he shrugged off two ethics scandals, one involving his attorney general, the other involving a political appointee to an obscure state commission whose members included Sarah Palin. Both scandals were political gifts to Palin.

The Alaska Oil and Gas Conservation Commission regulates technical details of how oil and gas fields are developed. It is supposed to prevent oil and gas from being wasted by short-sighted production methods. When an oil or gas field has multiple owners, the commission ensures each owner receives its proper share of production. As a technical agency, it is not the first place a governor might look for political patronage appointments. But a seat on the commission pays very well—about $120,000 a year—and professional staff do all the detail work. One of the three seats is reserved for a public member, and one seat goes to someone with expertise in the oil industry.

Conveniently for Governor Murkowski, the head of Alaska's Republican Party was also a petroleum engineer by trade. Randy Ruedrich had a brash personality and was a prolific fund-raiser for the party. Much of the money Ruedrich raised came from oil companies and their executives. A governor who worried about ethics and conflicts of interest would not have put his party's chief fund-raiser in a position of power over the party's chief source of funds—but Frank Murkowski did. He put Ruedrich on the oil and gas commission.

Murkowski also needed a way to reward Sarah Palin for her support during his election campaign. The not-terribly-well-known small-town mayor had made a surprisingly strong second-place finish in the Republican primary for lieutenant governor. Palin had dutifully campaigned for Murkowski, who faced a credible challenge from a woman, the capable but wonkish lieutenant governor, Democrat Fran Ulmer. Palin's support helped neutralize Ulmer's appeal to Alaskans who might have been tempted to vote for an accomplished younger woman instead of a sometimes inarticulate sixty-nine-year-old white male.

Although Murkowski wanted to find a suitable political job for Palin, there was a problem. Alaska's state capital is in Juneau, an isolated city in the state's southeast coastal rainforest, accessible only by ferry or air, 560 miles away from Palin's home in Wasilla. Murkowski expected his cabinet appointees to live in the state capital. Palin had children at home and turned down a high-level appointment because she didn't want to move to Juneau.

The public seat on the oil and gas commission was a perfect solution. Palin could work at the commission's office in Anchorage, just a forty-minute commute from her home. Although she lacked any expertise in oil and gas technology, and had little interest in developing any, she could rely on professional staff for information. And that $122,000-a-year salary was definitely attractive.[2]

So Sarah Palin, rising Republican star, and Randy Ruedrich, prolific Republican fund-raiser, found themselves working together on the oil and gas commission. Trouble soon followed.

Ruedrich was still head of the Republican Party, and to no one's surprise, he still devoted the same passion and energy to that political job. Ruedrich began doing some of that party work from his state-paid office, during business hours, while collecting his $118,000 state salary. Fellow commissioner Sarah Palin realized this and knew that it violated state ethics law. She reported the situation to Governor Murkowski's powerful aide, chief of staff Jim Clark.

At the same time, Ruedrich was drawing fire for publicly supporting a controversial development proposal, drilling for natural gas in shallow coal beds located in the rapidly growing communities north of Anchorage, even though his commission would have to regulate the project if it went forward. Ruedrich spoke at public forums, using information provided by gas developer Evergreen Resources. Ruedrich also gave the company's lobbyist a confidential legal memo that a state lawyer had prepared for the commission about the company's proposed development.

Despite steady public criticism about Commissioner Ruedrich's conflicts of interest, both as Republican party chair and advocate for Evergreen Resources' project, Governor Murkowski stood by his appointee for six months. But Democrats in the legislature continued objecting to Ruedrich's obvious conflict of interest. Sarah Palin publicly expressed similar concerns.

To quell the controversy, Ruedrich resigned in November.[3] But that did not necessarily render moot a potential case against him for violating state ethics laws. Prodded by Palin, Governor Murkowski reluctantly began an ethics investigation against Ruedrich. That process is confidential by law, and Palin was instructed to say nothing in public about how the potential ethics law violation was being handled. Frustrated by the gag order, Palin resigned after less than eleven months on the job. Her decision to quit in protest won her praise and statewide attention (it also freed her from a long commute to a job handling technical questions for which she had little expertise or interest). Ruedrich eventually paid a civil fine of $12,000 for breaking state ethics law—the largest penalty ever imposed in a state ethics case.[4]

With her handling of the Ruedrich affair, Palin looked like one of those rare public servants who put principle above personal interest. Alaskans saw her as an ethics crusader, courageous enough to blow the whistle on her own party's bosses. A maverick, one might say.

Later in his term, Governor Murkowski gave Palin another opportunity to enhance her reputation as an ethics crusader and political maverick. Attorney General Greg Renkes was one of Frank Murkowski's closest advisers, dating back to Murkowski's time in the U.S. Senate. Taking on unusual duties for an attorney general, Renkes was deeply involved in trying to entice a Taiwanese company to develop an Alaska coal deposit. It turned out that Renkes owned more than $100,000 of stock in a company, KFx, that hoped to supply clean coal technology for the development Renkes was pursuing. His holdings in KFx were an obvious conflict of interest.

At first, Renkes and Governor Murkowski tried to ride out the criticism that followed, and they shrugged off calls for Renkes to resign. One of the critics was former Murkowski appointee Sarah Palin. In December 2004, Palin joined a Democrat, State Representative Eric Croft, in filing a formal state ethics complaint against Renkes. It was an astute political move on her part. Once again, she showed she was willing to challenge her party's establishment, transcend party boundaries, and insist on high ethics standards for public officials.

For two more months, Governor Murkowski stood by his ethically compromised attorney general. During that time, Alaskans learned that Renkes had deleted thousands of e-mails from his state computer on the day the *Anchorage Daily News* broke the story about his conflict of interest. A mere "coincidence," Renkes said.[5] Governor Murkowski issued Renkes a reprimand, but critics questioned whether the state should have an attorney general who might face charges for obstructing justice.[6] A few days later, Renkes resigned.[7]

By allowing the controversy to fester, Murkowski had given Sarah Palin another two months of public attention as an ethics crusader who was willing to challenge her own party. Murkowski once again handed Palin a way to advance her political fortunes, and she took full advantage of it.

Murkowski also hurt his popularity by failing to deliver on his talk about getting Alaska's biggest development dream off the drawing boards. The state's vast North Slope oil fields are also full of natural gas, but marketing that gas requires a hugely expensive pipeline. The most likely route, through Canada to the Lower 48, will cost about $40 billion.

Murkowski had spent almost two years in secret negotiations with the state's biggest oil companies about the concessions they wanted before proceeding with the North Slope gas pipeline. He finally produced a deal that gave unprecedented, and probably unconstitutional, concessions—and it didn't even include a firm commitment to start work on the project. It also required him to ask the legislature to lock down the state's oil tax laws for the life of the gas pipeline, so the companies would have "fiscal certainty" against future tax increases on both gas and oil.

Murkowski's secret process had produced a brazenly bad deal, so bad that the Republican-dominated legislature never bothered to formally consider ratifying it. Murkowski hinted that he might implement the deal without the legislature's approval, which only provoked even stronger criticism of him as arrogant and out of touch.[8]

A year before he ran for reelection, a SurveyUSA poll showed Murkowski's approval rating was only 27 percent. That low rating opened the way for Palin to challenge him. Heading into the 2006 Republican primary, Murkowski's approval rating had sunk to 20 percent, second worst of any governor in the nation.

Palin blew Murkowski away in the Republican primary. In a three-way race, with a well-funded Republican Party establishment candidate, Johne Binkley, on the ballot, Palin got 50.6 percent of the vote. Murkowski finished third, with an embarrassingly low 19 percent.

Gregg Erickson, a Juneau-based journalist who has known all Alaska governors, wrote in 2008, "Murkowski was Alaska's worst governor . . . he was also its most incompetent. . . . Palin is lucky," Erickson continued. "Following Murkowski is the biggest break any governor could hope for."[9]

3

Fiscal Conservative or
Republican Robin Hood?

A s John McCain's running mate, Palin championed smaller government and less spending. To her supporters, she is a staunch fiscal conservative. But in Alaska, "fiscal conservative" doesn't mean what people in the rest of the country might think. Alaska has a big state government paid for largely by the oil industry, and Palin did nothing to change that basic arrangement. In fact, she passed the largest tax increase on the oil industry in the state's history.

The blog Conservatives4Palin.com said on June 2, 2009, that when it comes to budgets, it's "obvious" that Palin has "a stellar record." The last budget she passed, according to the blog, spent $1.1 billion less than the 2007 budget passed by her predecessor, a "whopping 9.5%" cut. Other fans point out that Palin vetoed several hundred million dollars of capital projects, showing that she was tough on pork barrel spending.

Palin's detractors note a different side of her record. They say state agency operating budgets steadily grew during her tenure. They point out that she persuaded the legislature to give every Alaskan—man, woman, and child—a check for $1,200 as an "energy rebate" when oil prices zoomed past the $100-a-barrel level. Daniel Larison of *American Conservative* magazine wrote during her vice-presidential campaign, "On her watch, she has increased spending considerably, as I suppose you might expect from a petro-state flush with revenues."[1] A profile in *Alaska* magazine, shortly after her first year in office, noted, "Others worry about the record-high $6.6 billion operating budget Palin passed in June and the near-record $1.6 billion capital budget she approved, despite making more than $235 million in cuts."[2]

It can be hard to sort out these conflicting claims about Palin's fiscal record. The annual budget bills almost always include unusual items or accounting gimmicks that make it difficult to compare year-to-year changes. Do the comparisons include federal money given to the state or just the state's own revenues? Did the previous year's budget deliberately short-fund programs one year to show an artificially low number, then cover the shortfall with a later supplemental funding bill? Does the comparison look only at spending on routine government operations, or does it include capital projects? (In Alaska, capital budgets routinely escalate when oil prices are high and shrink when oil prices fall.)

Deposits to Alaska's numerous savings accounts—sometimes billions of dollars worth—have to be reported in budget totals but politicians typically don't count them as "spending." Same goes for the dividends Alaska state government pays to each resident from the earnings on the state's oil savings account.

So it's true, for example, that Palin's first operating budget proposed an increase of $245 million.[3] But it's also true her overall spending plan for that year was $2 billion lower than the previous year. One billion of the difference came out of the capital budget; the other $1 billion was future money for K–12 schools that the 2007 legislature charged to the budget passed by the 2006 legislature. The 2007 legislature could do that, because oil prices had skyrocketed, bringing in $5 billion more than expected. That surge of money enabled Palin and the legislature to expand the 2008 budget and then show a drop in spending for 2009, when oil prices returned to more normal levels.

When you sort through all the claims and counterclaims, it's fair to say Governor Palin presided over a large and growing budget for state operations, while taking a harder line on pork items in the capital budget. In her first year, she vetoed $231 million of spending.[4] Only $5 million of those cuts were in the operating budget; the rest were capital projects. The following year, she vetoed $268 million, with only $32.5 million coming from the operating side of the budget.

In the last budget she handled before resigning, Palin went much lighter on the vetoes.[5] She cut only $80 million from all parts of the budget. Almost half—$35 million—stemmed from a technical issue, a disagreement about how much was needed to cover the state's oil and gas tax credits. Another $28.6 million was her controversial veto of federal stimulus money for energy conservation. After she resigned, the legislature overrode that veto.

In her press release about signing her last round of spending bills, Palin didn't claim to be a budget cutter. Instead, her release heralded the "conservative spending plan" and said "legislators agreed with us on the importance of slowing the growth of government."[6]

But in an end-of-session newsletter, six weeks before she resigned, Palin took credit for pursuing some typically liberal initiatives that expand the role of government.[7] Palin noted that she and the legislature agreed to help low-income adults who are on Medicaid by extending dental benefits that were due to expire and permanently writing those benefits into law. Palin also touted a $1.3 million funding increase to fight domestic violence and sexual assault. "The Legislature approved my administration's funding request of $2 million for a pilot preschool program," her newsletter said. She also mentioned that the budget increased state funding for K–12 education by $57 million. The $1.2 billion worth of capital spending, Palin noted, would mean 12,000 jobs.

Palin wrote that she was "disappointed" the legislature didn't raise income limits for pregnant women and children to get free health insurance from the state. Likewise, she was disappointed the legislature didn't pass a bill directing the state to divest any holdings of companies doing business in Sudan, as a way to protest the genocide in Darfur. That's the kind of "socially responsible" investing that fiscal conservatives normally oppose.

Palin portrayed herself as a leader in the movement against federal earmarks, the appropriations that members of Congress steer to favored home-state projects. At the national level, concern was growing that earmarks were helping drive out-of-control federal spending. In some cases, members of Congress were using earmarks to reward political supporters. Looking tough on earmarks was a way for Palin to burnish her image as a reformer and a fiscal conservative.

But in Alaska, U.S. senator Ted Stevens was legendary for his ability to bring home federal money. Alaskans loved Stevens for it—one civic group honored him as "Alaskan of the Century"—so Palin had to tread carefully. She did scale back the number of earmarks that the state of Alaska officially requested. But she was hardly a purist who rejected earmarks altogether. Under Palin, the state's federal funding requests dropped to $197 million in fiscal 2009, from the $350 million her predecessor had sought two years earlier.[8] She said her standard for requesting money was "when there is an important federal purpose and strong citizen support." Even with Palin's more measured approach, she was asking for more federal money, per capita, than any other state.[9]

In Wasilla, Palin had been the first mayor to hire a Washington, D.C., lobbyist for seeking federal money. The city got $8 million in federal funds from 2000 to 2003, and another $19 million came to the Wasilla area through the efforts of other groups, sometimes with the official support of Wasilla city government.

Alaska's most notorious earmark, the $400 million "Bridge to Nowhere" serving the town of Ketchikan (population 13,000), caused a political dilemma for Palin, the fiscal conservative. As a candidate looking to win over voters in Ketchikan, she led residents to believe she supported the project, which would connect the town to empty land. She posed for a photo with a t-shirt, "Nowhere, 99901" (Ketchikan's zip code), even though the Ketchikan bridge was the prime national example of earmark abuses.

After she was elected, it became clear that Congress would not fully fund the project and Palin abandoned it. Running for vice president, she said to the nation,

"I told Congress, 'Thanks, but no thanks,' on that bridge to nowhere"—without mentioning that she was for it before she was against it.[10]

Recently released state e-mails show Palin exploring whether the state could return the Ketchikan bridge money, especially in light of the bridge collapse in Minneapolis that killed more than a dozen people. "Why CAN'T we offer to return the 'B2N' [Bridge to Nowhere] earmark bc [because] the state can't afford the project, and the feds won't be paying for it?" she asked staff in an e-mail on August 2, 2007. "We should see that earmark redirected to Minnesota's tragedy bc [because] the Gravina bridge isn't going to happen on our watch anyway." Her staff explained that the money in question was Alaska's to use, according to a standard federal funding formula. The earmark had merely required the money to be used on the Ketchikan project. With the earmark removed, the money was Alaska's to use for other transportation projects, and that's what Palin did with it. The nonpartisan fact-checkers at Politifact.com reported, "Alaska took the bridge money, and then just spent it on other projects. Palin did make the final call to kill plans for the bridge, but by the time she did it was no longer a politically viable project. We rule Palin's claim is Half True."[11]

As President Obama and the Democratic Congress were putting together the stimulus package, Palin put Alaska in line for some of the money. Her January 12, 2009, press release said, "The governor has recommended five specific projects for the stimulus package, all of them in accordance with previous guidelines requiring that any individual spending requests must be in the national interest."[12] The five projects were a rocket launch facility on Kodiak Island and infrastructure needed for her proposed Alaska natural gas pipeline. "While the latest comment in D.C. suggest that no earmarks will be accepted," Palin's press release said, "the governor is hopeful that the extraordinary nature of these national-interest projects will allow their inclusion." Later, Palin would become a leading national critic of the federal stimulus—without mentioning that she'd asked that it include funding for Alaska projects.

■ ■ ■

In praising Palin's last budget, Conservatives4Palin didn't note something that might normally alarm fiscal conservatives—the state's spending plan exceeded the expected amount of revenue by roughly $1 billion. That gap was covered by drawing on reserve funds.

Balancing the state budget that way isn't unusual in Alaska. The state routinely uses savings accounts to fill budget gaps in years when oil prices are low. In the early 1990s, the legislature and voters amended the state constitution to create a special reserve fund for exactly that purpose. That constitutional budget reserve was down to its last $2.5 billion when Palin was elected. Some tough choices about budget cuts or new taxes were looming in a year or two, when that money ran out.

Palin caught a huge break from the gods that rule world oil markets—oil prices hit $140 a barrel during her second year in office. That astounding price, plus a stiff new oil tax she worked with Democrats to pass, produced extra billions of money for the state treasury. She and the legislature agreed to put billions of dollars from that surplus in the reserve account. It totaled $7.1 billion by the time she left office. "While other states currently experience crippling budget deficits, our savings have kept us relatively stable," she said in her spring 2009 newsletter.

In Alaska, "stable" government means big government. Measured by spending per resident, Alaska has by far the largest state government in the nation. In rankings compiled by the Tax Foundation, Alaska easily took first place, spending $13,508 per person in 2007—54 percent more than the next biggest-spending state, Wyoming. Only in Alaska could a self-described fiscal conservative run such a big-spending government. Palin was in charge of a state that draws almost all its spending money from oil, financial investments, and the federal government, not taxes on ordinary citizens. Alaskans pay no state sales tax or personal income tax. At the state level, ordinary citizens pay only relatively minor levies on alcohol, tobacco, gasoline, insurance policies, and vehicle tires. In fact, Alaska's state government is so wealthy, it sends each resident a check each year, just for breathing. The checks are paid from the earnings of state's oil savings account, the Alaska Permanent Fund.

What makes this lavishing of cash on ordinary citizens possible is an arrangement that former Republican governor Wally Hickel called "the owner state." (It's a nicer way of saying "socialism.") The state owns the land that has almost all of the rich oil fields on the North Slope. State government has leased the development rights to oil companies. In return, the state collects royalties on the oil that's pumped out—just as a private owner would. The state also collects several types of taxes on oil companies. A portion of that oil money has been put aside in the Permanent Fund, which is worth roughly $35 billion.

The Permanent Fund is essentially being run as a mutual fund for Alaskans. Except for a few minor expenses, all earnings are either reinvested or paid as dividends to residents. Each Alaskan effectively "owns" an equal share and collects an equal dividend. Residents who collected every payout since the first one in 1982 have received more than $30,000. The Permanent Fund dividend is understandably popular with voters. (Many Alaskans incorrectly think the official name of the state's savings account is the "Alaska Permanent Dividend Fund," emphasis on "*dividend*.")

Sarah Palin had the good fortune to be governor when the standard formula for those dividends produced a record-breaking payout of $2,069 for each Alaskan. Her energy rebate added another $1,200 to that year's check from the state. While other states were struggling to balance budgets and keep taxes under control, Sarah Palin was signing $2 billion worth of payments to individual Alaskans. "Some Alaskans see Palin as a modern-day Robin Hood who has returned money to taxpayers," CNN reported shortly after John McCain picked her to run for vice president.[13]

The Weekly Standard's Matthew Continetti lauded Palin in late 2009 as a standard bearer in the fight against President Obama and the Democratic Congress. "She understands that the Democrats want to increase the role that government plays in the economy and our daily lives," he wrote in a *Los Angeles Times* op-ed.[14]

Continetti didn't mention that Palin began her march to fame as governor of a state that depends so heavily on government spending, made possible by government ownership of most oil deposits. She did nothing to shrink the huge role state government plays in Alaska's economy. In fact, she raised taxes on the oil industry and then handed out more money to the people. You might say she was an Alaska version of Louisiana's rabble-rousing, Depression-era populist, Democrat Huey Long.

More than one observer has noted this irony: the self-proclaimed fiscal conservative who assails Barack Obama for his "socialist" agenda was governor of the most socialist state in the union.

4

Social Conservative,
But You Wouldn't Really Notice

Before becoming governor, Sarah Palin was well known to Alaskans as a staunch social conservative: strongly antiabortion and anti–gay rights. She'd won her first term as mayor of Wasilla by injecting the emotional issues of abortion and gun rights into the race for an office that dealt with neither.

When Palin ran for lieutenant governor in 2002 in the Republican primary, she complained it was a "kick in the gut" that her exemplary pro-life record didn't get her the endorsement of Alaska Right to Life.[1] (A more experienced antiabortion state senator got the endorsement—and he won the general election.)

In the 2006 race for governor, Palin made no secret of her socially conservative views.[2] On abortion, she was a pro-life fundamentalist. The only time abortion could be legal, she said, is to save the life of the mother: No exception for rape. No exception for incest. She said schools should teach both evolution and creationism. She opposed "explicit" sex education and praised the abstinence-until-marriage approach. She reminded Alaskans she'd supported the 1998 state constitutional amendment that banned gay marriage.

Yet one of Sarah Palin's first acts as governor was to veto a bill denying benefits to same-sex partners of state employees. She appointed a pro-choice woman to the state supreme court. She repeatedly refused to put abortion-restriction bills onto a special session agenda for the legislature. She did nothing to promote the teaching of creationism or intelligent design in Alaska schools. She took no steps to change how Alaska schools teach sex education.

At the *Anchorage Daily News*, we said this in an editorial during her vice-presidential race: "Sarah Palin's social views fall to the right of the American mainstream." But, the paper noted, "as governor, her opinions on abortion, same-sex health benefits and the like have stayed in the background. . . . She may even be a disappointment to her conservative base."[3]

A SURPRISING VETO

In October 2005, a year before Palin was elected governor, the Alaska Supreme Court ruled that the state could not deny benefits to the gay partners of state employees. Because the Alaska Constitution guarantees equal protection under the law, denying benefits that are available to heterosexual partners through marriage was illegal discrimination, the court said.

To Alaska's social conservatives, the ruling was an outrage. They complained about judicial activism and said judges were destroying the sanctity of marriage. Technical questions about implementing the gay benefits ruling kept it tied up in court for another year. But as Sarah Palin's rendezvous with voters in the November 2006 election approached, it was clear the court would require gay partner benefits to begin soon.

Just days before the November election, the man Palin beat in the Republican primary, Gov. Frank Murkowski, attacked the gay partner benefits ruling. He announced he'd convene a postelection special session of the legislature, dominated by conservative Republicans, to overturn it. Bringing up the issue so close to the election was expected to help drive social conservatives to the polls to vote for Palin. So after Palin won the governor's race, expectations were high that she'd welcome legislative action to reverse the court's gay rights ruling. By the time she took office in early December, the special session had passed a bill blocking the state from offering benefits for gay partners of public employees.

Palin's response surprised almost everybody.

She vetoed the bill because it was unconstitutional—which it was. Under Alaska's constitution, the only way to reverse a court's interpretation of a constitutional question is by constitutional amendment. In Alaska, that requires a two-thirds vote in each house of the legislature, not the simple majority that passed the anti–gay benefits bill. An amendment also requires ratification by voters in a statewide election. Palin issued a statement saying, "Signing this bill would be in direct violation of my oath of office."[4]

Socially conservative legislators were not happy with her decision. Sponsor of the vetoed bill, State Rep. John Coghill, said, "I would have like to have seen her stand up to the courts."[5] State Rep. Mike Kelly (R-Fairbanks) was even more blunt: "I was floored when she caved in without a fight."[6]

Palin was artfully vague on what she thought should happen next. "It is the Governor's intention to work with the legislature and to give the people of Alaska an opportunity to express their wishes and intentions whether these benefits should continue," she said in a statement.[7]

The special session had already passed a bill to hold an advisory vote, asking Alaskans if the legislature should approve a constitutional amendment to overturn the gay partner benefits ruling. The advisory vote would be held in a special statewide election that spring. Palin signed the bill.[8]

But a constitutional amendment to overturn the gay benefits ruling outright was not going to happen. Palin, along with anti–gay rights legislators, knew it would not get the two-thirds majority required to win legislative approval. The state senate was ruled by a bipartisan coalition that had agreed in advance to avoid divisive issues, even though coalition members included several hard-line social conservatives.

In early April, Alaska voters gave their advice on the issue. By 52.8 to 47.2 percent, they said yes, do amend the state constitution to deny benefits to partners of gay public employees.

Palin's reaction was strangely quiet. Media accounts of the election results did not include comments from her. The archive of her state e-mails sent while she was governor, released in June 2011, includes the period right after the advisory vote, but it has no e-mails discussing the results. Palin did not push the legislature to pursue the constitutional amendment. The effort would have been futile. Observers noted that if each individual legislator voted as advised by constituents in the special election, the amendment would not get the required two-thirds majority in the legislature.

Supporters of the anti–gay benefits amendment managed to bring it to a vote on the state house floor, but it fell well short of the two-thirds majority required to pass. The amendment would have faced even more difficulty in the state senate.

At the time, Palin was much more intent on pushing her top priority—legislation to promote the $40 billion Alaska natural gas pipeline. The idea of passing a constitutional amendment to overturn the gay benefits ruling—something Palin said she supported—just faded away.

"I'M NOT GOING TO JUDGE PEOPLE"

Unlike many of her fellow religious social conservatives, Palin used temperate, almost tolerant language when discussing gay issues. During the 2008 presidential campaign, she told CBS, "I am not going to judge Americans and the decisions that they make in their adult personal relationships. I have one of my absolute best friends for the last 30 years who happens to be gay, and I love her dearly, and she is not my 'gay friend,' she is one of my best friends, who happens to have made a choice that isn't a choice that I have made. But I'm not going to judge people."[9]

Contrast that with the language used by the man she nominated to be her second attorney general. In 1993, Wayne Anthony Ross had issued a public statement describing gays as "immoral" and "degenerates." After Palin selected him for attorney general, Ross was asked if he had changed his views, and he declined to take a softer line.[10] Palin never defended or repudiated her appointee's controversial views on gays. She touted him as a strong supporter of gun rights and developing Alaska's resources. Ross failed to win confirmation from the legislature. His attitude on gays and other social issues was just one of many controversies that led the legislature to reject him.

THAT PRO-CHOICE JUDICIAL APPOINTMENT

In March 2009, Sarah Palin appointed a former Planned Parenthood board member, Morgan Christen, to the Alaska Supreme Court. Palin made the appointment even though Christen had been vigorously opposed by one of Alaska's leading social conservative organizations, Alaska Family Council.[11] Her appointment of a pro-choice judge turned many heads among Palin's base of supporters, but her defenders pointed out that she didn't have much choice in the matter.

Alaska has an unusual, merit-based process for selecting judges. An independent panel screens judicial applicants and forwards the governor a list of the most qualified candidates. By Alaska's constitution, the governor must pick from the panel's list of recommendations.

In this case, six people applied, but only two passed muster with the Alaska Judicial Council. Christen was a well-respected state superior court judge. The other nominee given to Palin, Eric Smith, had been a lawyer for an environmental group before being appointed to a lower court. "From everything we could tell, even though he was probably not in line with our values, he was the lesser of two evils," explained Jim Minnery, of the Alaska Family Council, to the *Washington Times*. "We felt Morgan Christen was probably the one who would be most in opposition to our issues." But Minnery said Palin was "backed into a corner," and his group did not go after her for selecting the former Planned Parenthood board member.[12]

Palin might well have faced stronger criticism from more Alaskans if she had selected Judge Eric Smith. In Alaska, environmentalists are the bête noire of the political world. Alaska is a resource development state, and environmentalists are routinely accused of wanting to lock up the state and stifle all development. Faced with a choice between two judges who both had political leanings distasteful to her, Palin chose a woman.

Palin aide Frank Bailey made some headlines in early 2011 with a different explanation. In the then unpublished version of his memoir about working for Palin, leaked to the media by a rival author, Bailey suggested that his boss may have appointed Christen because she had ruled favorably in a child custody dispute involving Palin's sister. Her sister, Molly, prevailed over her ex-husband, Mike Wooten, who would eventually become famous as the trooper in Palin's Troopergate scandal.[13] "There is no question in my mind that Todd Palin became her champion because of how she ruled on that case," Bailey wrote in his manuscript, which was eventually published as *Blind Allegiance to Sarah Palin: A Memoir of Our Tumultuous Years*.[14] However, he noted that "Morgan Christen was a highly qualified candidate—and there is no evidence she ruled for Molly McCann [Palin's sister] to curry favor."

Yet when the Alaska court system was asked by the *Anchorage Daily News* to comment on Bailey's allegations in the unpublished manuscript, administrative director Christine Johnson pointed out several erroneous details. Christen had a very limited role in Palin's sister's case, Johnson said, and recused herself when she applied for the supreme court position.[15] After the court system wrote to Bailey's publisher, pointing out his errors, his book offered a revised account of his incendiary claim, which had already made news in Alaska. Todd was mistaken about Christen's role, Bailey said in the book. However, he went on to say, "There is no question in my mind that Todd Palin became her champion because of his misperception of her role in that case."[16]

Bailey faulted Christen for creating an awkward potential criticism of her appointment. Given that she would be applying for a future supreme court vacancy, likely during Palin's tenure as governor, Bailey suggested in the published version of his book that Christen should have avoided any potential conflict of interest by steering clear of Palin's sister's case. Bailey's book also faulted Palin for picking Christen. "In my mind," he wrote, "this is the complete inverse of Trooper-gate, with Sarah and Todd trying to hand out a plum job rather than taking one away, as they did to Walt Monegan."[17]

In announcing Christen's appointment, Palin did not complain about the dilemma she faced, having to choose between two liberal nominees. She issued a statement saying, "I have every confidence that Judge Christen has the experience, intellect, wisdom and character to be an outstanding Supreme Court justice."[18]

Alaska's social conservatives have long assailed the state's merit selection process for judges. They complain that it is skewed to producing liberal nominees to the bench. However, in this awkward case, Palin declined to embrace their cause. She chose not to challenge the judicial council, as her predecessor, the extremely unpopular Gov. Frank Murkowski, had. He balked at appointing from the judicial council's list, and requested more names. After the council stood by its original recommendations Murkowski gave in.

Palin did request the judicial council's entire files on the two nominees, Smith and Christen. That was an unusual step but hardly the forceful action some conservatives wanted. Family Research Council vice president Tom McCluskey told the *Washington Times*, "The fact she wasn't willing to stand up and fight this is something (they) will seriously question on the national stage."

INACTION ON ABORTION

The Alaska Supreme Court threw another hot social issue onto the legislative agenda during Palin's time as governor. In late 2007, the court struck down a law requiring a minor to get a parent's consent before having an abortion. Antiabortion legislators then tried to pass new versions of the restrictions on abortions for minors—and they didn't get as much help as they wanted from Governor Palin.

In 2008, the Alaska house passed a bill reimposing abortion restrictions on minors. Pro-choice legislators in the senate's bipartisan majority killed the bill by keeping it locked up in committee during lawmakers' regular session. Antiabortion legislators appealed to Palin for help. They asked her to put the house abortion-consent bill on the agenda for an upcoming special session of the legislature, along with a bill banning partial-birth abortions. One of the state's leading antiabortion groups, the Alaska Family Council, made a similar request.

Despite her staunch antiabortion stand, Palin refused. She wanted to keep the special session focused on her North Slope gas pipeline proposal, a $40 billion question critical to the state's economic future. (Dealing with that issue and other energy questions eventually took almost two full months of special session time.)

The abortion issue was also caught up in Palin's feud with the state senate president. Lyda Green was a staunchly conservative pro-life Republican from Palin's hometown of Wasilla. A veteran politician, Green had never warmed to the ambitious, attractive newcomer who had taken on the Republican Party establishment, and Palin felt no particular need to court her. Green won the Senate presidency by joining an alliance with the senate's Democrats. The Democrats' price for their support included an understanding to avoid divisive issues like abortion.

So when Senate President Green asked Palin to add the abortion restriction bills to a special session, Palin was not in the mood to cooperate with her hometown rival.[19] Palin replied in a letter chiding Senator Green for referring the bills to a committee, Judiciary, controlled by a pro-choice Democrat. Palin also noted that Senator Green and a fellow pro-life senator had voted against yanking the abortion restriction bills out of committee.[20] (In both cases, Senator Green was following standard legislative practice. Bills dealing with supreme court rulings go to the judiciary committee, and the majority never allows the minority to yank bills from committee.)

Palin also told Senator Green that the legislature can call itself into special session on the issue, by a two-thirds vote of its members. In her letter, Palin essentially told Senator Green: I won't put the abortion bills in play, unless you show me how you can get the bills through the pro-choice senators in your coalition.

There was no special session on the antiabortion bills in 2008.[21] Legislators who supported parental consent tried again in 2009. This time, Palin didn't stay on the sidelines. Her biggest legislative priority—the natural gas pipeline—had been resolved, and she had won the adulation of antiabortion voters during the 2008 presidential campaign. She held a rare press conference to trumpet her enthusiastic and very public support for a parental consent bill.

Once again, the legislation failed. It passed the state house, but another bipartisan majority had retained control of the senate and had again agreed to avoid divisive issues like abortion. Senate Majority Leader Johnny Ellis, a pro-choice Democrat, said at the time, "There was no appetite to tear ourselves apart over that issue."[22]

Palin's spokeswoman said the governor was "disappointed" the parental consent bill didn't pass and hoped the senate would try again early in 2010. (By that time, Palin would be gone from the governor's mansion, embarked on her new life as a nationally famous author and pundit.) Shortly after the legislature adjourned in 2009, supporters of the parental consent bill shifted tactics and started a voter initiative. Governor Palin helped their cause get into the headlines by publicly announcing her support. After she resigned as governor, though, Palin went MIA on the issue.

In late August, 2009, a month after Palin left office, she disappointed supporters of the parental consent initiative. They thought they had lined up the now ex-governor to appear at their megachurch event launching their petition drive. However, the day beforehand organizers learned Palin was not coming. Her spokeswoman said Palin had never heard anything about appearing at the event and was out of state. In his published memoir, Bailey said Palin had in fact confirmed the appearance and suggested she back out of it as political payback to one of the sponsors. The Alaska Family Council had opposed her appointment of supreme court justice Morgan Christen.[23]

The petition drive went on without Palin. The parental consent initiative made it onto the statewide ballot and passed in August 2010 by a 56 percent to 44 percent vote.

Palin's clearest statement on abortion as governor came in early 2009, after Planned Parenthood had invoked her as a bogeyman to raise money for its abortion rights work. Palin shrugged it off as political theater and went on to say this about Planned Parenthood:

> We agree on a mission here that we'd like to see fewer and fewer abortions. And I, embracing the culture of life, have perhaps a different approach in how I would like to see that goal reached. . . .The abortion issue has been with us for decades and has pitted well-meaning people of differing ideologies against each other. Where we can find common ground is in the belief that no one wants a single abortion. But when there is a clash of values, I always will come down on the side of life.[24]

A PARTING SHOT ON ABORTION

Endorsing the parental consent initiative was not Palin's last notable move on abortion issues. In the weeks before Palin quit, her administration imposed an antiabortion litmus test and forced out two well-regarded public health officials.

State public health director Bev Wooley was fired after she'd expressed personal reservations about the wisdom of forcing minors to involve parents in an abortion decision. She was fired even though she had pledged to support Governor Palin's contrary position in public testimony to the legislature. The state's chief medical officer, Jay Butler, vouched for Wooley, saying she was prepared to handle her personal conflict in a professional manner, but Palin's health commissioner fired her anyway. Butler shared some of Wooley's concerns about parental consent laws. When he was told he'd have to take on Wooley's duties, he quit. At the time, June 8, Palin sent a Twitter message, saying, "After 4 yrs of excellent service to State of AK, Dr. Jay Butler is returning to CDC. We wish him the best!" No mention of the abortion controversy that led him to quit.

Forcing out Butler and Wooley did not appear to be a calculated move to solidify Palin's antiabortion credentials. Palin sought no publicity on it—when asked about the abortion angle to the aides' departure, Palin declined to comment. The incident was handled by her health commissioner and only came to media attention about a month after it happened. Nonetheless, the purge cost Alaska the service of two capable professionals with solid records on public health.[25]

After John McCain picked Palin as his running mate, the *Anchorage Daily News* described her record on abortion this way: "Palin has not pushed that [antiabortion] agenda in her nearly two years as governor. She backed a couple of anti-abortion bills that died in the state legislature during the regular session, but didn't add them to the agenda during special sessions this summer."

But antiabortion activists in Alaska did not complain. "She's a woman of integrity and we trust her," Karen Lewis of Alaska Right to Life told the *Los Angeles Times*. "Sometimes you have to wait."[26]

Palin did not display her religious faith in her day-to-day work around the office, according to aide Bailey's published memoir. "I never saw Sarah read or carry a Bible on any of our frequent travels together," he writes. "Nor did she cite verses. We didn't hold prayers before meals or prior to meetings." But he says one key to "getting close to Sarah" was "have her believe you were a devoutly conservative Christian."[27]

SOCIAL ISSUES STAYED IN THE BACKGROUND

Social issues were not high in voters' minds when Sarah Palin won the governor's race. During the primary election on August 6, the *Anchorage Daily News* ran a story entitled: "Same-sex Unions, Drugs Get Little Play. Governor's Race: Gas Line Leaves No Room to Talk on Other Hot Issues."

Democratic gubernatorial candidate Tony Knowles tried to attack Palin for her hard-line view on abortion, allowing no exceptions for rape or incest. He didn't get very far with it. Voters were much more concerned with other issues: ethics, corruption, the failings of incumbent Gov. Frank Murkowski, and most of all, whether Alaska could achieve economic salvation by finding a way to jump-start a long-dormant $40 billion natural gas pipeline.

An adviser who was once close to Palin told me, "She's super-religious. Off the charts. She believes in signs, all that stuff. It's all part of a plan. And if the plan doesn't work, it's a sign the plan is not supposed to work."

But Alaskans didn't see much of that side of Sarah Palin. Sabra Ayres covered Palin's first legislative session for the *Anchorage Daily News*. She told me, "None of that stuff came up. There was no sense she went to evangelical churches or anything like that. Abortion, that didn't even come up for the session I was there." A November 2010 *New York Times* story noted that as a candidate for governor, Palin had said, "I don't wear my faith on my sleeve." And she had promised not to let her religious beliefs "bleed into policy—that is my commitment."[28]

At the *Anchorage Daily News*, we found that she made good on that promise. When Palin ran for vice president, we said in an editorial that she was "an extreme social conservative. She opposes abortion rights. She favors the teaching of creationism. She preaches abstinence-only sex education. She is open to the possibility of banning books from public libraries. She opposes gay marriage. She personally opposes benefits for gay partners of public employees."

However, our editorial noted, her extreme views "have not resulted in much action since she was elected. . . . She has rightly focused on ethics, oil taxes and gas pipeline legislation."[29]

5

Palin Triumphs over Big Oil, Round 1

Palin's predecessor tried to jump-start a $40 billion natural gas pipeline from Alaska's North Slope by offering Exxon, Conoco, and BP (formerly British Petroleum) unprecedented, multibillion-dollar concessions, with no guarantees of forward progress. To the dismay of Alaska's Big Three oil companies, Palin persuaded the legislature to take a different approach: competitive bidding for state incentives to pursue the mega-project.

■ ■ ■

In spring of 1968, Alaskans learned that drillers had discovered a mammoth oil field at a place called Prudhoe Bay. First estimated at nearly 10 billion barrels, it would become the nation's largest producing oil field for decades. Prudhoe Bay, and most North Slope oil, sits underneath land owned by the state of Alaska. Leasing these oil rights, and levying taxes on the oil operations, have netted Alaska's state treasury more than $100 billion dollars.

Before Prudhoe Bay, Alaska was an impoverished state, economically comparable to Mississippi or West Virginia, heavily dependent on federal money and seasonal industries like fishing and tourism. The prosperity brought by Prudhoe Bay vaulted Alaska into the ranks of the nation's wealthiest states. This oil money has allowed Alaska to fund a large state government without a personal income tax or statewide sales tax. University of Alaska economist Scott Goldsmith estimated that in 2006, oil revenues supplied each Alaskan with $13,150 worth of public services and government aid. The billions of dollars flowing from Prudhoe Bay oil helped make the oil industry the most powerful force in Alaska politics—a force Sarah Palin would eventually confront as governor.

THE NORTH SLOPE GAS LINE: A DREAM DEFERRED

Getting Alaska's oil to market had required an 800-mile pipeline to the state's ice-free southern coast—a project that required years of political struggle, a federal settlement of long-standing Native land claims, and another act of Congress to exempt it from recently passed environmental laws. The oil pipeline, completed in 1977, cost $8 billion, making it the nation's largest-ever private construction project.

Sitting on top of all that oil at Prudhoe Bay was a comparably huge reservoir of gas—a world-class deposit, about 26 trillion cubic feet. From the day Prudhoe Bay was discovered, Alaskans yearned for the gas to be developed along with the oil. Building a gas pipeline from the North Slope would cost as much as $40 billion, bringing Alaska another economic boom and pouring even more money into the state treasury.

Congress, in the late 1970s, passed a law giving controversial breaks and incentives for a gas pipeline from the North Slope through Canada to the Lower 48. Over the years, the companies that hold the gas and other pipeline promoters have spent hundreds of millions of dollars studying options for a gas line, but the project has never moved off the drawing board.

In part, this is because Alaska's gas is simply not as valuable as its oil. Many other big gas fields around the world don't need a $40 billion pipeline for getting the fuel to market. If Alaska's gas were brought into the Lower 48, selling such a huge amount at one time would flood the market and depress the price of gas already being sold by the same companies that hold Alaska's gas.

It also didn't help that Alaskans were divided about what route a gas pipeline should take. On one side were the Alaska-first partisans, who vehemently argued for an all-Alaska route, following the oil pipeline 800 miles to Valdez, where the gas would have to be liquefied and shipped in tankers to the Lower 48 or Asia. The other major faction thought the less-popular overland route through Canada was more practical, both politically and economically, even though the longer pipeline costs considerably more.

Most important of all, though, was this: Keeping the gas bottled up in Prudhoe Bay was more profitable to the lease-holding companies than producing it. In a field like Prudhoe Bay, leaving the gas in place helps maintain pressure in the oil reservoir and flush out more oil. Much of that gas comes out of Prudhoe Bay during oil production, but it's reinjected back into the field. Thanks to gas reinjection, and other enhanced recovery technology, Prudhoe Bay will produce about 40 percent more oil than originally estimated.

It's fair to say that if the multinational oil companies that hold Alaska's gas thought that producing it for the U.S. or world market would make them suitable amounts of money, they would have built a gas line by now. All three of the companies—Exxon/Mobil, ConocoPhillips, and BP—have extensive oil and gas holdings around the world. The prospects they developed were the ones that produced the most profit. Meanwhile, the companies could continue holding Alaska's gas until developing it rose to the top of their list of profitable projects. They could do so because they paid no price for holding on to the gas under their state leases, even though state leases require oil and gas to be produced when the deposit "is capable of producing hydrocarbons in paying quantities."[1]

As long as North Slope oil was flowing, and the state treasury was filled with oil money, Alaskans tolerated the lack of progress on a natural gas pipeline. But oil production has steadily declined since the late 1980s, to barely a third of peak levels. As oil production steadily fell, demands to develop Alaska's vast storehouse of gas grew stronger and stronger—especially when oil prices were low, causing state oil royalties and taxes to shrink. During those times, the state would tighten its spending and shore up the budget by dipping into rainy-day funds.

As the years went by with no progress on the gas line, more and more Alaskans began to accuse the industry of "warehousing" the gas—deliberately spurning what would be a profitable North Slope gas project merely because the companies could make even bigger profits by developing other projects around the world. In 2002, frustrated voters passed a ballot initiative creating a new state agency that would promote the all-Alaska version of a North Slope gas pipeline.

The same year, voters elected Frank Murkowski governor. His top priority was to get Alaskans a gas line. He spent nearly two years negotiating in secret with the big North Slope gas holders, and eventually produced a proposal offering the industry billions of dollars worth of concessions. His deal also signed away state sovereignty by barring any future oil tax changes for thirty years and gas tax changes for forty-five years. Murkowski further agreed to strip state courts of jurisdiction over any gas line disputes.

Such drastic concessions likely violated the Alaska Constitution—and the deal included no guarantees the project would move forward. Murkowski was essentially saying to Exxon, BP, and Conoco, "We're not going to make you build a gas pipeline, but if you decide to do it, here's the deal we'll give you."

Murkowski's deal was so flawed that his natural resource commissioner, Tom Irwin, privately warned the governor that it failed to comply with state law and the Alaska Constitution. For that bit of candor, Murkowski sacked him. Six of Irwin's senior staff then resigned in protest, including his chief aide on gas line policy, Marty Rutherford.

The mass departure of Murkowski's gas line team, thereafter known as the Magnificent Seven, drew criticism from leading Democrats, and from Sarah Palin, who by that time was running for governor against Murkowski. The public and Alaska lawmakers had so little confidence in Murkowski's gas line deal that the legislature never even considered ratifying it.

As the 2006 election approached, voters' frustration over the gas line escalated. Natural gas prices in the Lower 48 had spiked to record-breaking levels, and remained more than double the price from the 1980s and 1990s. Many Alaskans wondered why these high prices weren't enough for the gas holders to finally build the line. The November ballot would include a voter initiative, slapping a tax on the gas reserves at Prudhoe Bay as long as they remained undeveloped. With low oil prices and a big hole in the state budget, promoting a gas pipeline became the number one issue in the 2006 governor's race.

Palin flatly rejected Murkowski's approach, but she was vague about her alternative. She had supported the all-Alaska gas line voter initiative in 2002, as did most of the state's politicians. This time around, she stuck to general principles. "I want a competitive process that considers all viable options," Palin said in a mailer I received during the general election campaign. There would be no secret negotiations with the gas holders. "Our negotiations will involve the state legislature, producers and independent pipeline companies." She would not sign away the state's sovereignty over future taxes or court jurisdiction. If the state were going to offer concessions or financial incentives, Alaskans would get terms and conditions they wanted in return.

Palin opposed the reserves tax, as did the other major candidates for governor. The reserves tax was initially very popular with frustrated voters, and early in her campaign Palin supported it before changing her mind. She came to see it as the state's political establishment did—as a risky gamble with Alaska's largest industry.

In the Republican primary, Palin easily beat the deathly unpopular Murkowski in a three-way race. In the November general election, she faced former two-term governor Tony Knowles, a pro-oil Democrat. He was willing to continue negotiations with the gas holders and questioned Palin's ability to negotiate an appropriate deal.

During his time as governor, four years earlier, Knowles had argued that the state needed to offer the gas holders "fiscal stability" for their project. (That is industry code for "agreeing to lock in what the state's future tax system will be.") To many of the oil and gas industry's friends, Democrat Knowles looked like the better candidate. In late October, the Associated Press reported, "Normally stalwart Republican backers are shunning Sarah Palin and defecting to Democrat Tony Knowles in this year's gubernatorial race, with business and oil industry executives leading the way."[2]

It was ironic that in this Republican state, in this election, the candidate taking the harder line on the state's big oil and gas companies was the Republican, Sarah Palin.

PALIN CHARTS A NEW COURSE

Though conventional wisdom was that the gas reserves tax would easily pass, the industry spent $1.7 million to defeat it—a huge sum in a small state like Alaska. On the other side, supporters of the tax had little money for the vote-yes campaign. By the time election day arrived, the industry's advertising barrage had succeeded. Voters resoundingly rejected the reserves tax—but they did elect Sarah Palin.

Palin promptly began work on a new approach to promoting the gas line. She got her advice from the gas line team that had left the Murkowski administration in frustration. Before long, she brought Tom Irwin and Marty Rutherford into their old jobs. Palin's gas line advisers were determined the state should not repeat the mistake Alaska made with the oil pipeline. The same big North Slope companies that controlled the Prudhoe Bay oil fields also built and controlled the oil pipeline. By charging high shipping tariffs for sending oil in their pipeline, the big oil companies could prevent other competitors from succeeding in the North Slope oil patch.

One smaller oil company, Conoco, left Alaska in the early 1990s for exactly that reason. "All of the value of that property [on the North Slope] was taken away from us in the pipeline tariffs," Conoco CEO Archie Dunham said at the time.[3] (Conoco returned to the North Slope years later, when it acquired Arco, one of Alaska's Big Three oil companies, which owned part of the oil pipeline.)

The high shipping charges didn't hurt the big oil companies' overall profits, since they owned the pipeline. They were paying the overcharges to themselves, taking money out of one pocket and transferring it to another. The excessively high oil pipeline tariffs eventually drew the attention of the state utility commission. In looking at just one four-year period, the Regulatory Commission of Alaska found the pipeline owners had overcharged by 57 percent. Estimates of total pipeline overcharges, covering its thirty-four years of operation, range from $5 billion to more than $10 billion.[4]

Those excessive pipeline rates also cost the state treasury billions of dollars. Oil pipeline shipping fees are deducted from state tax and royalty calculations, so the high pipeline charges lowered the amount the companies had to pay the state.

When discussing the possibility of a gas pipeline, Exxon, Conoco, and BP repeatedly sounded a common theme: the state must offer them "fiscal stability"—a guarantee that the state would not raise taxes after the line goes into operation. One of the most controversial aspects of Governor Murkowski's discredited gas line deal was the thirty- to forty-five-year guarantee it provided against any tax changes. Palin was among those who criticized that concession.

After Palin took office, she released a memo that had been written by Murkowski's chief oil and gas adviser, who was bluntly critical of Murkowski's proposed deal. International oil consultant Pedro van Meurs had warned Murkowski: "This is a degree of fiscal stability that is normally reserved for highly corrupt and completely unreliable states. . . . There is absolutely no need to treat Alaska as a banana republic in order to secure the gas line."[5] Looking at the state's oil pipeline experience and Governor Murkowski's failed plan, Palin and her advisers decided on a different approach. They wanted to create a system of incentives that would prevent the gas holders from using control of a gas pipeline to lock up the basin and keep competitors out.

Palin and her team decided they would not negotiate in secret. The state would offer the same set of state incentives to any company, ask all companies to meet a common set of terms and conditions, take in proposals, and select the best one. The result was legislation known as the Alaska Gasline Inducement Act, or AGIA (uh-GEE-uh).

BIG OIL PUSHES BACK

Governor Palin introduced the Alaska Gasline Inducement Act (HB 177) on March 5, 2007. Exxon, BP, Conoco, and their allies strongly opposed it, but they had to tread carefully. The new governor was popular, and an oil industry corruption scandal was making headlines. Eventually Alaskans would learn that the state's most powerful oil lobbyist, Bill Allen, had bribed legislators when the legislature passed a new version of the state's oil production tax the previous year.

Exxon, BP, and Conoco knew that Governor Murkowski's solicitous approach to their gas line concerns had been repudiated. The legislature was going to have to pass some kind of new rules for a gas pipeline deal. The Big Three zeroed in on two points of attack: the new system should offer "flexibility" in what gas line arrangements the companies might propose, and the state should offer much stronger guarantees against future tax changes. Exxon official Marty Massey told the legislature, "Without stable fiscal terms I don't know how to make adequate investment decisions." In materials given to the House Resources Committee, Conoco's Wendy King wrote, the "AGIA structure hinders competition and creative alternatives . . . [the] State could pick the wrong winner and be tied up for over a decade. AGIA 'bid requirements' are too narrow, prescriptive, and could result in subsidization that may not even be in the State's interests." BP's Dave van Tuyl said AGIA "may create some unintended consequences that could jeopardize the vision of getting Alaska's gas to market quickly and at low cost. . . . [AGIA] would result in an exclusive winner before any real work is done and it awards state funds based on promises, not on results."[6]

The Resource Development Council for Alaska, the state's leading prodevelopment advocacy group, echoed the Big Three's concerns.

Palin stood firm. "It's no surprise that the producers and those independents wanting to do business with the producers, would acknowledge how good they had it, I guess, under the Murkowski administration, in terms of what was being given to them in order to induce them to perhaps, someday, build a gas line," she said at the time. "They're not comfortable, necessarily, with the process that we have laid out . . . because our process is a fair and transparent process where we're not going to be giving away the farm."[7]

PALIN'S GAS LINE PLAN PASSES

Industry lobbyists made virtually no headway with their work against Palin's gas line plan. Legislators did make one potentially significant change: the provision offering not to raise taxes for the first ten years the line was in operation was converted from an enforceable contractual guarantee to a pledge that could be revisited by a future legislature.

Palin argued against the change, but it was done on advice from legislative attorneys, who said an iron-clad, contractually enforceable guarantee would be unconstitutional. (The Alaska Constitution explicitly prevents the state from contracting away its authority to tax.) Palin cited advice from the attorney general that the constitution would allow an enforceable ten-year tax lock but legislators decided otherwise.

This change in AGIA later became a point of attack for Exxon, Conoco, and BP. Now, the guarantee AGIA offered for "fiscal stability"—no severance tax increases for the first ten years the gas line operates—was far too weak, they said. It was an ironic twist in the debate, because Exxon, BP, and Conoco's demand for a much longer and stronger guarantee on future taxes would be even more likely to violate the state constitution.

Despite strong lobbying from the Big Three oil companies, Palin's Alaska Gasline Inducement Act passed with just one legislator voting no. It wasn't quite as easy as it looked, according to Marty Rutherford, one of Palin's key aides on oil and gas issues. She told me that a significant number of legislators did not like Palin's approach. But a popular governor had offered a drastic course change from her discredited predecessor, and the political climate was rife with speculation about who would be indicted in the oil tax bribery scandal. For now, the oil industry was powerless to stop Palin's gas line plan.

"Opponents saw Palin's popularity and kept their powder dry for next go-round," Rutherford told me. Skeptical legislators would have another shot when they voted on whatever proposal came out of Palin's competitive bidding process. The one legislator who voted against was Anchorage Republican representative Ralph Samuels. After Palin resigned, he ran for governor, touting his skepticism of AGIA. He finished third in the Republican primary, with only 14 percent of the vote. He lost to Palin's successor, her Lt. Gov. Sean Parnell, who initially continued Palin's approach to the gas line.

An editorial in the *Juneau Empire* spoke for many Alaskans:

Oil companies know full well that they're getting stability in Alaska that they certainly don't have from other oil-producing entities, such as Angola or Nigeria. . . . The oil producers didn't like it [AGIA] because it lacked the giveaways to the industry that Murkowski was more than happy to include in his gas line plan.

We finally have leaders who are more willing to stick up for Alaskans and the resources they own.[8]

6

Palin Triumphs over Big Oil, Round 2

Her predecessor rammed through a controversial oil tax change in a process later found to be tainted by corruption in the legislature. Palin agreed the corrupt tax must be reformed—and worked with Democrats to pass the largest oil tax increase in Alaska's history. Fellow Republicans and the state's business establishment emerged as her strongest critics.

PRELUDE: A CORRUPTION SCANDAL ERUPTS

One week after Sarah Palin won the Republican nomination for governor, FBI agents raided the offices of six Alaska legislators. The agents were looking for evidence that legislators had accepted bribes from executives of Veco, an oil field service company whose owner, Bill Allen, was one of the state's most powerful influence brokers dating back to the 1980s.

The specter of oil industry corruption hung over that fall's election and helped Palin win. She had already earned a reputation as a reformer, and her Democratic opponent was a former two-term governor who'd been friendly with the industry, though he had a stellar ethical reputation and no connection to the corruption investigation. During the months after the FBI raid, Alaskans wondered who might be indicted for what corruption charges.

Those answers came the first week in May, just as Palin was finishing her first legislative session as governor. Three members of the 2006 state house were arraigned in federal court: a former house speaker, Rep. Pete Kott; former Rep. Bruce Weyhrauch; and current legislator Rep. Vic Kohring. The two men who bribed them, Veco owner Bill Allen and his chief lobbying aide Rick Smith, pleaded guilty to federal charges. The two lobbyists had bought legislators' support during 2006, when the legislature held a special session that produced a new version of the state's tax on oil production.

PALIN'S PREDECESSOR PUSHES A NEW TAX

The 2006 oil tax was part of then governor Frank Murkowski's effort to get a gas pipeline moving. The multinational companies holding Alaska's huge North Slope gas deposits said they would not build a gas pipeline unless the state guaranteed that it wouldn't raise oil and gas taxes for decades into the future.

Murkowski knew if he was going to lock in those taxes for thirty or forty years, the system badly needed an overhaul. Many of Alaska's oil fields were paying no severance taxes at all, thanks to a generous, and rapidly escalating, tax break that was intended to help small, marginally profitable fields. Alaska's severance tax imposed a nominal rate of 15 percent on the gross value of all oil produced. Thanks to the questionable tax break, the actual rate on North Slope fields averaged closer to 8 percent. One of the fields paying no severance tax was Kuparuk, the nation's second-largest field after Prudhoe Bay.

Governor Murkowski proposed shifting the severance tax to a new system based on profits, rather than the amount of oil physically pumped out of the ground. His idea of shifting to a tax on petroleum production profits, known by the shorthand PPT, was sound in concept. A tax based on gross oil production is regressive—it takes a huge share of the companies' revenue when prices are low and companies are struggling to make money. When oil prices spike upward, the gross tax takes a much smaller share of the windfall profits.

With a tax on oil production profits, the state shares the pain and shares the gains. In bad times, taxes are lower (and might even disappear). In good times, tax collections go up. The state's interests and the oil producers' interests are aligned. To ease the sting of the higher taxes in good times, Murkowski's tax plan offered generous tax credits for companies when they reinvested some of their profits in Alaska's oil and gas fields.

THE OIL TAX BATTLE OF 2006

In their gas line negotiations with Murkowski, Exxon, BP, and Conoco had asked Murkowski for a production profit tax rate of 12.5 percent, with a 25 percent tax credit for money they reinvested in Alaska.[1] Based on advice from international oil consultant Pedro van Meurs, Murkowski pushed for more. He let legislators know he'd propose a tax rate on profits of 25 percent with the investment credit at 20 percent.

When word reached the Big Three companies, they were stunned. A high-level delegation, including the CEOs of BP and Conoco, flew to meet Murkowski in Juneau. After the meeting, Murkowski announced he'd support lowering the tax rate to 20 percent. That concession stunned many legislators. It was one more stumble for Murkowski as the special session got under way.

His two years of secret negotiations had produced a gas line proposal built on multibillion-dollar concessions, with no guarantee of forward progress. For many reasons—ethics scandals, an arrogant attitude toward the perks of office, past budget cuts—his popularity with voters was plummeting.

While legislators were not eager to help Murkowski advance his gas line deal by making oil tax changes, most knew that the state's overly generous severance tax break was costing the treasury too much money and needed to be fixed. The legislature took Murkowski's tax proposal and debated how much bigger the tax increase should be. Lawmakers argued about increasing the tax rate on profits, whether to include an escalator for times of high oil prices, how big the investment credit should be, and what kind of deductions to allow.

Democrats pushed for a tax rate of 30 percent, but they were in the minority in both houses. They also sought a "progressivity" escalator that boosted the tax rate when high oil prices produced windfall profits.

The industry's allies were pushing hard in the other direction. Working from a Juneau hotel room where the FBI had a hidden camera, Veco's lobbyists, Bill Allen and Rick Smith, were using their clout, including bribes, to keep the oil tax rate as low as possible and include subtle tax breaks. In one notorious public display of his influence, Bill Allen sat in the visitors' gallery of the house and passed notes to friendly legislators right on the house floor.

Despite intense pressure from the house and Democrats for a higher rate, the Republican-run state senate insisted on a 22.5 percent base rate, with a modest escalator for high oil prices, and a host of other concessions that cut the industry's bill.[2] Each company, for example, got $73 million a year of automatic deductions. The effective date of the new tax was postponed, saving the companies an estimated $390 million. Leading the fight for the lower tax rate was Senate president Ben Stevens, whom Bill Allen later admitted to bribing.

PALIN INHERITS A TAINTED TAX

By the time Palin had settled in as governor, the state discovered the new oil production tax was bringing in much less money than expected—about $800 million less.[3] The industry's critics wondered if Alaska's oil companies were gaming the system, by inflating expenses and understating profits. So when the bribery scandal finally produced indictments in May, as the legislative session was ending, there were widespread calls to revisit the corruption-tainted oil tax.

Palin took her time deciding what to do. She waited nearly two weeks after the corruption arrests to announce that she would call a special session in the fall to reconsider the new oil tax. "Our oil tax formula was changed under a dark cloud of suspicion," she said. Her oil and gas advisers, led by Revenue Commissioner Pat Galvin and Deputy Natural Resources Commissioner Marty

Rutherford, spent the summer researching options for reforming the corruption-tainted oil tax, known by the initials PPT.

In August 2007, Palin issued the official call for a special session, to be held in October. "PPT just is not working as had been promised," Palin said. "Revisiting PPT . . . also allows legislators to basically start anew, to remove the taint of corruption and restore public trust."[4]

In running for governor, candidate Palin had supported returning to a tax based on gross oil production rather than profits. The gross tax is much simpler to administer, and it's harder for oil companies to play accounting games and short-change the state on tax payments. Many Democratic legislators also supported a gross oil production tax, for the same reasons.[5]

PALIN'S TAX PLAN

Marty Rutherford had initially supported the gross tax, too. Her department commissioned extensive analysis and modeling of options for fixing the corrupt oil tax. She remembers well when one of the analysts, Antony Scott, called to report that they couldn't accomplish what they were trying to do with any kind of tax on gross oil production. It just wouldn't work. His conclusion was such a stunning surprise that when he called with the news, "Antony asked me, 'Are you sitting down?'" Rutherford said. After reviewing the new findings, Palin's oil tax team was convinced.

Now, they had to convince Palin to switch. "She was very, very out there with [supporting] the gross tax," Rutherford told me. "We spent a lot of time explaining to her that it was not working. We finally convinced her. She said, 'If I've gotta take a bullet because that's what's in the state's best interest, I'll take a bullet.'"

Palin's proposal, known as ACES (Alaska's Clear and Equitable Share), put the tax rate on production profits back at 25 percent. It included a modest escalator boosting that percentage when oil prices hit high levels. Palin also wanted a minimum tax floor, based on gross oil production, for times of low oil prices, when a profits-based tax would bring in little to no state revenue. It included substantial tax credits for companies that invested money in exploration and new oil production.

Palin explained her thinking in a newspaper commentary published November 2 in the *Anchorage Daily News*:

> Keep in mind that the original oil tax rate recommendation was 25 percent. That's the same rate we are recommending in ACES. It has been reviewed by numerous economists with worldwide oil and gas experience. There is no dissention—25 percent is the right number.

The State of Alaska is currently the largest investor on the North Slope, having paid for 50 percent of all investments in 2007. Yet our share of net revenue, including royalties, property and corporate income tax, was about 40 percent. The "equitable share" component in ACES narrows this gap. Sticking to a tax rate of 25 percent helps accomplish that. . . .

The reality is we are a state very rich in natural resources. Currently, we do not receive fair value for our resources as they're extracted and sold for us, at a premium, to very hungry markets.[6]

The oil industry's allies blasted Palin's proposal. Jason Brune, director of the Resource Development Council, wrote in the group's newsletter: "If Governor Palin has her way, 68 percent of the value of every barrel of oil produced in Alaska will go to government. . . . If the tax rates rise yet again, these companies likely will, metaphorically speaking, throw their tea into the harbor by investing elsewhere."[7]

A BIG TAX INCREASE GETS EVEN BIGGER

But the Veco bribery scandal had cost the oil industry much of its political influence. It kept a low profile during the special session. Well into the session, House Speaker John Harris told the *Anchorage Daily News* he'd only had one visit from an oil industry lobbyist.

Record-breaking oil prices also hurt the industry's cause. Oil prices had doubled from the previous year, to around $80 a barrel. Exxon, Conoco, and BP were reporting huge profits to their shareholders. In Juneau, the debate was about how high the new tax should go. Palin's most reliable allies in confronting the oil industry—the legislature's Democrats—pushed for a much bigger increase.

Gregg Erickson, one of the state capital's most respected reporters on budget and tax matters, wrote a column noting this complaint from Chevron's John Zager, made two days before the session ended: "Across a broad range of prices (Palin's) bill was generally expected to raise $500 (million) to $600 million more than PPT [as the 2006 oil tax was known]," Zager said at the time. "The latest revisions to the ACES language, adding the more aggressive progressivity, have raised that number to $1.5 to $2.0 billion more than PPT."[8]

Palin didn't gripe about the legislature making the oil tax increase so much bigger. When the legislature passed its version, she said, "This bill strikes a careful balance. It assures a fair share of our oil's value for Alaska while encouraging producers to invest in new fields. . . . I know it is the right thing for the state."[9]

Democratic senator Hollis French successfully fought to get a much stronger version of her oil tax proposal through his Senate Judiciary Committee. French told me that "Sarah Palin invited me to her office for a short thank you. . . . She wanted me to know my work was appreciated."

Throughout the special session, Governor Palin kept a relatively low profile in both the legislative halls and the public debate. Revenue Commissioner Pat Galvin was the public face of her tax proposal, testifying again and again as legislative committees reviewed the bill. He was often joined by numerous legal and financial consultants with expertise in the oil industry. Their analysis provided a credible counterweight to the industry's claims that higher taxes would hurt Alaska by discouraging future investment.

Palin was not the kind of leader who delved into the details of legislation. One insider told me she would listen to and understand briefings on an issue but showed little evidence she had mastered the background materials involved.

Typically, a governor might talk to reluctant legislators about possible horse-trading arrangements—in a case like this, voting for the oil tax reform in return for, say, funding a project in their home district. But with the corruption investigation hanging over the oil tax debate, legislators were reluctant to come out and ask for deals like that with Palin. And she was not the type of governor to offer them. She had already made a name for herself by slashing hundreds of millions of dollars in "pork" from the capital budget. She could not turn around and start cutting deals for votes with capital projects.

Instead, she would explain what she considered to be the right thing, and expected them to do it. She relied on her political popularity—in effect on her "brand" as a trustworthy reformist leader—to carry her agenda. She did not wheel and deal with legislators to get what she wanted.

At one point, Palin did host a gathering of the Democrats in the house minority to discuss the oil tax reform. Like Palin, Democrats had started out in favor of returning to the much simpler tax on gross oil production, instead of modifying the corruption-tainted tax that was based on profits. She did have to help persuade the Democrats to shift gears and support a hybrid version of the profits-based tax.

Eventually she and the Democrats agreed on one that imposed strict limits on the deductions companies could take on the most profitable oil fields. A source close to that process told me that Palin herself cut the necessary deal with the Democrats—a surprise to her oil advisers. The pro-Palin Republican faction in the legislature took its cues from Palin. They knew Democratic support was critical to passing any oil tax reform, and she was doing what she had to do to keep the Democrats on board.

By the time the legislature was done, Palin's ACES tax proposal turned into the biggest tax increase in the state's history. Democratic senator Hollis French would later boast that official state figures showed the new tax brought the treasury an extra $4 billion during the first two years.[10] In early 2011, as oil prices returned to $100 a barrel, the state estimated that the new tax was bringing in an extra $3 billion a year.[11]

It was not the first time Palin pushed through a significant tax increase. One of her conservative admirers, Fred Barnes, pointed out a similar chapter of her history as Wasilla mayor in the July 2007 *Weekly Standard*: "Though Alaskans tend to be ferociously anti-tax, she persuaded Wasilla voters to increase the local sales tax to pay for an indoor arena and convention center."[12]

The final version of Palin's ACES oil tax increase passed the senate 14 to 5 and the house 26 to 13. It was a bipartisan vote: 16 Republicans and 24 Democrats voted yes. All but one of the "no" votes came from Republicans.

Palin had no qualms about signing this huge tax increase. In a column about Palin's oil tax victory, Gregg Erickson described her triumphant press conference:

> It was as if Gov. Sarah Palin asked the Legislature for a nice sensible winter jacket and they sent her a full-length mink parka with a wolverine ruff, seal skin trim, and a catalytic hand warmer in each pocket.
>
> A beaming Palin didn't seem to mind as she walked into the Capitol's third-floor conference room a couple of weeks ago to laud legislators for passing a bill boosting revenue by almost four times more than she had proposed in her Alaska's Clear and Equitable Share bill.[13]

At the *Anchorage Daily News*, we had endorsed Palin's opponent for governor, but our editorial called the final product a

> financially responsible fix to Alaska's corruption-tainted oil tax. . . . To pass any reform, Republican Gov. Sarah Palin needed cross-party support from Democrats. To the Democrats' credit, they backed away from plans to return to a tax on gross oil production instead of profits. To the governor's credit, she was flexible enough to accept significant enhancements in her initial proposal.[14]

DEMOCRATS DEFEND PALIN'S OIL TAX LEGACY

Major oil companies and their allies roundly condemned the new tax Palin pushed through. The Alaska Oil and Gas Association complained on its website that Alaska has "in essence more than doubled taxes on the industry, again."[15] In March of 2008, BP's top executive in Alaska, Doug Suttles, told the Anchorage Chamber of Commerce, "Today, by our calculations, Prudhoe Bay has the highest production tax now in the world."[16]

In Palin's 2009 state of the state speech, she staunchly defended the huge oil tax increase. "Our reformed oil production formula, ACES, helps them [oil companies] with strong incentives to keep capital reinvested, and it's working with new developments, as DNR [Department of Natural Resources] just announced a banner year for new companies entering our competitive oil and gas arena."

The oil tax investment credits were so popular, Palin and the legislature had to add another $100 million for them, for a total of $250 million the first year. In the following two years, the state allocated another $580 million—more than half a billion dollars—for cash rebates to oil companies whose investment credits exceeded the amount of tax they owed.

The incentives helped a newcomer to the North Slope, Pioneer, bring its Oooguruk field on line in just five years, roughly half the normal lead time on a new North Slope field. Another newcomer, ENI, used the state's investment rebates to bring its Nikaitchuq field on line in early 2011. *Petroleum News* noted a split within the oil industry in its December 20, 2009, issue: "While larger companies believe the increased tax rate is starting to harm investment in the state, pointing to the fact that several traditional explorers don't have work planned for this year, many smaller companies, particularly those without any production in Alaska, say the exploration credits make Alaska more attractive than other regions."

In *Going Rogue*, her memoir published in 2009, Palin speaks with pride about her huge oil tax increase: "We had struck that sweet spot where industry and the public interest were mutually served."[17]

In January 2010, six months after Palin left office, her Republican successor was trying to ease the sting of the new tax. The *Alaska Journal of Commerce* reported, "Alaska Gov. Sean Parnell has introduced legislation to expand investment tax credits under the state [oil] tax. Companies say this helps, but does not go far enough. Parnell so far is resisting a change to the high tax rate itself, created under the Alaska Clear and Equitable Share Act, or ACES."[18]

By the following year, Parnell had run his own race for governor and won. Apparently he felt that winning on his own gave him more freedom to depart from Palin's tough-on-oil-companies path. Heading into the 2011 legislative session, Parnell proposed a package of oil tax rollbacks and new breaks that critics said would cost $1.5 billion. Parnell pitched his plan in a newspaper column with rhetoric that might have come straight from the Tea Party, or from Sarah Palin's Facebook page: "History has shown that the more you tax something, the less you get of it," he wrote. "These companies will only invest if they are not punished by heavy taxation."[19]

When the House Resources Committee considered Governor Parnell's oil tax rollback, Claire Fitzpatrick, chief financial officer for BP Alaska, said that "Alaska is uncompetitive" with the current oil tax—the one Palin approved.[20]

In March 2011, the Associated Press reported, "Oil company executives . . . praised the [Parnell tax rollback] plan as making Alaska a more attractive place to do business." Mark Hamilton, a former University of Alaska president now working for a pro-business group called the Make Alaska Competitive Coalition, was quoted by public radio in Sitka saying this about Palin's oil tax:

> We are making a fortune off this new tax regime. An absolute fortune. We've repaid $5.5 billion into the constitutional budget reserve, there's another $7 billion assigned to general funds, we had a $3.4 billion surplus last year, and that didn't enjoy the highest spikes in the oil that we're seeing right now. We had the most popular governor in the history of the United States who, God bless her, had exposed grotesque corruption in the oil service industry. I think there was an atmosphere there that allowed us to pass a vengeful tax.[21]

The most vigorous defenders of Palin's oil tax increase have been Democrats. Sen. Hollis French touted his work on the new oil tax when he ran for governor in 2010. "I was surprised recently when my opponent in the Democratic primary began campaigning to discard this very hard-won victory," French wrote in a guest column for the *Anchorage Daily News*. "I'm proud of the bill we passed. We did it in the face of well-paid oil company lobbyists and knowing the industry would send campaign money to our opponents to punish us for our work."[22]

In early 2011, another Democrat, Anchorage state representative Les Gara, said, "It's worth reminding folks how 'abusive' Alaska's oil tax system has been to our producers. Eni and Pioneer have recently started production at two new fields, Ooogaruk [*sic*] and Nikaitchuq. . . . Conoco has proposed development there [National Petroleum Reserve-Alaska] under our existing tax system. Hard to argue that the current system deterred that development."[23]

Anchorage Democratic representative Mike Doogan blasted Governor Parnell's oil tax rollback proposal in a newspaper commentary: "The governor wants me to give a billion and a half dollars of your money to three of the wealthiest corporations on Earth. The governor's idea is that the tax reform . . . has so injured three of the wealthiest corporations in the world that they can't afford to explore for new oil, re-invest in Alaska operations or, most importantly, create jobs for Alaskans." Citing data from a status report produced by the governor's own Department of Revenue, Doogan wrote, "Since ACES became law, not only has the sky not fallen, but jobs, investment, participation and, oh yes, oil company revenue are all up."[24]

One of Palin's most surprising supporters on the oil tax issue was liberal blogger and media personality Shannyn Moore. Moore had assailed Palin during Troopergate and other ethics controversies. She also broke the story that when Palin was mayor of Wasilla, rape victims had to pay for the expensive kit used to gather evidence. But on oil taxes, Moore said in an April 2011 *Anchorage Daily News* commentary, "Sarah Palin was right. ACES has been fair and created jobs."[25]

So it is true, as PolitiFact pointed out during her vice-presidential campaign, that "with respect to taxes, Palin stood up to big oil companies."[26] Working with almost unanimous support from Democrats and liberals, and against the oil industry's Republican defenders, Palin delivered what turned out to be the biggest tax increase in Alaska's history.

7

Palin Triumphs over Big Oil, Round 3

Alaska's Big Oil companies boycotted the competitive bidding for the state's gas pipeline incentives and worked to derail the process. After an exhaustive review by technical experts and the public, Palin recommended the legislature sign a contract with an independent pipeline company that has built more than 30,000 miles of pipelines in Canada and the United States.

Two of Alaska's Big Three oil companies launched a competing pipeline initiative and worked hard in the legislature to kill Palin's proposal. After meeting in special session for almost two months, the legislature narrowly approved Palin's proposed deal with the independent pipeline company. Once again, Democrats were her most reliable allies. She faced more criticism from fellow Republicans and the state's business establishment.[1]

■ ■ ■

In her first victory over Big Oil, Palin got the legislature to approve her basic approach to promoting a gas pipeline. Instead of negotiating concessions up front with the multinational oil companies that hold the huge North Slope gas reserves, Palin and the legislature agreed on a drastically different strategy. Through competitive bidding, the state would offer up to $500 million in reimbursements to a company that pursues a gas pipeline on the state's preferred terms.

This new process was so different, whether it would work was not at all clear. How would the state structure the competitive bidding? What companies (if any) would apply? (The major gas holders, Exxon, BP, and Conoco, indicated they would not.) How would the state pick the best proposal? And if the state could strike a deal, would the legislature and public approve it?

Unlike Palin's first-round victory on the gas pipeline issue, which came with only one dissenting vote among sixty legislators, this stage of the battle provoked much stronger resistance. The president of the state senate, a fellow Republican, was staunchly opposed. So was the speaker of the house, another Republican. Alaska's largest and most politically powerful companies—Exxon, BP, and Conoco—all fought to block the path Palin was pursuing.

WHAT PALIN WANTED ALASKA TO GET

When she ran for governor, Palin promised an "open and transparent" process for pursuing a new kind of gas line deal, in contrast to the two years of secret negotiations her predecessor had conducted with Exxon, Conoco, and BP.

As requested by Palin and approved by the legislature during her first year, the state would openly solicit proposals from any interested, capable party. An evaluation of each bid would be subject to public review and comment. Bidders would have to agree to pursue a project that met the state's criteria, known as must-haves. Those must-haves included elements missing in Governor Murkowski's previous gas line deal. Most notably, with Palin's plan, there would now be benchmarks for obtaining Federal Energy Regulatory Commission approval of the project.

The state also required five take-off points in Alaska, so some gas could be made available to local use. Shipping rates would be based on distance, so gas delivered to Alaskans would pay lower transportation charges than gas moving all the way through Canada. The gas line would have to offer "open access," so the owners could not lock out new companies that might discover gas in the future.

But one condition in particular especially rankled the companies holding North Slope gas. The state required the project developer to support a method of calculating shipping charges that's known as rolled-in rates. With rolled-in rates, all shippers share the cost of expanding the pipeline system. This prevents a two-tiered pricing system, where new gas drillers have to pay much higher shipping rates to get their gas into the pipeline—a key concern for Palin and her gas line team. They had seen how control of the Alaska oil pipeline had allowed existing oil producers to squeeze out potential competitors. Rolled-in rates are the general rule on the Canadian segment of the project, but on the U.S. side, it was a deal breaker for Alaska's major oil and gas companies.

The Big Three gas holders also complained that the state's offer of "fiscal certainty" was too short and too weak. They wanted a much longer, legally enforceable guarantee against future tax increases on the pipeline. However, the Alaska Constitution prevents such a long-term guarantee, since it prohibits signing away the state's power to tax.

The Big Three gas holders didn't like the financing terms Palin convinced the legislature to set, either. The state said the gas pipeline should be built with at least 70 percent borrowed money, with no more than 30 percent equity financing from the builders' own corporate coffers. That's because under federal regulations, equity investments in pipelines are riskier, and earn a higher rate of return, which drives up financing costs and produces higher shipping rates.

High shipping charges discourage further gas development. They also cut the revenue the state collects in royalties and taxes, which are based on the net price of gas after shipping costs are deducted. But oil companies are in a high-risk, high-return business, and they generally prefer to earn the higher returns that are possible when they finance investments with their own money.

In return for meeting the state's conditions, Palin's plan offered up to $500 million in state reimbursements for advancing the pipeline project. The state agreed to repay 50 percent of expenses for the expensive, detailed engineering needed to produce a construction cost estimate. Solid cost numbers are required so the pipeline can tell potential shippers the rates, or tariffs, they would be charged.

Once the pipeline project solicited customers who want to ship gas, a stage known as open season, Palin's plan would commit the state to pay 90 percent of the cost of following through to get federal approvals needed to build the project.

THE BIDS COME IN

In the fall of 2007, the Palin administration received five gas pipeline proposals. The major gas holders, Exxon, BP, and Conoco, all boycotted the bidding. Conoco submitted an alternative proposal, outside the state's formal process. It did not meet all of the state's required criteria, most notably for rolled-in rates, and Conoco wanted a longer guarantee of fiscal certainty.

Two proposals came from government development agencies in Alaska; neither was prepared to do the full project the state requested, through Canada to the Lower 48 markets. The other two bids came from small companies that also failed to meet all the state's conditions. (One of them planned to partner with Sinopec, a company owned by the Chinese government, and supply the gas to China.)

Many observers were surprised at who did not bid. Mid-American, a pipeline and energy holding company controlled by Warren Buffet's Berkshire Hathaway company, had been considered a leading candidate. A big Canadian pipeline company, Enbridge, didn't bid, either.

The one complete bid came from the only major independent pipeline company that responded, TransCanada. It had more than 30,000 miles of pipelines in North America, including a network heading south of Alberta to the Midwest United States. The company also had rights to a corridor through northwestern Canada, so it would not have to start from scratch in the time-consuming process of negotiating easements with Canada's aboriginal First Nations.

The Palin administration put TransCanada's application out for sixty days of public comment, including twenty public "town hall" meetings in communities around the state.

THE BATTLE BEGINS

The political resistance from opponents of Palin's approach began almost immediately. In February, Alaska's powerful senior U.S. senator, Ted Stevens, expressed sympathy for the major gas holders' complaints about Palin's approach. In Stevens' annual address to the legislature, the *Juneau Empire* reported, "Alaska's senior senator seemed to side with oil companies, such as ConocoPhillips, which have called for 'certainty' in tax rates."[2]

Palin stood firm. Noting that the state offered a tax lock for the first ten years of operation, she responded to Stevens' criticism, "We're very confident we are on the right course." The gas holders want forty or more years of tax stability, she said, and that's not acceptable.[3]

Palin's team continued an intensive review of TransCanada's bid, including the public comments, during the spring of 2008. Drawing on the expertise of national experts, the gas line team commissioned hundreds of pages of technical, legal, and financial analysis, all of which was posted on the Internet.

As with oil taxes, the gas pipeline was a case where Palin hired good people and got out of the way. She brought back the high-ranking experts that had quit or been fired from the Murkowski administration because they didn't support the concessions he had made in his secretive, discredited pipeline deal. Finance and money questions fell to Revenue Commissioner Pat Galvin. Natural Resources Commissioner Tom Irwin handled issues relating to state oversight of its oil and gas leases and related development questions. Day-to-day operations were handled by Irwin's deputy resources commissioner, Marty Rutherford, head of the gas line team.

I dealt with Irwin, Galvin, and Rutherford multiple times on the gas line and oil tax questions. Unlike many Alaska politicians and officials, they did not just assume that what is good for Big Oil was good for Alaska. They recognized that they were handling matters worth billions of dollars, and that their job was to get their bosses, the people of Alaska, the best possible deal.

They also realized they were going against savvy negotiators at multibillion-dollar, multinational corporations—people whose sole job was to vigorously pursue the interests of their worldwide shareholders. Palin's gas line team knew that the major oil companies never open negotiations with their bottom line. They knew that what Exxon, BP, and Conoco say in public might just be posturing designed to weaken the state's bargaining position.

I spoke with Tom Irwin when he was being accused of having personal animus toward Exxon, which at the time was trying to hold onto development rights at the state-owned oil and gas field at Point Thomson. Irwin shrugged it off. Exxon does what's best for Exxon, he said, and he tries to do what's best for Alaskans. You're not trying to be liked, he said. "It's just business."

OPPOSITION BEGINS TO GROW

To keep her pipeline plan moving forward, Palin would have to overcome opposition from two different flanks.

Supporters of the politically popular all-Alaska pipeline route, which would require shipping the gas from the port of Valdez on tankers, won an early skirmish in the state legislature. The house and senate rushed through a resolution asking Palin to let the legislature consider bills on an in-state pipeline during the special session that would be held to review TransCanada's bid.[4] Democratic representative Beth Kerttula of Juneau thought the resolution was just a "smokescreen" from opponents of Palin's deal. Promoting the smaller in-state pipeline, she said at the time, was a way to supply the political cover they needed to keep Palin from moving ahead with TransCanada.[5]

The other challenge for Palin also came in early April, just five weeks before Palin was due to make a final decision on TransCanada's proposal. With great fanfare, BP and Conoco launched a competing project, boasting that they would spend $600 million on it and did not want state subsidies. (They also didn't want to meet the state's required pipeline terms, but they stayed quiet about that.)

Palin's Republican opponents were quick to tout the BP/Conoco project, which the two companies shrewdly gave the iconic Alaska name "Denali."[6] The chair of a key senate committee, Charlie Huggins, said, "The companies are not asking for $500 million of state money, instead they are going to spend $600 million of their own money."[7] He was one of many basically saying, "Why pay TransCanada to do the pipeline, when BP and Conoco are doing it for free?" (The "it" they were offering, however, didn't include all the state's required conditions. That's why the state offered financial incentives to a competing project.)

Conservative columnist Dan Fagan, a frequent critic of how Palin handled the oil industry, crowed, "The birth of the Denali Alaska pipeline obviously means the death of AGIA [Palin's pipeline plan]. . . . BP and Conoco are betting $600 million the people of Alaska will not let their pea-brained politicians hold up the project by refusing to negotiate fiscal terms. So will our governor let AGIA die and allow the free market to do its thing?"[8]

Palin stuck with her plan. She got support from Democrat Hollis French, a key ally of Palin in her other battles with the oil industry. "I hope Alaskans are viewing this with the skeptical eye it deserves," he said. What BP/Conoco announced was an "illusion," French said, to undercut political support for TransCanada's proposal.[9]

Illusion or not, it's fair to say, as U.S. senator Lisa Murkowski did, that Palin at least deserved credit for finally getting the gas holders to propose a pipeline of their own. "By her tough stance over the past two years, she has brought the companies around to building [*sic*] a gas line now," Murkowski said.[10]

Alaskans had waited almost thirty years to get to this point, where major North Slope companies said they would move ahead with a gas pipeline. But the question remained: was the BP/Conoco project for real, or was it just for show, to kill off TransCanada as a competitor?

In late May, Palin's gas line team completed its analysis, which included sophisticated Monte Carlo simulations across a wide range of scenarios. Only in the most extremely unlikely cases—a "perfect storm" of adverse events—would the project be uneconomic. Compared with what BP and Conoco were proposing, the analysis showed, the state would come out further ahead pursuing the TransCanada proposal, with more revenue and more gas development. Given the project's economic strength, and TransCanada's expertise, the gas line team concluded TransCanada could succeed.

Palin recommended the legislature approve TransCanada's bid. "Everything we asked for in AGIA to protect Alaska's interests is in the TC Alaska project. In fact, because of the competitive process, TC Alaska's proposal is a better proposal than we'd even hoped for, and everything in its proposal is binding and enforceable," said Palin.[11]

ON TO THE LEGISLATURE

When the legislature convened in special session to consider Palin's recommendation, both the house speaker and senate president were opposed. Skeptics of the deal took charge of the legislature's review. The *Juneau Empire* noted that "the process appeared to be tilted against TransCanada, with mostly outspoken opponents chairing the meetings in which the license was considered."[12]

For the first few days, legislators heard from Palin's in-house experts, outside consultants, and TransCanada. All the homework Palin's gas line team had done would soon pay off. According to a *Juneau Empire* story just a few days into the session, "Senate Majority Leader Johnny Ellis, D-Anchorage, said he thinks most legislators have been convinced of the merits of TransCanada's AGIA application, and are now just watching the debate." Sen. Con Bunde, a Republican from Anchorage, was impressed. "If we were on the floor, I'd call the question," he said.[13]

But inside the legislature, and in the court of public opinion, pro-oil-industry Republicans were still resisting. One of Palin's most dogged critics was Republican representative Jay Ramras of Fairbanks. Aggressively questioning witnesses from Palin's staff and TransCanada, Ramras referred to their testimony as "propaganda" and said, "This is a fool's errand that we're on."[14]

After hearing from experts and officials, legislators decided to hold hearings around the state. Palin's supporters agreed, hopeful that the hearings would build public support by explaining the deal and bringing citizens into the process.

For opponents, holding many hearings fit with their strategy of dragging out the review as long as possible. If the legislature didn't approve the deal within sixty days, it would die. By filibustering the deal, opponents might be able to run out the clock.

LINES OF ATTACK

Opponents used several lines of attack against Palin's pipeline deal. They claimed TransCanada had a crippling legal problem known as withdrawn partners liability. Supposedly, TransCanada would owe billions of dollars to partners that still had Alaska gas line rights dating back to the congressionally approved project that failed in the early 1980s. TransCanada eventually produced waivers from the "withdrawn" partners that were still viable entities. The company also agreed not to use any of the work that the decades-old venture had produced, to ensure it would not owe anything to its past partners.

Critics repeatedly claimed TransCanada's project would fail, because "TransCanada doesn't have any gas." But TransCanada is not a gas driller or producer—it's a pipeline company that somehow managed to build 36,000 miles of pipelines without controlling any of its own gas production.

Critics also said Palin's deal with TransCanada would cripple efforts to build what Alaskans really wanted, namely, an all-Alaska version of a gas pipeline. They pointed out that, under Palin's deal, the state would be on the hook for triple damages if it helped a competing pipeline project.

However, the critics failed to note that TransCanada agreed to offer shippers the all-Alaska option to Valdez as part of its proposal, with a line running south from Fairbanks, instead of branching off to Canada. Also, the triple-damages threat doesn't apply to a small in-state pipeline, such as the possible "bullet line" that would go directly to the state's most populated areas. A line no bigger than 500 million cubic feet a day, large enough to supply in-state markets, but roughly one-ninth the size of the big line through Canada, would be exempt from triple damages.

Critics did make some inroads with the complaint that TransCanada was a "foreign" company that would take Alaska money to create jobs in Canada. Exxon, BP, and Conoco were not exactly homegrown Alaska businesses. But they spend lavishly on lobbyists and campaign contributions and public relations in Alaska, unlike TransCanada. As a matter of corporate policy, TransCanada declined to play the American-style, big-money political game, explaining that it wanted to keep overhead costs low. It agreed to open an Alaska office, but much of the work would be done from Calgary.

The Canadian angle helped provoke one former Alaska governor, Republican Wally Hickel, into opposing Palin's pipeline deal. As a die-hard, Alaska-first advocate, Hickel could not abide sending Alaska's gas through a foreign country.[15]

Another former governor, Democrat Tony Knowles, also opposed Palin's plan. Known during his tenure as an oil-friendly Democrat, Knowles said the legislature should postpone action so the competing ventures could negotiate about merging into a single project.[16]

In early July, to neutralize criticism from advocates of an in-state pipeline, Palin announced a politically useful, but practically dubious, plan. She said the state would work with Alaska's biggest natural gas utility on a much smaller pipeline to get gas to the state's most populated areas, including Fairbanks and Anchorage. The line might run from the North Slope, or it might run the opposite direction from the much smaller (and declining) gas fields south of Anchorage in Cook Inlet. She even raised the possibility of investing state money in the $3 billion project, to be led by Enstar Natural Gas, with gas flowing by 2013.[17]

It turned out to be little more than a useful political feint. Enstar would fail to get state authority to start billing customers for construction before the line went into service. Not long after, the company shelved the project.

In the legislature, review of Palin's proposal went on and on, day after day. Opponents used hearing after hearing to float critical arguments and try to produce negative news coverage.

VICTORY NEARS

On the forty-eighth day of the special session, Palin's deal faced its first vote. The House Rules Committee sent the measure through to the full house, even though four of its seven members recommended "do not pass."

The next day, the house voted. The same bipartisan coalition that passed Palin's oil tax increase held together. In the 24–16 vote, all but one Democrat voted yes, along with eight Republicans.

Republican representative Gabrielle LeDoux of Kodiak complained that with the deal, "We give half a billion dollars to a foreign company to ship gas to a foreign country." Palin-friendly Republicans and Democrats defended the TransCanada license as a worthwhile investment, which would help prevent the major oil companies from locking up Alaska's North Slope gas. Democratic minority leader Beth Kerttula said, "This is the way out of the monopolistic system Alaska has been living under for many years [with the Trans-Alaska oil pipeline]."[18]

In Alaska's largest city, voting for Palin's pipeline deal was not a politically popular stand. As the senate vote neared, one Anchorage Democratic senator told me that Palin's plan was the least popular option with his constituents. They preferred the all-Alaska pipeline to Valdez, which Alaska voters had endorsed in 2002, or wanted the state to pursue the Conoco-BP proposal.

Palin's aide Joe Balash e-mailed her on July 25, saying, "We have been getting lots of pressure from senate dems that are with us, but who want 'cover' because they are getting calls and e-mails against AGIA." In response, Balash had rushed out an e-mail alert in Palin's name, urging, "Call Your Alaska Senator Today!" with a Top 10 list of reasons to approve the TransCanada deal. Slight problem: He had neglected to clear the idea with Palin. Upon getting a copy, she e-mailed her staff, "Huh??? This is from WHOM? And WHY???" Once Balash explained, Palin let the matter drop.

On July 31, with just days left to win legislative approval, Palin's plan had its closest call. The senate's special twelve-member energy committee approved it on a vote of 7 to 5. Opponent Lesil McGuire, R-Anchorage, floated several killer amendments but withdrew them and said she'd bring them up instead when the measure hit the senate floor. Seeing the news on her BlackBerry, Palin e-mailed her key staff: "Thank you Lord. And you guys."[19]

Time was running short. With a drawn-out debate in the senate, Palin's deal might be killed by running out the clock. Senators could also sink the deal by amending it. Since the bid came through a competitive process, the state could not make approval conditional on new terms that had not been offered to other bidders.

Opponents had reached their high-water mark in the senate committee. On August 1, the full senate easily defeated McGuire's amendments in test votes. On final passage, fourteen senators—eight Democrats and six Republicans—voted yes. Four of the five votes against Palin's pipeline deal came from her fellow Republicans.

Responding to a congratulatory note from her natural resources commissioner, Tom Irwin, Palin called it "an awesome victory" and jokingly credited him by saying, "The Irwin Line will happen!"[20]

Palin and her bipartisan coalition had overcome what the *Juneau Empire* called "strenuous opposition" from Exxon, BP, and Conoco. Opponent Charlie Huggins, a Republican senator from Palin's home region, complained to the *Juneau Empire*, "This is the largest public project in the history of our country, and we're fixing to outsource it."[21]

A TAINTED DEAL?

Later, during her vice-presidential race, Palin would face an accusation in the national press that her pipeline agreement was a tawdry deal, tilted from the start for TransCanada. The Associated Press story noted that Marty Rutherford, head of Palin's gas line team, had a potential conflict of interest. At one point she had worked at a lobbying firm on behalf of TransCanada—a detail the AP claimed was not shared with legislators reviewing the state's deal with TransCanada.

The Associated Press report was done by an AP team sent in from outside the state. Alaska media debunked the AP's claim, and Palin's chief character witness was a Democratic legislator, Beth Kerttula. According to the *Juneau Empire*:

Kerttula said that not only was Rutherford's past employment well known, it was years ago and did not amount to a conflict of interest.

"I'm really unhappy about it," she said.

"I don't believe Gov. Palin should become vice president, but I don't think this story was fair and accurate," she said.[22]

At the *Anchorage Daily News*, we agreed. I wrote an editorial saying much the same thing, even though we had endorsed the Obama/Biden ticket over McCain/Palin. Our editorial said the AP story gave readers "no grounds for judging whether there were sound public policy reasons for those terms [the state required pipeline bidders to meet] or if they reflected the nefarious agenda implied in the story." It was a "skewed account" offering "little new" and relied heavily on complaints that were "fully aired" during the legislature's special session, we wrote. "Bottom line," our editorial said, "Alaska's bidding process for a gas line license was not flawed."[23]

THE OPPOSITION DOESN'T GIVE UP

Palin's critics persisted with their attacks on the deal. Andrew Halcro was one of the most vocal. A Republican who ran for governor as an independent against Palin and got only 9.5 percent of the vote, Halcro is one of the most strident "Palin-can-do-no-right" critics.

During his brief time in the legislature, Halcro won respect for his courage in taking unpopular stands and bucking his Republican party elders. Later, he wrote some thoughtful columns for us at the *Anchorage Daily News*. But when it came to Palin, he just couldn't seem to get over the fact that he'd lost to a candidate he viewed as his intellectual inferior.

Just five months after the legislature's vote, and before TransCanada could do much state-reimbursed pipeline work, Halcro wrote a blast on his blog, asking, "How long will the Palin administration continue this charade?" Like many other critics, Halcro insisted that the Palin administration should sit down with Exxon, BP, and Conoco and negotiate the long-term fiscal certainty the companies are demanding.

State Revenue Commissioner Pat Galvin repeatedly said such talks would be premature. The pipeline is economically worthwhile for them under current state rules, he said. If there comes a point where the companies can show otherwise, Galvin said, then the state can talk about concessions that might be needed.

In the first legislative session after lawmakers approved Palin's TransCanada deal, Republican house members Jay Ramras and Craig Johnson introduced a resolution (HCR12) calling on Palin to reconsider the deal and redo the analysis that led the legislature to approve it. Ramras contended that the 2008 financial market crash and glut of Lower 48 gas were a "tectonic change" that justified another look.[24]

Galvin responded that the state was sharing a big chunk of the cost with TransCanada for exactly this reason—so that work would proceed despite temporary downturns in the project's prospects. "It's ironic that we're in this short-term dip in gas prices that makes AGIA so necessary," Galvin said. He noted that with the state's deal, TransCanada has "a contractual obligation to keep moving forward."[25]

Around the same time, famed author Joe McGinniss joined the attack on the state's gas line deal. In an article for *Portfolio*, McGinniss said it was Sarah Palin's fault a pipeline wasn't being built already. He cited Republican state representative Mike Hawker, who claimed "The only thing standing in the way of an Alaska gas pipeline is the Sarah Palin administration."[26] (Hawker's wife works for Conoco, TransCanada's competitor on the Alaska gas line.)

EXXON JOINS; CONOCO AND BP BAIL OUT

Meanwhile, TransCanada continued to move the project through the preliminary stages, with the state sharing the costs. Palin's approach began to look better that June, when Exxon signed on as a partner with TransCanada. Asked why Exxon did so, rather than joining the project pushed by its fellow gas holders BP and Conoco, Exxon official Marty Massey said TransCanada's project "has the best chance of success and is the best way to get all parties together."[27] Noted Alaska business reporter Tim Bradner called Exxon's announcement a potential "game-changer" for the gas pipeline.[28]

Exxon said it still wanted the state to settle fiscal terms for the pipeline. However, Exxon apparently realized that the issue of fiscal certainty could be addressed later in the process, when it was closer to the time for making a go/no-go decision on building the project. That point is still, as of this printing, a couple of years away.

Exxon's move caused resentment among many Alaskans, who were not happy watching the company line up to collect a share of the state's pipeline subsidies. For almost twenty years, Exxon had angered Alaskans by fighting a court ruling requiring it to pay $5 billion in damages for the 1989 Valdez oil spill in Alaska. Yet other Alaskans, like Democratic state representative Beth Kerttula, realized that getting Exxon on board was essential if any pipeline was going to be built.[29]

In the spring of 2010, TransCanada held its "open season," the formal process of soliciting customers who want to ship gas in the pipeline. Building that line would cost between $26 and $41 billion, depending on whether it goes to a port at Valdez, Alaska, or overland to an existing natural gas hub in Alberta, Canada. At the end of the open season, in July, TransCanada announced: "We've received multiple bids from major industry players and others for significant volumes."

BP and Conoco held their open season as well, with a cost estimate of $35 billion for a line going to Alberta, Canada. As is normally the case, the bids for both projects carried important conditions. Some of those conditions are under the pipeline company's control. But two big ones—a state guarantee of fiscal terms, and what company will get the development rights to the state-owned North Slope gas field known as Point Thomson—would also need to be worked out. After open season, TransCanada/Exxon and BP/Conoco each spent months in confidential negotiations with potential shippers.

By September 2010, the *Financial Times* of London reported that Conoco would "reassess" its Alaska gas line project, because so much gas was coming into the market from Lower 48 sources. By early 2011, the BP/Conoco project had cut its staff from a core team of eighty to ninety people to around thirty or forty. In May, the two companies officially canceled the project, saying they could not secure customers.

WORK CONTINUES UNDER PALIN'S APPROACH

As of this printing, TransCanada has continued its work with the state subsidies it won through its competitive bidding process. However, it has not obtained definite customers or made a commitment to begin building a pipeline.

The lack of definitive progress frustrated Alaskans, and gave ammunition to critics of Palin's gas line deal. Republican state senator Bert Stedman, for example, argued that TransCanada would have to produce shipping commitments by summer 2011. If there were no deal by then, Stedman said, it would be time to try another tack.

The *Anchorage Daily News* called for patience. In an editorial on January 31, 2011, the paper said, "We'd guess most aren't ready to pull the plug on AGIA (Alaska Gasline Inducement Act) just yet; they'd rather wait to hear what comes of the negotiations in both the state-sanctioned TransCanada-Exxon project and the competing Denali Project of BP and Conoco Phillips."

That's the course Palin's successor, Gov. Sean Parnell, pursued. But to defend this part of Palin's legacy, he had to fight members of his own Republican Party. House Speaker Mike Chenault pushed a bill aimed at declaring the TransCanada-Exxon project "uneconomic," so the state could back out of the deal. "There is support here to just scrap the whole AGIA process," Speaker Chenault said. He trotted out a poll "saying 61 percent of the 400 Alaskans polled believe the state should cut its losses and not provide any more money," according to the *Anchorage Daily News*.[30]

Again, the legislature's most reliable defenders of Palin's pipeline deal continued to be Democrats. In March 2011, Juneau state representative Beth Kerttula wrote a strong defense in the *Anchorage Daily News*, saying, "TransCanada has done everything it was supposed to do so far."[31] "Everyone agrees a major gas pipeline wouldn't be economic at today's depressed gas prices," she wrote. "The project will succeed or fail based on the expected price of gas in 10 or more years." Meanwhile, she pointed out, Palin's deal with TransCanada and Exxon is a way "to force progress on essential pre-construction work before we have final commitment from the North Slope producers to ship gas. That's why we are paying 90 percent of their expenses now. . . . We've been stuck at the starting gate for 30 years," Kerttula wrote. "What AGIA has done is finally move us out of the gate."

But where that gate leads is not yet clear. Despite Palin's efforts to bring Alaska a gas pipeline, the *Daily News* editorial noted, "Alaskans are running out of patience. . . . Not to mention running out of affordable natural gas."[32]

8

Palin Triumphs over Big Oil, Round 4

Exxon had sat on a lucrative Alaska oil and gas deposit for more than twenty years. Palin and her oil and gas team forced Exxon's hand (with a boost from her predecessor). Exxon decided to play the Alaska gas pipeline game according to the rules Palin established.

■ ■ ■

Governor Palin inherited one fight with Big Oil that she was happy to continue: the struggle to force development of the state-owned oil and gas field at Point Thomson.[1]

Exxon and other companies had long ago found huge deposits of oil and gas at the field, where the first state leases were issued in the late 1960s. Those state leases require the companies to develop any oil or gas found in commercial quantities. Even though Point Thomson has 8 trillion cubic feet of natural gas and hundreds of millions of barrels of liquid hydrocarbons, Exxon refused to put the field into production.

In 2005, then governor Frank Murkowski got serious about demanding that Exxon and its partners develop Point Thomson. Exxon continued to claim there would be no market for the gas until a gas pipeline were built from the North Slope. The company also claimed that technical issues with the high-pressure gas deposits made it too difficult to produce the field.

In order to hold onto the leases without producing the oil or gas there, Exxon had to submit a plan to the state each year, explaining the work it would do to "develop" the field. Every year, Exxon would submit a plan that made it look like it was moving forward—promising just enough activity to keep the state from cracking down and taking back the leases. Exxon was essentially "warehousing" the gas and oil sitting underneath its state leases until such time as it suited the company's purposes to develop the field.

Governor Murkowski decided Alaska had waited long enough. (It was one of the rare instances in which Palin's predecessor stood up to Big Oil.) His administration, led on this issue by his natural resources commissioner, Mike Menge, rejected Exxon's twenty-second plan of "development." It was the first step in a legal process that would allow the state to take back the Point Thomson leases for failure to produce from them.

The Murkowski administration told Exxon that the field "contains hundreds of millions of barrels of hydrocarbon liquids. These hydrocarbon liquids could be produced using mostly existing oil pipelines without construction of a North Slope gas pipeline." Exxon would have to begin production by October 1, 2009, and it had ninety days to submit an acceptable plan for doing so.

Exxon refused, and just before Murkowski left office, his administration terminated many of the Point Thomson leases.

ENTER THE PALIN ADMINISTRATION

With Palin taking office, Exxon filed one last formal appeal through the administrative process.[2] Palin's acting commissioner of natural resources, Marty Rutherford, refused to reverse the Murkowski's administration's decision.

Exxon then took its case to state court. In December 2007, State Judge Sharon Gleason issued a split ruling. The state had proper ground for rejecting Exxon's plan of so-called development at Point Thomson, she decided. However, she ruled that the state had to give Exxon and its partners one last chance to remedy the deficient plan before the state could terminate the leases.

In classic Palin fashion, she issued an exaggerated claim of victory. Her press release about the ruling carried the headline: "Judge Gleason Rules in Favor of State; Court Affirms DNR Actions on Pt. Thomson."[3]

Well, not exactly. Judge Gleason didn't affirm the state's decision to take back the leases. She ruled that the state was trying to revoke the leases without giving Exxon and its partners a fair and legally required chance to remedy their failures in a way that would let them keep the leases.

By state law, Exxon would get its chance in a quasi-judicial proceeding where the "judge" of Exxon's plans would be Palin's natural resources commissioner, Tom Irwin. Irwin was a strong, no-nonsense commissioner—passionate about seeing Alaska resources developed, but only on terms that are good for his "shareholders," the people of Alaska. He definitely did not accept the notion that what was good for Exxon was automatically good for Alaska.

Irwin's strong commitment to that vision had led him to break with his previous boss, Gov. Frank Murkowski, when Murkowski offered up his wildly unpopular gas pipeline deal with Exxon, BP, and Conoco, offering billions of dollars' worth of concessions without getting the companies' commitment to build the project. Palin liked Irwin's feisty Alaska-first attitude and brought him back as her natural resources commissioner.

Irwin took almost a full week to hear Exxon and its partners explain what they would do to keep the Point Thomson leases and why it was good enough. He was not impressed. In a ruling issued a month later, in April 2008, Irwin concluded that the state was simply being offered more of the same empty promises, with no penalties for failing to keep them. He was offended at Exxon's claim that the lack of nonperformance penalties showed how serious they were about actually doing the work this time.

Irwin was especially upset with Exxon's lead official, Craig Haymes. "I did not find Mr. Haymes to be a credible witness," Irwin wrote in his ruling. Further, Irwin wrote, "If Appellants [Exxon and its partners] do not recognize that they have failed to follow through on commitments in the past, I cannot trust them when they promise to follow through on commitments in the future. And if Appellants truly believe that they have always followed through on promises to DNR," Irwin ruled, "then they lack the ability to understand what a commitment is and I cannot trust them to responsibly develop Point Thomson's resources." He added, "I am not persuaded that this long-standing pattern of broken commitments will change." Irwin declared that the state would take back the Point Thomson leases.[4]

At the time, I wrote an editorial for the *Anchorage Daily News* saying, "Commissioner Irwin, backed by Gov. Palin, has made it clear: The state won't play the patsy at Point Thomson any more."[5]

Bloomberg.com published an analysis comparing Palin to Venezuela's socialist leader Hugo Chavez: "Alaska Governor Sarah Palin, a former beauty pageant winner, is succeeding where Venezuela President Hugo Chavez, a former paratrooper and military coup leader, so far has failed. Palin threatened to evict Exxon Mobil Corp., the world's biggest oil company, and partners BP Plc, Chevron Corp. and ConocoPhillips from a state-owned gas field." Bloomberg reminded readers that Palin had also "raised taxes on oil profits by $1.5 billion a year and rejected industry ownership of a $25 billion (gas) pipeline." Palin told Bloomberg that when it comes to dealing with Alaska's oil companies, "We've got to play hardball."[6] (Note, though, that both Bloomberg's numbers are on the low side. By 2011, Palin's tax increase was bringing in $3 billion extra a year and the cost of a gas pipeline was estimated in the $26 to $41 billion range.)

EXXON MAKES A $1.3 BILLION CONCESSION

After Irwin's ruling, Exxon appealed to state court again. During that process, Palin's team negotiated an interim compromise. In January 2009, the state told Exxon it could keep two of the leases and the company would drill wells on each of them by 2010.[7] By 2014, Exxon and its partners would produce at least 10,000 barrels a day of hydrocarbon liquids from Point Thomson. The facilities would be designed so they could easily be expanded to ramp up future production. To make it all happen, Exxon and its partners agreed to spend $1.3 billion.

This time, Exxon did what it promised to do.

While that work went forward, Exxon, its partners, and the state would continue fighting over whether the state could terminate the other Point Thomson leases. As part of an earlier set of promises to the state, Exxon had agreed to surrender eight leases in the field. To keep those leases in 2002, Exxon had said it would drill at least eight wells or pay a $20 million penalty. Exxon didn't drill the wells and paid the penalty, but initially claimed it should be able to keep the eight leases. The state countered that the 2002 agreement provided that failing to drill those eight wells terminated the leases. Exxon eventually agreed to surrender them.

After Palin left office, the state lost another round in court over the remaining Point Thomson leases. Judge Gleason ruled that Commissioner Irwin's week-long hearing was not adequate due process and told the state it had to start a brand-new proceeding.[8] The state appealed, and as of 2011, the case was still on hold at the Alaska Supreme Court while the state tried to negotiate a settlement with Exxon and its partners.[9]

A KEY PRECEDENT?

At 10,000 barrels a day, the Point Thomson field is not very big by Alaska standards—it will increase state production by only about 1.5 percent. But it marked the first time the state forced one of the Big Three gas holders to develop a state-owned resource before it suited their own financial purposes to do so. And if the state can do that at Point Thomson, maybe it can do likewise with the North Slope natural gas pipeline.

That's the theory behind Palin's decision, ratified by the legislature, to partner with the independent pipeline company TransCanada. It's true the state can't afford to spend billions in subsidies and magically make an uneconomic $40 billion pipeline pay off for private investors. But if a project is financially feasible, Point Thomson shows that it is possible to change the internal judgments of multinational oil companies about how profitable a project must be before they decide to pursue it.

Perhaps it's just coincidence that five months after Exxon agreed to drill the two wells at Point Thomson and committed to start production by 2014, Exxon joined forces with TransCanada on the state-sponsored version of the North Slope gas line project. Rather than join the competing project that BP and Conoco had proposed and then eventually canceled, Exxon has decided to pursue the gas pipeline on the terms set by the state.

Skeptics would note, correctly, that Exxon has yet to make any commitment to produce the huge deposit of natural gas that's at Point Thomson. And the company has said that the state will at some point need to work out some kind of guarantee about future taxes for the natural gas pipeline.

However, the state, first under Palin and then under her successor, has made clear that Exxon's 10,000-barrel-a-day project is not enough to justify letting the companies keep all the other Point Thomson leases. The prize at Point Thomson is gas, not oil. And all analysts agree that if there is going to be enough gas to supply a North Slope gas pipeline for thirty or more years, some of the gas will come from Point Thomson.

Will the state of Alaska's current course, set by Sarah Palin, produce a natural gas pipeline? It's too early to say it will. But it's also too early to say it won't.

9

This is the Record of a Tea Party Favorite?

As a candidate for vice president, Sarah Palin drew huge crowds with the fiery rhetoric of a hard-line, small-government conservative. As governor of Alaska, Sarah Palin ran a big-government state and had a record on many issues that would strike most people as pretty liberal.

She poured state money into bailing out a socialist enterprise, a failing, state-owned dairy, even after state managers moved to close it. She convinced the legislature to put more than $95 million into renewable and alternative energy, with a goal of supplying half the state's electricity from those sources. When prices for gasoline and heating oil soared, Palin got the legislature to give every man, woman, and child a payment of $1,200 as an energy "rebate."

Palin tried to increase state-funded health insurance for children and pregnant women. She asked the legislature to require divestment of state holdings in companies linked to genocide in Darfur. She proudly touted her successful efforts to increase funding for K–12 education. She sought to add money to Head Start, the preschool program for poor families, and to experiment with publicly funded preschool for four-year-olds.

Environmentalists were pleased when she reversed her predecessor's controversial move to weaken state review of development permits. And in a little-noticed change, the Palin administration restored some prison rehabilitation efforts that had been curtailed in tighter times.

She never challenged, or even questioned, public employee collective bargaining rights. Her work as governor gave no clue she would head to Wisconsin in 2011 and praise Republican governor Scott Walker for taking on the unions representing state workers.

PALIN'S CONTROVERSIAL BAILOUT ATTEMPT

As Palin came into the governor's office, the state of Alaska owned the dairy industry's only major milk-processing operation. The state had taken ownership of the Matanuska Maid dairy co-op in the mid-1980s, after it fell into bankruptcy. The Mat Maid dairy was a textbook socialist enterprise—the state government owned the means of production. The government's goal was to keep local dairy farmers—about 120 of them at the time—afloat. They needed a place to sell their milk, or they would have to dump the unsold milk and slaughter their cows.

Alaska's dairy farms began as a social experiment from the New Deal era. In the 1930s, the federal government encouraged struggling farmers from the Lower 48 to make a fresh start in the fertile lands just north of Anchorage. The Matanuska Maid dairy, serving those farmers, was always a marginal operation. It was stuck running low volumes for a small market that had high fixed and operating costs. As the market grew, the dairy imported most of its milk from the Lower 48 because the imported milk was cheaper than local supplies. However, the dairy still marketed its products as Alaska-made and expected customers to pay more for them. It was not a formula for economic success.

As the dairy struggled, critics said the state should sell it off to private enterprise. Farmers, however, feared that privatization would merely exchange one problem for another. The profit motive might force private owners to import cheaper milk from the Lower 48 instead of buying from local farmers.

Six months after Palin took office, the dairy's management recognized the inevitable and moved to shut it down. In southcentral Alaska, there were only four dairy farms left. Faced with a failing state-owned business, what did Sarah Palin, the avowed advocate of small government and free market economics, do? She poured state money into the failing operation and tried to keep the state-owned enterprise going. Palin's handling of Mat Maid demonstrates some familiar themes in her time as governor: a soft spot for hometown causes, a strong reaction to a personal slight, less-than-stellar personnel appointments, and distribution of dubious information.[1]

When management moved to shut down the state-owned dairy, farmers panicked. With neighbors and supporters, they soon staged a small but emotional demonstration. By then Palin was already moving to help them. The same day management recommended closing Mat Maid, Palin had decided to show up for a visit at the dairy's Anchorage plant. Nobody knew she was coming, and she was told to wait for the CEO, who was across town in a meeting.

Big mistake. Tired of waiting, she left before the CEO got there.[2] And within a month, the CEO, Joe Van Treeck, was gone. Palin couldn't directly fire him. The dairy is overseen by a nominally independent body, the state creamery board.

However, the creamery board is appointed by the state board of agriculture, which serves at the pleasure of the governor. So Palin replaced the agriculture board with her own appointees. The new members then took over the creamery board and began overseeing dairy operations.[3] One early item of business was firing the CEO.[4]

Palin supporter Red Secoy had been watching the dairy's struggles, and he warned against firing Joe Van Treeck. "He has already done miracles keeping Mat Maid operating for last 25 years," Secoy e-mailed to one of Palin's aides. "If Joe Van Treeck can't keep Mat Maid going then no one can."[5] (Van Treeck eventually filed suit for wrongful discharge and won a settlement from the state.)

Not surprisingly, the team Palin brought in did not fare any better. The new chair of the state agriculture board was Kristan Cole, a real estate agent who had been a grade-school classmate of Palin's. To run the state division of agriculture, Palin picked Franci Havemeister. The *Anchorage Daily News* account of her appointment described her as "a Matanuska-Susitna Borough local who married into a well-known farming family." The *New York Times* later noted that "Ms. Havemeister cited her childhood love of cows as a qualification for running the roughly $2 million agency."[6] After sacking the dairy's CEO, Palin dispatched an economic development aide, Joe Austerman, to run the operation. He'd been a schoolmate of Palin's and founded a Mailboxes, Etc. franchise.

The dairy's new management combed through records, looking for problems and gold-plated expenses, but they didn't find much. They cut all spending on travel and advertising, but those were hardly extravagant—about $320,000 a year for a $15-million-a-year business.[7]

Meanwhile, the new management actually increased costs by boosting payments to local farmers, one of dairy's biggest expenses—even though local milk already cost more than importing milk from the Lower 48. The new management surprised everyone by showing a profit of $62,000 for the month of June. Favorable headlines suggested a cause for optimism at the struggling state-owned dairy. "Two months ago, the state-owned Matanuska Maid dairy was in such dire financial straits its managers moved to shut down the company," the *Anchorage Daily News* reported. "It's a different story today."[8]

But not long after, Palin's new managers had to admit those rosy results were illusory. Revised results showed that the dairy's profit for the month was just a few thousand dollars. The *Anchorage Daily News*, citing agriculture board chair Kristan Cole, reported that "the company also needs to correct a June report that showed a profit of more than $60,000. The actual profit was only a couple of thousand dollars because of expenses mistakenly omitted."[9] That same report noted that in July, the first full month of operation under Palin's new team, losses reached a record-breaking level of $300,000 a month. By the time it was over,

Palin's intervention to keep the dairy open cost another $600,000 to $800,000 of state money.

One of Palin's harshest critics, Andrew Halcro, summed it up this way: "Palin appoints her friends and neighbors to take over running a state dairy and they end up running it further into debt." (Halcro, a former legislator, never got over losing to Palin in the governor's race. He spent much of Palin's time in office time writing a highly critical blog with extensive postings on her latest actions. On the Mat Maid issue, though, Halcro was probably the best-informed critic in the state.)

Palin's handling of the Mat Maid dairy did stem from some legitimate concerns. Suddenly deprived of a dairy to buy milk, farmers would have to dump it and slaughter their cows—a terrible waste. She aimed to buy time for the farmers while a private operation worked on cobbling together enough state and private funding to launch a smaller dairy capable of sustaining itself. It might not have been such a scramble, if she had heeded e-mails from her staff warning about the dairy's troubles some two months before management announced the shutdown.

Ultimately, Palin did what a liberal governor might have done: The government intervened to help shield people from the real pain that is often inflicted by the pitiless workings of capitalism. She used government money to temporarily help a handful of farmers and about fifty dairy workers.

That's no different in principle from what President Obama did with the bailout of Chrysler and General Motors. Obama bailed out the nation's auto industry. Palin bailed out Alaska's dairy industry. The difference is simply a matter of degree. Obama's bailout accomplished something that Palin's didn't: It saved the enterprises in question. GM is still in business. Chrysler is now part of Fiat. Matanuska Maid is history. Its large plant in the middle of Anchorage is now a storage warehouse.

Palin can take credit for keeping her hometown area's dairy farms going. They now have an outlet for their product: Matanuska Creamery, a small dairy that sells boutique, 100 percent Alaska products. The new creamery, whose startup funding included federal economic development aid, got some of its equipment cheap from the state's failed operation.

Palin's record with Matanuska Maid did not keep her from criticizing federal bailouts. Speaking to a meeting of Republican governors shortly after the 2008 election, she decried those who "may be standing in line with their hands out despite, perhaps, some poor management decisions on their part," and she asked, "When is enough enough?" Bailouts create an addiction like opium, she said. In this case the opium is "other people's money."[10]

She didn't mention how she was happy to use other people's money to keep Alaska's state-owned dairy going for a few more months. In doing so, she disregarded friendly advice early in the process from Red Secoy, a supporter in the heart of Alaska's dairy country. In an e-mail June 18 to her aide Joe Balash, Secoy wrote:

> With the ethanol growth the price of feed is going to put a squeeze on even the best run dairy's [*sic*] in lower 48. . . . I don't want to see Sarah get into something which will backfire and haunt her for the rest of her administration. . . . I do not believe that the dairy can once again operate without lots of government dollars. If she goes and puts 2–3 million dollars into [it] to save livelihood of 4 or 5 farmers it will not set [*sic*] very well with a lot of people in the state. Also by axing board members that aren't yes men she puts other state directors into the position of maybe not being quite candid enough so as not to lose their jobs.

With the Mat Maid dairy, Palin's small-town loyalties triumphed over her small-government principles. The state's dairy farms are in her home region, the Matanuska-Susitna Borough. People she knew personally were affected. There were no hordes of Tea Party protesters objecting to "socialism" and telling her to "get government out of the dairy business." It was another case where running the most socialist state in the union conflicted with the conservative principles she would later highlight for a national audience.

ALASKA CONSERVATIVES BEGIN TO COMPLAIN

By the end of her first year in office, Palin was hearing from disaffected conservatives. Arthur Corliss of Anchorage e-mailed her this complaint:

> You managed to get an absurd tax increase passed with ACES [her new oil tax]. Let's put more money into fat and bloated government. We (my whole family voted for you) sent you to Juneau to clean house and reign [*sic*] in an abhorrent government that has the highest per-capita costs of any state government. . . .
> At this point of your administration I have seen nothing that would compel me to vote for you a second time. . . . You've increased taxes . . . done virtually nothing to downsize government with your first budget, and screwed up the Mat-maid situation beyond belief. . . . We were sold a bill of goods with you.[11]

Linda Wood e-mailed Palin a similar complaint just before John McCain chose her to run for vice president. The resident of Eagle River, a conservative bedroom suburb of Anchorage, complained Palin had not done more to promote school vouchers, home schooling, and "private, military, and christian [sic] schools." In her August 21, 2008, e-mail, Wood wrote, "There are times you act more like a socialist then [sic] a Republican. Another Eagle River resident, Larry Hart, had e-mailed a similar complaint on July 31: "If you are not going to act and make decisions as a conservative republican, pleasse [sic] leave the party. I will no longer support you unless you change back to the reaons [sic] why you were elected.

From the other side of the Alaska political spectrum, Palin got this e-mail from John Burton in Juneau on July 28, 2008: "This State employee, despite the fact that I am a Democrat, thinks you are doing a great job. Don't change the way you look after Alaskans."

At the same time, Palin was receiving a steady stream of e-mails from out-of-state conservatives who were hopeful that John McCain would pick her as his running mate.

A SURPRISING SHIFT ON HEALTH CARE

Sarah Palin's fans among antigovernment Tea Party supporters would probably be surprised by one aspect of her record on health care. After running for vice president, she came back to Alaska and proposed expanding government-paid health insurance for children and pregnant women.[12] She did so even though oil prices had plummeted, meaning the state would have to use reserve funds to balance the budget.

Health care was an issue where she started out on fairly traditional conservative ground and moved in a more liberal direction. As candidate for governor, Palin said she would work on "solutions that will lead to more affordable health care for Alaskans. I support flexibility in government regulations that allow competition in health care." Her goal in doing so was to "drive down health care costs and reduce the need for government subsidies."[13]

Palin appointed a health care commission but no major initiatives came out of it. On health care, the issue she pushed the hardest was a failed effort to repeal the "certificate of need" program.[14] It requires state permission for making expensive investments in new health care facilities. The idea is to prevent redundant investments that drive up costs, because providers will be tempted to order more procedures to pay for their equipment. Repealing this state government rule was consistent with Palin's free market principles. However, each side could point to some evidence from other states in arguing that repeal would help, or actually hurt, efforts to cut health care costs.

Repeal was favored by entrepreneurial doctors who want to grab potentially profitable business from hospitals. They could do so by undercutting the hospitals' prices on high-volume procedures. And they had an ally in the Palin administration. One of her informal advisers was a former campaign volunteer, Paul Fuhs, a paid lobbyist trying to kill the certificate of need program.

Hospitals wanted to keep the program, saying this kind of competition from doctors was unfair cherry-picking. Unlike hospitals, the doctors' facilities are not required by law to give free emergency care to patients who can't pay.

Palin's push to repeal the certificate of need was controversial, and it helped sink legislation with other potentially helpful elements, such as creating a state health commission, and a website with health care information for consumers.[15]

However, her priorities as governor lay in areas far beyond health care. One high-ranking appointee told me that health care and education "were starving for her attention." Oil and gas issues and ethics complaints consumed big chunks of her time. And as her close aide Frank Bailey noted in his book, *Blind Allegiance*, she spent huge amounts of time responding to every new utterance by her critics.[16]

In her last year, Palin made a surprising switch on one health care issue. She endorsed a modest expansion of Denali KidCare, the government-paid health insurance for low-income kids and pregnant women. Her predecessor and Republican conservatives had cut access to the program during an earlier budget squeeze caused by low oil prices. To qualify, a family's income had to be no more than 175 percent of the federal poverty level, down from 200 percent.

Restoring that cut to children's health care was endorsed by the health care policy council she formed in 2007. Palin, though, refused to support legislators (mostly Democrats) who tried to pass that recommendation in 2008. As an *Anchorage Daily News* story noted in 2009, "Palin last year opposed the push to increase coverage—even though the state was enjoying a huge surplus at the time from high oil prices." The change would add coverage for about 1,300 children and 225 pregnant women.

Why the switch? Palin, pressed on why she had now changed her position, kept repeating that it was an opportunity for more children to be covered, according to the *Daily News* story.[17] (Juneau fisheries and business journalist Bob Tkacz told me, "She stuck to 'the message' more than anybody I ever covered. You'd ask her a follow up question and she'd give the same response, almost literally word for word.")

Conservative Republicans again blocked the extra children's health care coverage. It wouldn't be fiscally responsible to do what Palin wanted, they said, and to add government services when state oil income had drastically shrunk. The expanded health care coverage would have to be paid from the state's multibillion-dollar reserve fund, built up through her oil tax increase.

MORE HEAD START, MORE PRESCHOOL

In the Tea Party universe Palin now inhabits, someone who wants to expand Head Start for poor families and offer free public education to four-year-olds would no doubt be called a "big government liberal." Or maybe even a "socialist." Odd, then, that Palin proposed exactly that in her last year as governor. "Palin also called for an $800,000 increase in Head Start preschool programs and another $2 million for the state Department of Education & Early Development to try a pilot program for half-day preschool," the *Anchorage Daily News* reported in covering Palin's last budget proposal.[18]

She got the preschool money. In her March/April 2009 newsletter, Palin reported, "One exciting new development is that the legislature approved my administration's funding request of $2 million for a pilot preschool program." Sarah Palin could boast about expensive initiatives to expand government without angering Alaska taxpayers, since almost all the state's spending money comes from the oil industry.

TAX AND REDISTRIBUTE

Misusing the power to tax leads to government moving into the role of some believing that government then has to take care of us.
—Sarah Palin, vice-presidential candidate, Des Moines, Iowa,
October 25, 2008

When oil prices zoomed past $100 a barrel in 2008, Palin decided that government should take care of Alaskans who were suffering from high energy prices. She proposed giving Alaskans an extra $100 a month to help pay higher energy bills. She had the money to do so because she had passed the largest tax increase in state history, a multibillion-dollar boost in the state's levy on oil production.

"Alaskans are feeling the pinch of high energy costs," she said. "The state treasury is swelling, while family checkbooks are evaporating. The right thing to do is to return surplus monies to the resource owners through energy relief."[19] (When she says "resource owners," she means Alaskans. Most oil development in Alaska occurs on state lands, owned by state government in trust for the benefit of Alaskans. It's an Alaska version of socialism.)

One of Palin's most dogged critics as governor, the arch-conservative radio talk show host Dan Fagan, blasted her: "Gov. Sarah Palin's massive entitlement program announced this past week to help with rising energy costs will hand out millions of free cash to Alaskans, increasing their dependency on government." He called her a "populist" whose main worry was looking good to the liberal media.[20] (Ironically, our editorial at the supposedly "liberal" *Anchorage Daily News* criticized her idea of giving energy rebates to every man, woman, and child in Alaska.)

Eventually the legislature decided to offer energy cost relief as a one-time $1,200 cash payment, not the $100 a month Palin originally proposed. In a newsletter to constituents issued on August 20, 2008, Palin said, "I'm pleased to report to Alaskans that in early August, our Alaska Legislature agreed to approve a one-time resource rebate that returns part of our resource wealth to Alaskans—the owners in common of these resources."

While she and John McCain were criticizing Barack Obama for wanting to "share the wealth," Palin was sharing the wealth with Alaskans through a $1,200 "energy rebate" made possible by taxing the state's oil companies.

DIVEST FROM DARFUR?

During her vice-presidential debate, Sarah Palin surprised many people, including me, by making this statement: "When I and others in the legislature found out we had some millions of dollars in Sudan, we called for divestment through legislation of those dollars to make sure we weren't doing anything that would be seen as condoning the activities there in Darfur."

Socially responsible investing is the kind of cause usually embraced by liberals, not by fiscal conservatives. Divesting from Darfur was being pushed by one of the Alaska legislature's most liberal members, Les Gara (D-Anchorage).

The man in charge of Alaska's $30 billion oil savings account, the Alaska Permanent Fund, warned against the course Gara was pushing. "We believe that the prudent course of action," Mike Burns told a state house committee earlier in 2008, "is to make investment decisions on strictly economic grounds, and we do not believe that investment decisions made for social or political reasons are in the best interest of the permanent fund."[21]

Palin was a late convert to the cause of divesting from Darfur. She was first asked to do so in November 2006. By February 2008, in the same hearing where Burns warned against a divestment mandate, Palin's deputy commissioner of revenue also spoke against divestment. Brian Andrews told the house committee, "[T]he desire to make a difference is noble, but mixing moral and political agendas at the expense of our citizens' financial security is not a good combination." It's a tribute to Gara's intense lobbying, which included a parade of passionate Darfur activists, that Palin reversed course and agreed to support the divestment legislation. Despite her support, which came late in the legislative session, it failed to pass.

NOT A TOUGH-ON-CRIME CONSERVATIVE

Rehabilitating prisoners is another cause that is typically associated with liberals. During the tight budget times Alaska suffered under Palin's predecessor, the state cut back on rehabilitation and treatment programs. But by 2008, the state had more money to work with, as oil prices spiked and Palin's huge oil tax increase began to fill the state treasury.

In her 2008 State of the State speech, Palin said, "We're implementing realistic plans to deal with overcrowded prisons, including rehabilitation and work requirements for the 95 percent of inmates who will re-enter society instead of just 'warehousing' them." Palin was definitely not a "tough-on-crime" conservative.

Her budget proposal included increases for treatment of sex offenders and substance abusers. It also had money to add two chaplains who would, according to the budget documents, "enhance prisoner rehabilitation by encouraging responsible behavior, promoting spiritual growth and moral development while focusing on improving the quality of relationship with God, family, self, and community."[22]

A CRISIS IN RURAL ALASKA

One area where Palin could have shown more leadership and concern was in rural Alaska. Outside the state's limited road system, Alaska has scores of small, isolated communities afflicted by poverty, unemployment, social problems, and brutally high energy costs. All supplies have to be flown in on small plane or delivered by barge during a few ice-free months. Despite the challenges, residents, mostly Alaska Natives, feel a deep connection to the land, where their traditional cultures have endured for centuries.

In an editorial about Palin's return to Alaska after the national election, we at the *Anchorage Daily News* wrote:

> Rural Alaska is another challenge awaiting Palin, and it needs more of her attention than it has gotten. Remote communities had to buy a full winter's worth of fuel at this summer's record-high prices. Residents got some help from the state's one-time $1,200 a person energy rebate, but the crushing cost of energy and generally weak rural economy mean the future of Alaska's remote, largely Native communities is precarious.[23]

Few communities were hit harder by that crushing cost of energy than the Yupik Eskimo village of Emmonak, located close to the Bering Sea, 400 miles off the state's road system. Heating fuel cost $7.83 a gallon and that price was going up toward $9 a gallon, as supplies had run out and replacement fuel was flown in by small plane. A bitterly cold winter had gripped the village for months. Making matters worse, the economic mainstay of the community, its commercial king salmon fishery, had failed that summer. Elder Nicholas Tucker wrote an open letter to the outside world, asking for help: "I am forced to decide buying between heating fuel or groceries," he wrote. He detailed the stories of twenty-five other struggling families, identified only by their initials. "So many in this village are in hunger, without fuel, and other essentials and uncertain about their future."[24]

After his eloquent plea made statewide and national news, Palin was widely criticized for a slow and seemingly uncaring response by the state. She refused to declare an economic disaster, saying a past change in state law prevented her from doing so. At first, she refused to let state aircraft help in the numerous charity food lifts that were being organized. Eventually, she decided to make a high-profile charity visit to the vast, impoverished region, traveling with the conservative evangelical organization Samaritan's Purse and its famous leader, Franklin Graham. Traveling with Franklin Graham helped her look good to the nation's religious conservatives. She didn't look so good to rural Alaskans, though.

For some reason, Palin and the entourage did not go to Emmonak and meet with Nicholas Tucker. He had to travel 100 miles to another village to get five minutes in the middle of a noisy crowd with her.[25] Palin's decision to bypass Emmonak, seeming to avoid the elder who had brought attention to the crisis, was considered a huge slight. Even worse, she suggested to Tucker that he and others might improve things by electing better leaders in their villages.[26]

Palin did send state outreach workers to make sure the region's residents were enrolled in all available assistance programs. Some of her senior staff made trips to the region. In the end, thanks largely to the aid supplied by charities, the immediate crisis passed—but the small and struggling remote villages throughout Alaska saw no improvement in their long-term prospects during Palin's time in office.

10

Al Gore, She's Not

When it came to environmental issues, Palin was a fairly typical Alaska conservative. She reliably promoted development of Alaska's oil, minerals, and timber. She sided with hunters who wanted aerial wolf hunting to cut down their four-legged competition for moose and caribou. She questioned whether polar bears are at risk from global warming and challenged whether beluga whales in Cook Inlet qualify for protection under the federal endangered species act. When a voter initiative that would have tightened antipollution rules for the state's mining industry appeared on the ballot, she opposed it. "A staunch believer in Alaska resource development—and generally skeptical of measures that she thinks could slow or block development" is the way we put it in an editorial at the *Anchorage Daily News* when she was running for vice president.

No surprise there. To win statewide office in Alaska, a candidate must enthusiastically promote development of the state's oil, gas, minerals, and other resources. (Oil production drives one-third of the state's economy.) In Alaska's statewide politics, having the endorsement of "greenies" is like running for office in Boston and bragging that you're a New York Yankees fan.

Palin supported oil drilling in Alaska's Arctic National Wildlife Refuge, a motherhood-and-apple-pie issue that has been deadlocked in Congress for thirty years. Democrats took control of Congress the year she was elected, so there wasn't much Palin could do to help. Democratic leaders made sure the refuge remained protected. One of their few Republican allies on the issue was the man who picked Palin to run for vice president, John McCain. His stand on drilling in the refuge was awkward for her, but Alaskans seemed to hope she could persuade a President McCain to change his mind.

Palin also supported offshore drilling in the Chukchi and Beaufort Seas, the stormy, ice-choked waters off Alaska's northern coast, and on land in the National

Petroleum Reserve. These areas are also owned by the federal government, which controls Alaska's best oil prospects. No doubt Palin would have opened more state government lands to oil drilling if she could have, but the state long ago threw open the doors to oil exploration on the land it owns.

NO AREA NEED BE OFF LIMITS

In Palin's view, no area of Alaska was so special that it needed to be off-limits to drilling, mining, or logging. Like most of Alaska's political establishment, Palin favored "responsible" development, and showed little interest in protecting areas open to intensive exploitation.

She couldn't bring herself to oppose the giant Pebble Mine, a copper, gold, and molybdenum prospect proposed in the headwaters of Bristol Bay, the world's largest wild salmon fishery, the one where she and husband Todd fish every summer. As a candidate for governor, she went to the region and told voters, "I am a commercial fisherman; my daughter's name is Bristol. I could not support a project that risks one resource that we know is a given, and that is the world's richest spawning grounds, over another resource."[1]

Bristol Bay voters may have thought those words meant she'd join them in opposing the Pebble Mine. But her artful wording left herself room to maneuver. As governor, she stayed officially neutral on the project, even though the mine's developers talked about creating an open pit two miles across and more than a thousand feet deep. At one point, plans indicated the mine would likely require the largest dam in state history—600-feet high, creating a lake miles-long to store potentially toxic mine tailings, all in a known earthquake zone.

Palin said the Pebble Mine should be allowed to see if it can get the necessary environmental permits through the state's normal regulatory process. That just so happened to echo the exact argument the mine owners were using to deflect attempts to kill the mine outright.

She also joined the mine's advocates in opposing a ballot measure designed to protect salmon streams from mining pollution. Pebble Mine was the prime example used to promote the initiative, which made the August 2008 primary election ballot. Palin appeared in ads, financed by the mining industry, saying that Alaska's existing laws were strong enough to keep mining pollution from becoming a problem. That argument, and a multimillion-dollar mining industry advertising campaign, led Alaska voters to defeat the stronger mining pollution rules in Ballot Measure 4.

However, Palin's assertion that existing laws were adequate was called into question by developments after the vote. Owners of the state's largest mine, a zinc operation known as Red Dog in the northwest part of Alaska, agreed to an expensive fix for its chronic water pollution problems. TeckCominco said it would build a 55-mile-long pipeline to dump its wastewater far away from a local Native village, where water supplies were being contaminated. Teck also agreed to install water filtration systems in every home in Kivalina, the village downstream from the mine.[2]

KILLING WOLVES IS OK

Probably Palin's most controversial environmental policy was her strong support for killing wolves and bears to boost the number of moose and caribou available to hunters.

According to *High Country News*, a respected journal that covers environmental issues in the western United States: "From the time Palin became governor in 2007 until she resigned in July of 2009, she took bold action against not only black bears, but also wolves and grizzlies. . . . She tried to reinstate a wolf bounty and aerial gunning of grizzlies (efforts that failed); she also authorized the gassing of wolf puppies in their dens using poisonous carbon monoxide (which is still allowed today)."[3]

Killing wolves from airplanes or letting hunters chase down bears from aircraft wasn't a popular policy with Alaska voters. Twice in the decade before Palin was elected, in 1996 and 2000, Alaskans passed ballot measures to restrict aerial "predator control." But urban sports hunters had powerful allies in the Republican-dominated legislature, and they were able to get hunters back in the air, killing off their four-legged competition. (Laws passed by voter initiative in Alaska can be repealed after just two years.)

On predator control, Palin aligned herself with urban sports hunters, especially the Alaska Outdoor Council. When making appointments to the state board of game, which manages wildlife, she chose only hunters and trappers, never someone whose main interest was wildlife watching. Palin's appointees continued her predecessor's controversial wildlife policies, which also included bear baiting. Alaska law lets hunters put out food or garbage at isolated sites to attract black bears (not grizzlies) and then shoot them.

In the 2008 primary election, Alaskans voted down a ballot measure putting new limits on aerial killing of bears and wolves. Thanks to Palin and allies in the legislature, the state spent $400,000 to "educate" Alaskans about the benefits of "predator control" before the vote.

Palin has pointed out that Alaskans are unusual, because many residents, especially the state's Native peoples, rely heavily on moose and caribou for food. Natives and urban sports hunters have fought for decades over who gets priority to hunt for Alaska's game animals, but they could agree they wanted to limit competition from bears and wolves. Instead of fighting over how to divide up rights to take Alaska's game animals, they united on a policy for increasing the supply of game for hunters.

A SHIFT ON GLOBAL WARMING

During Palin's term, it was becoming obvious in Alaska that global warming is a real phenomenon. Here was another case where she staked out liberal ground early then shifted to a more conservative stance. In her early talk about global warming, Palin did not exactly sound like Al Gore, but she took it seriously. Nine months into her term, in September 2007, she issued an order creating a subcabinet working group on climate change, noting:

> Scientific evidence shows many areas of Alaska are experiencing a warming trend. Many experts predict that Alaska, along with our northern latitude neighbors, will continue to warm at a faster pace than any other state, and the warming will continue for decades. . . .
>
> As a result of this warming, coastal erosion, thawing permafrost, retreating sea ice, record forest fires, and other changes are affecting, and will continue to affect, the lifestyles and livelihoods of Alaskans.[4]

She asked her new subcabinet for "a strategy to identify and mitigate potential impacts of climate change" and help "in evaluating and addressing known or suspected causes." Her 2007 order gave no sign she would later become a vigorous opponent of efforts to reduce greenhouse gas pollution. On the contrary, her executive order asked her subcabinet to look at "the opportunities to reduce greenhouse gas emissions from Alaska sources."

While governor, Palin generally avoided the question of what is causing global warming. "The causes and effects are more diverse, complex and scientifically debated than is recognized in the [federal] reports," is the way she put it in a 2007 press release.[5] Over time, she expressed more doubts about the scientific consensus that human activities are a significant cause. During her vice-presidential race, *Time* magazine noted a recent interview in which she said, "I'm not one though who would attribute it to being man-made." [6]

Five months after leaving office, she wrote in the *Washington Post*, "While we recognize the occurrence of these natural, cyclical environmental trends, we can't say with assurance that man's activities cause weather changes."[7]

Palin's subcabinet on climate change offered no significant new policies or legislation. It was mainly a forum for discussing ways to respond to the damage inflicted by global warming, rather than preventing greenhouse gas pollution.

She was not eager to pursue large sums of federal money to help Alaska cope with climate change—something Alaska's famed bring-home-the-bacon U.S. senator Ted Stevens, tried. Seeking federal money would conflict with her rhetoric about shrinking the federal government and shunning federal earmarks.

Her top priority was making sure that global warming concerns would not inhibit the development of Alaska's fossil fuels.

Palin fought the federal listing of the polar bear as a threatened species—an issue in which even the very pro-oil Bush administration admitted that the science was so strong that it had to take action. Alaska's polar bears require large areas of sea ice for hunting their prey, and sea ice is rapidly disappearing as the arctic steadily grows warmer. In a *New York Times* op-ed about the polar bear controversy, Governor Palin accused environmentalists of seeking the endangered species listing as a way "to force the government to either stop or severely limit any public or private action that produces, or even allows, the production of greenhouse gases."[8] She didn't want greenies to get another legal tool for harassing Alaska's oil and energy industries. "There is insufficient evidence that polar bears are in danger of becoming extinct within the foreseeable future," she asserted. In a press release, she said, "Polar bears survived prior warming periods greater than the current one."[9] In her op-ed Palin asserted that her stand "is based on a comprehensive review by state wildlife officials of scientific information from a broad range of climate, ice and polar bear experts."

Note that she said state wildlife "officials," not state wildlife "biologists" or "scientists." She refused to release any information about what the state's scientific experts told her wildlife "officials." When a federal Freedom of Information Act request pried loose copies of e-mail sent by state biologists, it showed that they accepted the federal scientists' analysis. Palin's "wildlife officials" had overruled the state's scientific wildlife experts.

In her December 2009 commentary for the *Washington Post*, she wrote, "I got clobbered for my actions by radical environmentalists nationwide, but I stood by my view that adding a healthy species to the endangered list under the guise of 'climate change impacts' was an abuse of the Endangered Species Act. This would have irreversibly hurt both Alaska's economy and the nation's, while also reducing opportunities for responsible development."

By November 2010, she was even more acerbic in attacking concerns about global warming. A long *New York Times Magazine* profile of her by Robert Draper reported that "human-induced climate change [was] a concept she derides as a 'snow job' and this 'global warming Goregate stuff.'"[10]

AS WITH POLAR BEARS, SO TOO WITH BELUGA WHALES

Beluga whales were another case where Governor Palin's enthusiasm for development led her to downplay well-established scientific concerns.

In Cook Inlet, the large body of water jutting into Alaska from the north Pacific Ocean, the beluga population had crashed and stayed stuck at low levels for years. Most likely, the crash was caused by overhunting. (It's legal for Native subsistence hunters to take the whales.) Even when hunting stopped, the whales had not recovered, so the federal government listed them under the Endangered Species Act. It was another case where the science was so clear that the very pro-development Bush Administration had to act.

Again, Palin challenged the science for political reasons. Her administration questioned whether the whales were a genetically separate population that qualified for legal protection, and whether the federal government was accurately counting them. Her fish and game commissioner said, "An ESA listing is not appropriate or necessary at this time. The population is stable and beginning to recover."[11] In a press release, Palin claimed that existing state and federal laws offered the whale enough protection: "While challenging the listing, we will continue to protect beluga whales," she said.[12]

Her main concern was the possibility that environmentalists could use the beluga listing to challenge development projects. Among the projects at risk, according to advocates of development, were the expansion of the Anchorage port, a proposed bridge north from Anchorage to huge tracts of undeveloped land, and oil drilling in Cook Inlet.

However, the Bush administration listed the beluga in the fall of 2008, and three years later, no environmental lawsuits have been filed using it to block projects.[13] As of early 2012, the only lawsuit pending was the one Palin launched, challenging the federal decision to protect the whale.

SOME MODESTLY GREEN MOVES

Palin did make one high-profile decision that pleased conservationists. She reversed former governor Frank Murkowski's decision to eliminate the habitat protection division from the state fish and game department. Murkowski claimed the habitat division was an extra layer of bureaucracy that slowed or killed development proposals. He moved it to a more pro-development state agency.

Palin took her time deciding whether to restore the habitat division—about a year and a half into her term. And by that time, one of the former biologists told me while I was at the *Daily News*, the habitat division's expertise had been severely compromised. Its most knowledgeable staff, he said, had either retired or gone to work for higher pay with the federal government.

During Palin's time in office, the oil company BP had a series of embarrassing pipeline leaks on Alaska's North Slope. The leaks were due to bad maintenance of aging equipment, because the multibillion-dollar company was pinching pennies even as oil prices and profits were strong.

To her credit, Palin took the incidents seriously. She was especially offended that BP could shift some of the repair costs to the state through the tax rules in place at the time. "My administration ramped up oversight of the oil industry and created a petroleum-systems-integrity office," Palin explained in a Facebook posting on April 30, 2010. "There was proof of some improper maintenance of oil infrastructure which I believed was unacceptable. We instituted new oversight and held British Petroleum (BP) financially accountable for poor maintenance practices."

Palin faced resistance from fellow Republican legislators in pursuing those goals. "The legislature is tearing the rug out of my efforts to prove our ability and committment [sic] to the oversight that's needed," she wrote in an e-mail to her press staff on February 25, 2008.

Although Palin eventually got the funding for more oversight, $5 million, three years later, Alaska didn't have much to show for it, according to Richard Fineberg, one of Alaska's most diligent oil industry watchdogs. "The first two years and first million dollars were largely wasted on preliminaries," he wrote in late 2009. A comprehensive study of oil industry risks, the centerpiece of Palin's effort, had yet to begin. Facing criticism of the study design from experts, the state "put the project on hold and severed its working arrangement with its managing contractor," Fineberg wrote. "During those two years, one is hard-pressed to find any indication that Palin followed through to insure that the mission she had launched stayed on course to accomplish its stated purpose."[14]

The result? More spills—just when Palin was touring the country to promote her memoir. "The series of spills in Alaska during the last six weeks of 2009 undermined Palin's attempt to portray herself as an effective environmental protector," Fineberg wrote. He condemned what he called "Palin's misleading and superficial brags concerning her environmental performance."[15]

One surprise on the environmental front was seeing the governor of an oil state make a big push for renewable energy and energy conservation. During her tenure, the state put at least $95 million into alternative energy projects and allocated $200 million to help Alaskans make their homes more energy-efficient. She announced a goal of getting 50 percent of the state's electricity from renewable sources by 2025. Thanks to several existing hydroelectric projects, the state was already halfway to that goal when she took office.[16]

Palin's top development priority, a North Slope gas pipeline connecting to the North American pipeline grid in Alberta, Canada, was not a point of conflict with environmentalists. It is one traditional energy project where Sarah Palin and President Obama are on the same side.

The gas pipeline would generally follow the TransAlaska oil pipeline and the Alaska Highway, so it wouldn't invade what is now pristine country. And the natural gas needed to fill the line has already been drilled on the North Slope—it's being reinjected because there's currently no market for it. Burning natural gas produces only half as much greenhouse gas as burning coal—a point Palin has repeatedly made. As long as Alaska's gas isn't used to steam the oil out of Alberta's huge tar sand deposits, most environmental groups don't object to the project.

President Obama has supported federal efforts to get Alaska's gas line going and did so as a candidate as well. In early August 2008, an aide informed Palin that Obama had endorsed the project. She e-mailed back, "He did say 'yay' to our gasline. Pretty cool. Wrong candidate."[17]

ENERGY EXPERT?

In her vice-presidential campaign, Palin boasted about her experience with energy issues. She repeatedly claimed Alaska produced "nearly 20% of the nation's domestic energy." According to the nonpartisan organization factcheck.org, that claim is "Not true. Not even close."[18] The group found that "Alaska did produce 14 percent of all the oil from U.S. wells last year, but that's a far cry from all the 'energy' produced in the U.S. Alaska's share of domestic energy production was 3.5 percent, according to the official figures kept by the U.S. Energy Information Administration." Palin was only off by a factor of five.

Leaving aside her inflated boast, Palin's energy initiatives brought no relief to Alaskans who have to cope with painfully high energy prices. In the small, isolated communities of Alaska's bush, where all supplies arrive by plane or summer barge, gasoline and heating oil can cost $7 or $8 a gallon. The state's second-largest city, Fairbanks, also pays a stiff price for relying on costly oil to heat buildings in its frigid winter climate. Alexander Gajdos, a businessman trying to bring affordable natural gas to the region, said in 2011, "Ever-increasing energy prices have forced Fairbanks and the Interior into economic dire straits."[19]

A growing shortage of natural gas in the Anchorage area, where most of the state's population lives, is driving up the price of what used to be low-cost energy. The area is eager to get gas from the big North Slope pipeline that Palin promoted, but that project is looking more and more unlikely, and it wouldn't bring relief for a decade.

In the meantime, Palin flirted with other ways to get North Slope gas to Fairbanks and Anchorage. They included a "bullet line," a smaller pipeline that would serve only in-state markets, not the Lower 48. Her efforts were largely for political cover, and she didn't push hard for an in-state-only line. Alaska's markets are too small to support such a stand-alone pipeline, which would still cost several billion dollars. Getting North Slope gas to Anchorage would depend on whether the big gas pipeline through Canada was built, in which case a spur line might be able to serve the state's largest city with affordable gas.

Alaska's urban gasoline prices still run about 35 cents a gallon higher than the national average, even though the state's gas tax is among the lowest, 8 cents a gallon.[20] The part of the state where most people live, known as the Railbelt, still has an inefficient, balkanized electricity system served by six different utilities. In the Lower 48, an area of comparable size would support only one utility. Palin made a half-hearted effort to force the Railbelt utilities to consolidate some operations,[21] with no success.

It was the kind of boring but potentially important issue that Gov. Sarah Palin didn't spend much time on.

11

From Ethics Crusader to Ethics Target,
Part I: Troopergate

On July 11, 2008, Gov. Sarah Palin's chief of staff informed Walt Monegan that he was no longer Alaska's commissioner of public safety. Monegan was offered a lower-ranking position, and he declined. He was, effective immediately, out of a job.

Before Governor Palin made any formal announcement, Monegan informed his fellow commissioners he was no longer public safety commissioner. Soon, the media learned about his departure and started asking questions. Monegan told the *Anchorage Daily News* that the firing came "out of the blue. . . . If the governor was upset with me for one thing or another, it had never been communicated to me."

Asked by the paper to explain, Governor Palin's spokesperson, Sharon Leighow, offered little in the way of specifics: "The governor feels that the department of public safety could be better served under new management."[1]

Thus began the controversy that became known as Troopergate.

It got that name because of one Mike Wooten, a state trooper who had been married to Sarah Palin's sister. Before Palin became governor, Wooten and Palin's sister, Molly McCann, went through an ugly divorce and continued to have disputes about their children. Wooten had behaved in a way that led Sarah and Todd Palin to fear for their family members' safety and to question why he was fit to remain a trooper. Their complaints about Wooten continued after Palin became governor, and Wooten knew it.

So when Palin failed to provide much of a reason for firing Walt Monegan, Mike Wooten was ready to supply one. He gave his explanation to the prominent anti-Palin blogger, Andrew Halcro. Halcro, a former legislator who had run against Palin for governor as an independent and got less than 10 percent of the vote, used his blog to criticize Palin on almost a daily basis. (It was as if he felt compelled to tell Alaskans how dumb they were to elect a lightweight like Palin instead of a smart guy like him.)

After talking to Wooten, Halcro posted a long item titled, "Why Walt Monegan Got Fired: Palin's Abuse of Power." Most of the post discussed disputes Monegan reportedly had with Palin over funding for his department. But, Halcro wrote, "More alarming than any budget battle, Monegan said no to firing a State Trooper who had divorced Governor Palin's sister because the guy was being maliciously hounded by Palin's family."

Halcro portrayed Wooten as the innocent victim of a Palin family vendetta, with Commissioner Monegan suffering collateral damage. Halcro's portrayal of Wooten was odd, as Alaskans would soon learn that he was not exactly Trooper of the Year material. After the Palins' complaints, Wooten had been suspended for five days for a variety of inappropriate incidents. Most notably, Wooten had made a threat that Palin's father would "eat a f*cking lead bullet" if he hired a lawyer to help his daughter divorce Wooten.

The trooper investigation, which remained confidential until Wooten released his own personnel file, also found that he had illegally shot a moose, drunk beer in his patrol car once, and used his trooper-issued taser on his stepson (because the kid was curious and wanted to know what it was like). Palin's sister also obtained a domestic violence restraining order against Wooten.

After Halcro's blog posting about Monegan's firing, Governor Palin fired back. She released a statement saying, "To allege that I, or any member of my family, requested, received or released confidential personnel information on an Alaska State Trooper, or directed disciplinary action be taken against any employee of the Department of Public Safety, is, quite simply, outrageous."[2]

Her denial was accurate, since it used the words "directed disciplinary action be taken." Eventually, Monegan would agree that neither Palin nor her husband was quite so blunt when talking about Wooten. But Monegan did respond to Palin's statement by saying he felt "pressured" to fire Wooten.

And with that remark by Monegan, the controversy spun out of Palin's control.

SO, WHY DID SHE FIRE HIM?

Her lack of another substantial explanation for firing Monegan didn't help. In talking about a new direction and better management for the department, it sounded as if she were holding him accountable for issues he didn't have control over—such as the difficulty in filling trooper vacancies in hard-duty, remote bush outposts, and other administrative problems stemming from tight funding in his department.

At the *Anchorage Daily News*, we asked in an editorial July 20, 2008, "If dealt the same hand, how will a new commissioner do better?" Two days later, our paper ran a long analysis asking, "Is the 'new direction' for the Department of Public Safety really new?"

Palin went on the attack against Monegan, with a press release entitled, "Palin Responds to Latest Falsehoods."[3] Contrary to what Monegan was saying, she asserted that she had supported more funding for public safety and spent plenty of time with Monegan during many meetings and trips. The release included quotes from several other cabinet commissioners saying how accessible Governor Palin is. However, her counterattacks did not quell the controversy.

On July 28, the legislature's interim governing body, the legislative council, agreed to investigate Troopergate and hire an independent counsel. The vote was unanimous, 12–0, eight Republicans and four Democrats. Republican state house majority leader Ralph Samuels said, "Monegan was so popular with the troops. . . . Legislators are upset about Monegan. That has really stoked some fires."[4]

Rep. David Guttenberg, a Fairbanks Democrat on the Legislative Council, said, "There's something that doesn't quite smell right."[5] The council's vice chair, Republican representative Nancy Dahlstrom, said, "We've had a cloud over our body the last few years since the [federal corruption] investigations have occurred. For the overall good of our state, we just need to get to the bottom of this."[6]

A spokeswoman for the governor said Palin "doesn't see a need for a formal investigation." But, said Sharon Leighow, "The governor has said all along that she will fully cooperate with an investigation and her staff will cooperate as well."[7]

In helping Leighow prepare that response, Palin e-mailed her on July 29, complaining that the legislature was "spending $100g on a fishing expedition." "I invite the investigation," Palin wrote, "but it's obvious to me we could get to the bottom of it all if leggies and reporters would just ASK me further questions." She just didn't understand why an informal process wouldn't be good enough. (Answer: people, including she, might have good reasons to be less than candid about what happened.) In any event, Palin's pledge of "full" cooperation would last only until John McCain picked her to run for vice president. She never answered questions from the legislature's investigator.

AN AIDE CAUGHT ON TAPE

On August 13, the Troopergate crisis escalated. Governor Palin released a tape in which a key aide, boards and commissions director Frank Bailey, talked to a trooper official about Wooten on February 29, 2008. Bailey, not realizing he was talking on a trooper line where every call is recorded, said,

> But you know, Todd and Sarah are scratching their heads. You know, why on Earth hasn't—why is this guy still representing the department? He's a horrible recruiting tool, you know. . . . I mean, from their perspective, everybody's protecting him . . . she really likes Walt a lot. But on

this issue, she feels like it's—she doesn't know why there is absolutely no action for—for a year on this issue. It's very, very troubling to her and the family, you know. I can—I can definitely relay that.[8]

Palin distanced herself from Bailey's action. "I am truly disappointed and disturbed to learn that a member of this administration contacted the Department of Public Safety regarding Trooper Wooten," Governor Palin said in a press release. "At no time did I authorize any member of my staff to do so."[9]

Bailey said he was acting on his own initiative, that neither the governor nor her husband had directed him to go after Wooten. "It is apparent that comments I made to a Department of Public Safety official regarding Trooper Wooten improperly and incorrectly implied that I was acting on behalf of the governor and/or her husband. That was wrong," Bailey said in that same press release.

Not wrong enough to cost Bailey his job, though. Palin put him on paid administrative leave, and within a month, he was back on the job. His "punishment" was basically a paid vacation.

By early 2011, Frank Bailey had grown disillusioned with Palin and wrote a highly critical, tell-all account of his time working for her. He initially had trouble selling the manuscript, which was leaked by the much more famous author of a competing book on Palin, Joe McGinniss. In Bailey's memoir, he expressed regrets about hounding Wooten on Palin's behalf.[10] He doesn't claim Palin knew of his tape-recorded call in advance, or directed him to make it, but he says the get-Wooten operation was a Todd Palin production.[11]

"He was, in fact, the source of every tidbit of Wooten intelligence I possessed," Bailey wrote. He told Palin's chief of staff, Mike Tibbles:

Mike, it came from Todd. Every file, letter, photo, and accusation . . . every bit of information on Wooten came from Todd . . . My actions were always on behalf of Todd and Sarah, no matter what they say now or in the future. . . . At the time [the tape of Bailey was released], I questioned how much she actually knew. After many months, I became convinced she knew much more than she let on."[12]

He makes clear: Todd's anti-Wooten work was not a rogue operation—Sarah Palin shared his concerns and did nothing to rein him in.[13]

At the press conference where Palin released the Bailey tape, she acknowledged that members of her staff had contacted troopers about Wooten roughly two dozen times. Palin acknowledged the obvious: "The serial nature of the contacts understandably could be perceived as some kind of pressure presumably at my direction," she said.[14]

But the next day, Palin contradicted her own admission. In an interview with the *Anchorage Daily News*, she said if Monegan had felt pressured, "I'm sure Monegan would have come to me and said, 'Call off the dogs, I'm feeling pressure.'" As to Bailey's call and the many queries about Wooten from her staff, Palin said, "If that's pressure, then [after] years in law enforcement, how do they do their job if that's perceived as pressure?"[15]

In an August 15 e-mail to some of her staff, she continued denying that all the Wooten-related contacts in the public safety department amounted to "pressure."

> Date: Fri, 15 Aug 2008 09:40:57
>   To: Sharon Bill
>   Cc: Talis 2
>   Subject: Press conf on Wednesday
>   I still don't believe there were ANY Monegan-pressured calls and the closest to that would have been Bailey's tape (but it wasn't to Monegan), or Todd's inquiry (but that wasn't "pressure" on Monegan—it was following Law's website instruction to bring trooper concerns and complaints to the DPS Commissioner, and following Security Detail's request that Todd bring forth his concerns to the Commissioner—it wasn't a "pressure" call). . . . I totally disagree with Walt's assertion that Bailey and Krietzer and Todd and Tibbles specifically "pressured" him. And Talis' call wasn't pressure either.

ENTER JOHN McCAIN

Shortly thereafter, Republican presidential candidate John McCain chose Sarah Palin as his running mate. The Troopergate controversy burst into national headlines and set off political spin wars and partisan combat.

In Alaska, Palin's bipartisan governing coalition began to fracture. Democrats, who had almost unanimously supported Palin's major initiatives, didn't want to see her win national office against their party's ticket. Republicans, especially those who had resisted Palin's initiatives during her first twenty months in office, ran the risk of looking disloyal to their national party. They grudgingly began to say nice things about Palin.

McCain and Palin attacked the legislature's investigation as a partisan witch-hunt because it was being overseen by a Democratic senator, Hollis French. They didn't mention that the investigation had been launched with unanimous, bipartisan support from a legislature where Republicans held a majority of seats. Or that French had joined several Republicans in a bipartisan coalition running the senate. Or that the legislature hired an independent investigator who was a well-respected former state prosecutor, Steve Branchflower.

A week after McCain brought Palin into the presidential race, she managed to arrange a competing Troopergate investigation, on more favorable terrain. She essentially filed an ethics complaint against herself with the state personnel board, whose three members are appointed by the governor. Two members were still serving terms begun under Palin's Republican predecessor, and she had reappointed the third. As required by state ethics law, the personnel board picked an independent counsel to investigate—criminal defense lawyer Tim Petumenos. Palin agreed to waive the confidentiality that would normally keep the entire process secret.

After opening this new track, Palin's lawyer, an aggressive bulldog named Thomas Van Flein, demanded the legislature drop its investigation. But legislators in both parties had supported the investigation and continued to do so. They said the legislature had the right to investigate if it so chose, in addition to the personnel board proceeding.

The state initially agreed to pay Palin's lawyer in the matter. Once she entered the vice-presidential race, though, it looked as if the state would be paying a highly partisan expense. Palin was left to pay her own legal bills—an issue that would prove significant in her decision to resign. Having started an alternative investigation through the state personnel board, Palin now had a political shield for resisting the legislature's inquiry.

The Senate Judiciary Committee subpoenaed nine of Palin's staff and her husband, Todd. At first, the state department of law said the state officials would cooperate and subpoenas were unnecessary, but the attorney general, a Palin appointee, soon countermanded that offer. Two aides and Todd Palin disregarded the subpoenas and declined to show up at the hearing for which they were summoned. Seven other aides filed suit challenging their subpoenas. The seven refused to show up at a later legislative hearing where they were supposed to testify.

What followed was a confusing two weeks of lawsuits. Six of Palin's Republican allies in the legislature sued to block the legislature's investigation. That case was combined with her aides' suit challenging the subpoenas. Within a week, the state superior court rejected both challenges.

While the Alaska Supreme Court considered urgent appeals in both cases, the seven Palin staffers agreed to answer written questions. They responded a day before the state supreme court dismissed both challenges. The next day, the legislature's investigator handed in his report. He admitted that it was not based on any information Palin's nine aides had supplied at the last minute. Neither Governor Palin nor Todd Palin spoke to the legislature's investigator.

ABUSE OF POWER

Investigator Steve Branchflower concluded there was probable cause Palin violated state ethics law.[16] Repeatedly complaining or inquiring about why Wooten was still a trooper, as she and Todd both did, was, essentially, pursuing a personal benefit (in this case, settling a family score), and that amounted to an abuse of her power as governor. "The evidence gathered during my investigation clearly establishes that Public Safety Commissioner Walt Monegan was pressured directly by Todd Palin to fire Trooper Michael Wooten," Branchflower reported.[17]

The Palins' pursuit of Wooten was not done out of fear for their safety, as Governor Palin had publicly claimed, according to the Branchflower report. Todd Palin did not mention fear of Wooten in his many complaints and inquiries about him. During her term, Palin reduced her security detail and often went without trooper protection. Branchflower wrote, "I conclude that such claims of fear were not bona fide and were offered to provide cover for the Palins' real motivation: to get Trooper Wooten fired for personal family related reasons."[18] "Although Walt Monegan's refusal to fire Trooper Michael Wooten was not the sole reason he was fired by Governor Sarah Palin, it was likely a contributing factor," Branchflower concluded.[19]

Nonetheless, Branchflower found Palin had the right, under the broad powers the Alaska Constitution gives a governor, to fire her commissioner.[20] He documented some concern among Palin's inner circle that Monegan was not a team player on budget issues and plans for his department.[21]

Palin's press aide Bill McAllister claimed that the report "vindicated" her—blithely ignoring the finding that she violated the ethics law.[22] In later interviews with the press, Palin touted the report's conclusion that she was within her rights to fire Monegan.

But she went on to make a claim that astounded those who understand the plain meaning of the English language: "Well, I'm very, very pleased to be cleared of any legal wrongdoing, any hint of any kind of unethical activity there. Very pleased to be cleared of any of that."[23]

It was the most brazen, contrary-to-fact assertion from a public official that I encountered during my twenty years in journalism. Anyone who read the report knew that what Palin said was not true. Her claim provoked a cascade of criticism in the national media. CBS, ABC, the *Washington Post*, the *Kansas City Star*, the *San Francisco Chronicle* all pointed out that what she claimed was flatly contradicted by what the report actually said.

At the *Anchorage Daily News*, we wrote an editorial saying,

> Sarah Palin's reaction to the Legislature's Troopergate report is an embarrassment to Alaskans and the nation.
>
> She claims the report "vindicates" her. She said that the investigation found "no unlawful or unethical activity on my part."
>
> Her response is either astoundingly ignorant or downright Orwellian.

Page 8, Finding Number One of the report says: "I find that Governor Sarah Palin abused her power by violating Alaska Statute 39.52.110(a) of the Alaska Executive Branch Ethics Act."

In plain English, she did something "unlawful." She broke the state ethics law.

If she had actually read it, she couldn't claim "vindication" with a straight face.

Palin asserted that the report found "there was no abuse of authority at all in trying to get Officer Wooten fired."

In fact, the report concluded that "impermissible pressure was placed on several subordinates in order to advance a personal agenda, to wit: to get Trooper Michael Wooten fired.[24]

An interesting personal detail surfaced in the Branchflower report. Here's how the *Anchorage Daily News* described it: "Before the 2008 Police Memorial Day ceremony, Monegan sent Palin a photograph to sign and present at the event, but failed to realize that it was actually a picture of Wooten." We'll never know for sure what role this awkward incident played in her decision to fire him—Frank Bailey doesn't mention it in his very detailed account of Troopergate—but it is the kind of personal slight that someone like Palin would find hard to forgive.

Bailey attributed Monegan's doom to another personal slight. On June 30, eleven days before he was fired, the commissioner sent Sarah Palin an e-mail saying, "We have received a complaint that had you driving with Trig not in an approved infant car seat; if so this would be awkward in many ways." She denied doing so and demanded to know who reported it. "In that moment, both Sarah and Todd reached their breaking points," Bailey wrote. When Monegan sent the e-mail—at 9:30 at night, no less—"Monegan's fate was sealed," according to Bailey.[25]

A PRE-ELECTION PRESENT FOR PALIN

On November 3, just one day before the nation made its choice between Obama-Biden and McCain-Palin, personnel board investigator Tim Petumenos issued his report on Troopergate: Not guilty on all counts. No ethics law violation, no abuse of power.[26] Palin's communications with Monegan did not cross a legal line, Petumenos concluded. She never asked Monegan to fire Wooten. Her complaints to Monegan about Wooten were made in discussing other legitimate issues.

As for the governor's husband, Petumenos said he had a First Amendment right to complain about Wooten. Even if she knew exactly what her husband was saying and doing, under the state ethics law, the governor can't be held legally responsible for what her husband does as a private citizen.

Petumenos's interpretation was as generous as Branchflower's was strict. Petumenos ignored the serial pattern of contacts and took each incident by itself. If the account was disputed, Petumenos dismissed it as evidence. On the undisputed contacts, each one, taken by itself, did not amount to a smoking gun—not even Frank Bailey's taped phone call.

Monegan's lawyer, Jeff Feldman, later questioned why Petumenos ignored the cumulative weight of the circumstantial evidence, which could easily have supported a different conclusion. In a long critique of the report, Feldman noted that prosecutors routinely make cases where the proof comes from presenting an entire pattern of actions, which, if taken individually, might look much more innocent.[27]

Governor Palin did send at least two e-mails, directly addressing Monegan about the Wooten case. However, she did it artfully, not mentioning the name "Wooten." She started with a brief discussion of a pending public safety issue and then complained at length about how somebody who'd done what he did was still a trooper, in one case noting he only got a "slap on the wrist."

But Governor Palin's e-mails didn't come right out and say, "Fire Wooten," and Petumenos explained them away. The ethics act, he wrote, "does not go so far as to prohibit mentioning one's personal frustrations and experiences in the course of discussions about matters having nothing to do with such interests."[28]

However, there was one element of Petumenos's report that didn't get much attention at the time. While exonerating her based on the available evidence, he said he wasn't sure he saw all the relevant evidence. Some of it may have disappeared:

> We are concerned about the use by the Governor and some of her staff of private e-mail accounts for government business. . . . This is not illegal. But the practice, along with what we found to be bad advice that was apparently received within the Governor's Office, does not give us the assurance that we were able to locate all of the e-mails. [The "bad advice" was that her use of private e-mails didn't violate the state's record retention policy.] In particular, the Governor and Frank Bailey conducted government business on private accounts. . . . Independent Counsel cannot say that any e-mails were destroyed that were pertinent to this inquiry. Neither can it be said that they were not.[29]

Petumenos also reported that the state's e-mail search and retrieval system was extremely primitive. Some key e-mails might be missing, he said.

NOT IN DISPUTE

Given the evidence that did turn up, some key aspects of Troopergate are not disputed: Well before she was governor, Sarah Palin e-mailed and talked to troopers with reports about Wooten's behavior. She complained about multiple incidents that, in her view, proved he was unfit to remain a state trooper.

Wooten was no Boy Scout. At least four substantial allegations made by the Palins were upheld in the trooper's investigation and he was suspended for five days before Palin became governor. The head of the state troopers at the time, Col. Julia Grimes, wrote this assessment to Wooten on March 1, 2006, eight months before Palin was elected governor:

> The record clearly indicates a serious and concentrated pattern of unacceptable and at times, illegal activity occurring over a lengthy period, which establishes a course of conduct totally at odds with the ethics of our profession. . . . This discipline is meant to be a last chance to take corrective action. You are hereby given notice that any further occurrences of these types of behaviors or incidents will not be tolerated and will result in your termination.[30]

That disciplinary action was secret until Wooten himself disclosed it in the early days of Troopergate. Coming into the governor's office, Sarah and Todd Palin had not been officially informed of what action, if any, troopers took in response to their previous complaints, since state personnel matters are confidential. However, aide Frank Bailey offers e-mail evidence that the Palins were aware that Wooten had been disciplined. He notes in his memoir that Sarah Palin sent an e-mail on April 11, 2006, to *Anchorage Daily News* reporter Lisa Demer, saying, "Rumor has it that Wooten was suspended for two weeks with pay," for some of the incidents the Palins had reported, though Palin complained in the e-mail that "all other citizen complaints against this trooper were swept under the rug."[31]

It is undisputed that, as governor, Palin wrote e-mails directly to Commissioner Monegan, making clear she was unhappy that Wooten was still a state trooper. Her close aide, Frank Bailey, was caught on tape telling a trooper official, "She [Palin] doesn't know why there is absolutely no action for—for a year on this issue. It's very, very troubling to her and the family, you know. I can—I can definitely relay that."

Palin admitted that her staff had made inquiries about Wooten some twenty times.[32] It is undisputed that Todd Palin also made numerous contacts with various state officials about Wooten's conduct as a trooper—a fact even the favorable report by Petumenos confirmed. Todd's efforts scored success on one count: he documented that Wooten rode a snowmachine in rugged rural country while he was supposedly unable to work normal duty as a trooper and was receiving workers' compensation. Upon receiving that information, the state reevaluated Wooten's case and he returned to regular work.[33]

The troopers' union suggested that the Palins may have inappropriately accessed Wooten's workers' compensation file, but both investigations, Branchflower and Petumenos, found no irregularities in how the case was handled.

Two other key points are not disputed: Monegan agrees that Palin never straight-out asked him to fire Wooten. And, Palin had the authority to fire Monegan because the Alaska Constitution gives the governor wide latitude to fire cabinet appointees.

TROOPERGATE TAKES ITS TOLL

From a strictly legal perspective, whether Palin violated state ethics law in Troopergate was a close question. If ever litigated in court, a judge probably could have ruled either way. Branchflower's report was essentially a brief for the prosecution, and the exoneration offered by Petumenos was essentially a brief for the defense.

In the court of public opinion, Alaskans rendered a mixed verdict. The McCain-Palin ticket carried Alaska by 1.6 percentage points less than Bush-Cheney did four years earlier: 59.42 percent vs. Bush-Cheney's 61.07 percent. Considering that her approval level as governor had approached 90 percent at one point, the McCain-Palin ticket's failure to do better than Bush-Cheney was a big surprise. McCain, however, had alienated Alaskans during his Senate career by fighting with U.S. senator Ted Stevens over the billions of dollars in federal earmarks (a.k.a. "pork") that Stevens steered to his home state. McCain also opposed oil drilling in Alaska's Arctic National Wildlife Refuge, considered the state's best prospect for another big oil discovery.

After her run for national office, Palin's approval level in Alaska steadily fell. In his book, Bailey cited an e-mail in which Palin bemoans a May 2009 poll showing "my astounding drop in poll #s. To go from 80+ percent to 50 percent is dramatic."[34] By the time she resigned in July 2009, FoxNews.com noted, "Her approval ratings in the state have skidded in recent months."[35]

It's impossible to say how the courts or an Alaska jury might have come down on the question of whether Palin broke the law. More telling is what the whole controversy revealed about Palin's character and the workings of her administration.

On the plus side, it showed her and Todd's fierce loyalty to family—an admirable thing. Alaskans might well have forgiven her that, if she had asked them to. As Republican state senator John Cowdery said, after the legislature's investigation was released: "I can't put a lot of fault on their trying to defend their family. I'm not sure they went about it in the right way." (Cowdery probably wasn't the best person to comment on doing things "the right way." He was indicted as part of the FBI's corruption investigation.)

Palin got advice in a similar vein from a prominent social conservative, Debbie Joslin, known for her work with the Eagle Forum Alaska. In a confidential e-mail July 27, Joslin wrote,

> IF you did fire WM [Walt Monegan] in part or in whole because of the brother in law, just admit it and make it right. Hire him back if that makes sense and even if it doesn't, just say that you are sorry you let personal feelings get in the way and move on. People will forgive you . . . even if you did make a mistake, we all stand ready to get past it. You have high enough approval ratings that this will just be a little bump in the road.

Palin, of course, could not admit she'd made a mistake. She e-mailed Joslin the same day:

> I'd be the first to admit if I made a mistake two weeks ago in offering Walt a different job aside from Commissioner. Replacing him (as has happened in Walt's last two jobs) had absolutely nothing to do with problems from 2005 with a former brother-in-law.
>
> I never asked, nor pressured Walt in any way to fire Trooper Wooten, as he admitted to reporters once he realized the suggestion had been made. When first elected, my security detail asked that I forward on concerns to Walt about the one and only threat I've known of against me and my family (that was Wooten's). It was appropriate that I did so. I have no regrets in forwarding the concerns to him, as any citizen would do.
>
> No personal feelings ever influenced my recognition that DPS needed a lot more action and results in dealing with some horrendous activities in rural AK, and needed action to fill the dozens of vacant trooper positions that have sat empty for more than two years now.

Troopergate was a chance for Palin to show her mettle in her first real test handling a political crisis. Instead, it revealed grave weaknesses—issues that would become even more evident in the months leading up to her decision to resign. She simply did not tell the truth about what the legislature's investigation found. She said the Branchflower report found no violation, no ethics problem, when in fact it found just the opposite.

Early on, her administration had pledged to cooperate with the legislature's investigation—an admirable, stand-up reaction. But John McCain came calling and Palin switched to stonewall mode.

She filed an ethics complaint against herself to start a competing investigation and give her cover for reneging on her pledge of cooperation. At least two of her aides and her husband did not comply with a legitimate state senate subpoena, one they never bothered to challenge in court. Palin herself never talked to the legislature's investigator. Though candidate Palin had promised to run an "open and transparent" administration, she refused to release the transcript of her three-hour interview with the personnel board investigator who exonerated her.

It was not the first, or the last, time she made a dramatic shift because it was politically advantageous to do so—in this case, to help her ambitions for national office.

Her legitimate concerns as a citizen about one particular public employee consumed an inordinate amount of her administration's time and attention. In his book, Bailey said the Wooten case ate up "hundreds and hundreds of man-hours" of staff time.[36]

The senator who handled the legislature's Troopergate investigation, Hollis French, told me, "Frank Bailey's book absolutely vindicated what Steve Branchflower found: that she abused the power of her office by letting Todd pursue a personal vendetta." Of Branchflower's report, French said, "He was dead-smack on."[37]

Bailey wrote of Troopergate, "This saga, unfortunately, epitomized the worst of Sarah's dysfunctional psyche and administration, including the compulsion to attack enemies, deny truth, play victim, and employ outright deception."[38]

Palin had no ability to see the Wooten situation, and the controversy that engulfed her, from another, less personal, more detached perspective. In an editorial I helped write at the *Anchorage Daily News*, we said of the Palins, "Their passion blinded them to any other considerations. They had no sense that the power of the governor's office carries a special responsibility not to use it to settle family scores. They had no sense that legal restrictions might prevent the troopers from firing Wooten. They had no sense that persistent queries from the governor's office might be perceived as pressure to bend state personnel laws."[39]

An editorial by the *Fairbanks Daily News-Miner*, a much more conservative paper, took a similar view:

> Of course, Mr. Palin had every right as a resident to petition his government, as Petumenos asserted. But, let's be realistic—the governor's husband is not an average resident. When he knocks, a commissioner is going to answer the door, repeatedly. Todd Palin shouldn't have been the one knocking; he put state employees in a very awkward spot. If the governor felt the Wooten issue needed a review, she could have ordered a careful, legal process to do so.[40]

After the critical Branchflower report came out, our editorial in the *Anchorage Daily News* drew this conclusion:

> Has Gov. Palin committed an impeachable offense? Hardly.
> Is what she did indictable? No.
> But it wasn't appropriate, especially for someone elected as an ethical reformer. And her Orwellian claims of "vindication" make this blemish on her record look even worse.

A KNUCKLE-RAP AND A QUESTION LEFT HANGING

After Palin lost her bid for national office and returned to Alaska, neither side was eager to continue the Troopergate fight.

The state senate was not happy that Palin's aides refused to comply with the legislative subpoenas, even though most of the aides eventually provided written statements. Early in the 2009 session, it passed a resolution to that effect on a 16–1 vote. Senate Resolution 5 said, "While the witnesses who did not appear as required by their subpoenas committed contempt, under the totality of the circumstances, the Senate imposes no penalty for their failure to appear."

And that was the last thing the legislature did about Troopergate. But as the legislature and Palin moved on, one potentially explosive question was left hanging.

Here's how an editorial in the *Fairbanks Daily News-Miner* described it: "Palin and Monegan disagree about whether two conversations concerning Wooten ever occurred. Monegan said they did; the governor said they didn't. Someone isn't telling the truth, but the investigator [Petumenos] could not determine which person."[41]

So either the man who was Alaska's commissioner of public safety was lying, or Governor Palin was lying.

On that question, Frank Bailey is a powerful inside witness against her. His book refers to an e-mail Palin sent to Commissioner Monegan on September 27, 2007, in which she alludes to previous discussions she'd had with Monegan. The e-mail, which was among the thousands the state publicly released to the media, discussed a controversy involving another trooper named Spitzer. Palin's e-mail described Spitzer as someone "who had a bad reputation, *along with his fellow trooper whom we've talked about before*" [emphasis added]—phrasing that sounds like Palin's classically indirect way of referring to Trooper Mike Wooten. The e-mail appears to be evidence that Palin was lying when she denied talking about Wooten with Commissioner Monegan.[42]

In Bailey's memoir, he said Palin lied on another important point in Troopergate. "While it is fair to say that Wooten was not Sarah's exclusive beef with Walter Monegan, it is a flat-out untruth to say—as she did under oath in the Petumenos Report, dated November 3, 2008—"*that the Wooten matter played no role in her decision to terminate Mr. Monegan.*"[43] (emphasis in original)

It would have been interesting to see both Palin and Monegan speak to the matter, in public, under oath, so people could judge for themselves who was more credible. However, the legislature did not have any interest in provoking such a high-stakes confrontation, and Alaskans did not insist on it.

Troopergate was over. It was time to move on.

12

From Ethics Crusader to Ethics Target, Part II: Oops! Not All Those Ethics Complaints Were Frivolous

Troopergate was just the first of many ethics controversies for Gov. Sarah Palin. But before Palin ever won the governor's race, she had to deal with an ethics problem that came to light during the Republican primary for governor—one that might have sunk a lesser candidate. Though it never resulted in a formal complaint or charge, Alaskans learned that she had used her office for partisan purposes when she was mayor of Wasilla.

In recapping the story during the 2006 gubernatorial campaign, the *Anchorage Daily News* wrote,

> Public-record requests of the City of Wasilla revealed Palin campaigning for lieutenant governor in 2002 on city time. The records . . . showed Palin arranging campaign travel from the mayor's office and using her administrative assistant to write thank-yous to campaign donors. . . . Palin responded by calling the accusations exaggerated. . . . She said she apologized for any mistakes. Mostly, she dismissed the charges as last-minute smears by desperate opponents.[1]

It was the same offense that Republican Party chair Randy Ruedrich had committed when he worked at the Alaska Oil and Gas Conservation Commission. The person who blew the whistle on Ruedrich was none other than his fellow commissioner, Sarah Palin.

The Ruedrich case catapulted Palin to statewide fame as an ethics reformer. From there, she built a strong image as the crusading champion of high ethical standards. Her image was so strong that she easily withstood the news that she had used her public office in Wasilla for inappropriate partisan activity.

It was the first in what would be many contradictions in her record on ethics—and after Troopergate, her critics were eager to point them out. That scandal had revealed that the paragon of ethics reform was less than perfect in her own behavior. Politically, the once highly popular governor was now vulnerable. For her critics, it was open season. Upwards of twenty other ethics-type charges were formally filed against her or aired in public.

Most of the official cases were quickly dismissed—some were downright frivolous. But in a few, an investigation found some legitimate grounds for concern—even as she was claiming she "won" all of them. In the process, she began to look more and more like the kind of politician she once railed against—the type who takes advantage of the perks of office and, when caught in questionable behavior, invokes the classic defense: "But I didn't break any law."

COMPLAINTS APLENTY

Alaska law makes it easy to file a formal ethics complaint. It is also easy to make a media splash about filing one, because there is no penalty for violating the confidentiality that is supposed to apply to the process. And file complaints her critics did.[2]

One claimed she broke the ethics law because she publicly said she would vote no on an antipollution initiative appearing on the state's August 2006 primary ballot. (Apparently the complainer thought a governor has to surrender the right to free speech on a ballot measure.)

Another claimed that she improperly used her office for political purposes by talking to reporters about her unsuccessful vice-presidential campaign while sitting in her state office. (As if she were supposed to step outside into the Juneau rain to answer their questions.)

A third one claimed that the ethics law somehow barred her from campaigning for Georgia U.S. senate candidate Saxby Chambliss in late fall 2008.

One complaint asserted, without any evidence, that Palin had been paid to do radio and TV interviews after she lost the vice-presidential race. (That one was so sloppy it was dismissed almost immediately.)

There was even one complaint supposedly filed by "Edna Birch," which as the Associated Press later pointed out, was "a busybody character on the British soap opera Emmerdale." That one was dismissed after Palin's lawyer reported there was no record of any Alaskan by that name.

Another ethics complaint took Palin to task for going to a Right to Life event in Indiana, just as the Alaska legislature was finishing its work in 2009. Sondra Tompkins alleged that Palin should have stayed in the state capital and was essentially moonlighting for her political action committee, SarahPAC. That one was quickly dismissed by an investigator, who said Palin's travels may have been politically unwise, but they were not illegal. If voters wanted a remedy, the investigator said, it would have to come at the ballot box, not through the ethics law.

In yet another case, Palin was accused of improperly advancing her own political career by using state funds to appear in ads promoting Alaska seafood in national publications. Palin's only involvement was to give permission to use her picture, and the ads were arranged before she was recruited to run for national office, so the complaint was dismissed. However, it certainly didn't hurt her political ambitions to have state money spent getting her name and photo into national media.

Some complaints had more substance. When Palin's husband was running the Iron Dog snowmobile race, Palin showed up in logo gear from her husband's sponsor, Arctic Cat. Palin said she didn't get any money for wearing the company's clothes, and the resulting ethics complaint was dismissed.

However, Todd Palin was a professional snowmobile racer, and his Arctic Cat sponsorship was worth $7,500 in 2007. It's not hard to imagine an astute sponsor trying to take advantage of having a racer whose wife is nationally prominent and parlay a small sponsorship of her husband into much more valuable publicity. And indeed, Governor Palin appeared in a *Sports Illustrated* online photo wearing Arctic Cat gear. It was the kind of situation a politician setting the highest possible ethical standards would avoid. But that was not the kind of politician Palin was. In a snarky press release condemning the entire episode, she said,

> Yes, I wore Arctic Cat snow gear at an outdoor event, because it was cold outside, and by the way, today, I am wearing clothes bearing the names of Alaska artists, and a Glennallen Panthers basketball hoodie. I am a walking billboard for the team's fundraiser! Should I expect to see an ethics charge for wearing these, or the Carhartts I wear to many public events?[3]

One of Palin's most dogged critics was Andree McLeod. She filed at least half a dozen ethics charges, including one after Palin announced her resignation but before she actually left office. McLeod was originally a Palin supporter but soon grew disenchanted with her. Palin and her team said it was because Palin wouldn't hire McLeod for a job in her administration.

Andree was well known to journalists in Anchorage for many years. She liked being in the middle of political controversy, pushing her grievance of the moment. I viewed Andree as a gadfly who occasionally had gripes that were worth checking out. Whether or not she was a disgruntled job seeker, McLeod had a well-honed sense of righteousness that Palin somehow offended. She went after Governor Palin with the same passionate obsession Todd Palin showed in going after trooper Mike Wooten.

McLeod's first complaint scored a small tarnish on Palin's squeaky-clean ethical image. A Palin supporter named Tom Lamal had been seeking a state job, but his qualifications didn't quite fit the position as advertised. Palin's staff, particularly Frank Bailey, helped get the position redefined so Lamal could be hired. An investigation found no violation of the ethics law, but found some e-mails in which her staff made comments that proved politically embarrassing. The investigator recommended that Bailey, Palin's director for political appointments, get formal ethics training.

Palin would later seize on this incident to attack Bailey's credibility, after he published his tell-all memoir, which accuses her of being untruthful, along with many other sins. She told *Fox News Sunday* on June 5, 2011, "Frank Bailey has some ethical problems of his own." Of all the 24,000 employees in her administration, she said, "It was only Frank Bailey who was ordered to undergo ethics training." She conveniently neglected to mention how she had put Bailey on paid leave for a month, instead of firing him, after he was caught on tape pressuring the state troopers to fire Palin's ex-brother-in-law.

In Palin's defense, some of McLeod's complaints were nit-picky. She filed one asserting that the governor's official website should not have posted this brief statement about her selection as vice-presidential candidate: "It is a great privilege to be John McCain's running mate and to be considered by the American people for the Vice Presidency. This honor is a testament to the reforms and progress we have made together in Alaska. Now is the time to take that spirit of reform to Washington."

In the same complaint, McLeod said Palin's state-paid spokesperson, Bill McAllister, should not have answered media questions about whether Palin would be attending a partisan political event in Washington, D.C. Both allegations were dismissed.

TEA PARTY, TAKE NOTE

Some of McLeod's complaints raised interesting questions—the kind that might resonate with antigovernment Tea Party critics who don't like a system that's tilted in favor of incumbents and helps them stay in office.

Was it OK for the governor to collect her state salary when she was campaigning full time in the Lower 48? An independent legal analysis of McLeod's complaint on this score said yes. It ruled that state law explicitly allows Alaska's governor to run for a different office and still collect a state salary. Complaint dismissed. Tea Party, take note: on Palin's home turf, taxpayers have to subsidize the ambitious politician aspiring to higher office.

Was it OK for a key Palin aide, Kris Perry, to travel on state time, at state expense, with Palin to partisan functions in the Lower 48? Perry had taken personal leave to accompany Governor Palin to the Republican National Convention. But later, Perry stayed on the state payroll when she went with Palin on the national campaign trail and to other Republican events after the election. A review by the attorney general's office found Perry did not violate the ethics law. Alaska governors traveling outside the state, even to partisan events, typically take along staff to help conduct official state business. That, the investigator found, is what Perry was doing. Perry had formally asked for ethics guidance and received clearance to take the travel assignment.

In the Kris Perry case, an elected official's partisan ambitions caused additional expense for Alaska taxpayers. Both cases involving Palin's political travels out of state show the advantages that incumbents enjoy once they get into office—a common subject of complaint from the antigovernment conservatives who so enthusiastically support Palin.

Another situation that was legal ended up causing Palin considerably more embarrassment—and financial pain. During her vice-presidential campaign, the *Washington Post* reported that Palin collected state travel payments—per diem for meals—while living at her Wasilla home and commuting to the governor's office in Anchorage. She collected almost $17,000 covering 312 nights.[4]

A month before she left office, a critic filed an ethics complaint about that, seeking reimbursement of the money. Palin contended the meal charges were legal, because her official duty station was Juneau, so when she was at home she was officially on "travel" status. It was another instance in which Palin looked like a politician taking full advantage of the perks of office. She eventually had to pay back taxes on the income from the meal money, which the state payroll office had never included on her W-2.[5] Palin had a similar back-tax problem from using a car the state provided to her as part of her job. The IRS considered it a taxable benefit, but the income never appeared on her state-issued W-2.[6]

Her unreported, untaxed free-ride income was the same tax problem that cost former U.S. Senate Democratic leader Tom Daschle the chance to work in the Obama administration. Daschle hadn't paid taxes on the value of his employer-sponsored ride. (His ride, in a limo complete with chauffeur, was much better than Palin's.) Unlike Daschle, Palin weathered this tax problem easily. She simply turned in her state car, paid the taxes (as far as we know), and went on her way.

But she wasn't happy about it. In the unpublished version of his manuscript, Frank Bailey included this e-mail from Palin:

> I paid taxes off the W2s the state provided me—this was an inconvenience for other ex branch officials (not just me) and I was never hiding anything, in fact we've been asking for months what the conclusion was. . . .

> The whole story is about me. Its [*sic*] as if I did something wrong.

. . . I swear I've been banging my head against a wall trying to get answers on housing, travel, First Family, etc for TWO YEARS and no one could give me answers. Anyway—it sucks to be made to look like I've done something wrong when we,ve [*sic*] been sacrificing family time, resources, etc in order to do it right.[7]

Less than a week before Palin left office, her nemesis, McLeod, filed another complaint, this time alleging Palin had received various gifts without disclosing them. McLeod pointed to a big backlog of unopened mail, possibly including gifts, in the governor's office. Members of Palin's extended family, McLeod claimed, took unspecified free trips that required disclosure. Citing news clips, McLeod claimed that Palin should have disclosed that she accepted political advice from John Coale, a politically connected lawyer in Washington, D.C. (It's unclear whether the advice was the kind Coale would normally charge for, or the kind a friend provides. Coale is married to Palin-friendly Fox broadcaster Greta Von Susteren.)

The last-minute complaint was classic Andree McLeod: a mix of the petty (unopened mail) and the potentially significant (free family travel)—but she didn't provide any evidence of the latter. It's unclear what became of that complaint. All we know is that it did not produce a finding of probable cause that Palin violated the ethics law. (That is the stage at which the confidentiality of the process is lifted.)

As a short-timer in office, Palin was already starting to bypass the mainstream media, using the safe, no-follow-up-questions communication outlets of Facebook and Twitter. She blasted McLeod's last complaint in seven tweets on July 20, 2009, including these: "In violation of Ethics Act more allegations were filed today by serial complainer; gave to press be4 we could respond; ridiculous, wasteful . . . it costs political critics NOTHING to file/play their wasteful game; They should debate policy in political arena, not hide w/process abuse."

WE WON THEM ALL?

Over the past nine months I've been accused of all sorts of frivolous ethics violations—such as holding a fish in a photograph, wearing a jacket with a logo on it, and answering reporters' questions. Every one—all 15 of the ethics complaints have been dismissed. We've won!
                 —Sarah Palin, resignation speech, July 3, 2009

Palin and her staff also have been misstating the outcome of at least two known investigations. . . . To claim an unbroken string of victories, Palin had to exclude the legislative investigation that found she had abused her power, a Personnel Board case in which she reimbursed the state

for questionable travel expenses, and another Personnel Board case in which a staff member was referred for ethics training.
                                        —*Juneau Empire*, July 26, 2009

Speaking strictly in legalistic terms, Governor Palin was correct at the time she spoke on July 3: all fifteen complaints formally filed against her under the Executive Branch Ethics Act were dismissed, without any formal admission or finding of guilt.

However, the Troopergate case had produced a mixed verdict—a different investigation, launched by the Republican-dominated legislature with unanimous, bipartisan support, found she had in fact violated the state's ethics law.

As for the complaint involving her children's state-paid travel, the *Juneau Empire* noted that it's a stretch to say the outcome qualifies as a "victory." Palin agreed to repay the state for ten cases of questionable billings for trips her children took with her, more than $6,800 worth.[8] One of those trips involved a $700-a-night hotel room in New York. Another saw her daughters spend several nights at the Ritz-Carlton in Philadelphia. The state had also paid to fly daughter Piper to see her dad start his long-distance snowmobile race, the Iron Dog, and to attend her mother's political speech that evening.

More disturbing, Palin did some after-the-fact alterations to the travel records in order to better justify taking her children along. According to an October 22, 2008, Associated Press report:

> After Republican presidential nominee Sen. John McCain chose Palin as his running mate and reporters asked for the records, Palin ordered changes to previously filed expense reports for her daughters' travel.
>
> In the amended reports, Palin added phrases such as "First Family attending" and "First Family invited" to explain the girls' attendance.

For Piper's trip to see her dad's snowmobile race, the AP reported, "Palin later had the relevant expense forms changed to describe the girls' business as 'First Family official starter for the start of the Iron Dog race.' . . . Some organizers of these events said they were surprised when the Palin children showed up uninvited, or said they agreed to a request by the governor to allow the children to attend."

E-mails between Palin and her administrative assistant, Janice Mason, dated August 1, 2008, show them discussing how the travel authorizations (referred to as TA's) were "retyped" to "more fully explain each trip/event."

As a candidate, Palin said she would do things differently from other politicians—and in the case of her children's travel she did. The AP story noted that the only other recent governor with school-aged children, Tony Knowles, never billed the state for their travel. "I cannot recall any instance during my eight years as governor where it would have been appropriate to claim they performed state business," Knowles told the AP.

When Palin announced the settlement of the children's travel complaint and her repayments, she went into full spin mode. She said the investigation found "that I broke no laws or ethics rules . . . there is no fault to be ascribed to me." The problem was not her judgment; she said it was "the lack of clarity in the formal guidance regarding travel."[9]

Here, as in the other ethics cases, facing questions about her behavior, she invoked the typical politician's defense: "I didn't break any law."

THE "VICTORY" STRING ENDS

After Palin's resignation speech, her unbroken string of dismissed ethics complaints was broken. Investigator Tom Daniel found "probable cause" that a trust fund set up for Palin, and formally endorsed by her when she was still governor, violated state ethics laws. Taking money from the fund, Daniel found, "will violate the Ethics Act prohibition against a public officer accepting gifts intended to influence performance of official duties."[10] To avoid a violation and end the case, Palin could refund the money or agree not to take it. Daniel noted that the trust fund solicited money for her legal bills, but it was not limited to that use.

Palin and her allies fought back against Daniel's preliminary ruling. They said there wasn't any ethics violation—yet—because she hadn't actually accepted any money from the fund. Her supporters also charged investigator Daniel with bias, even though he had handled five other ethics cases involving Palin and dismissed them all. Daniel had given money to Democratic candidates and was part of a large national law firm that had represented the Obama campaign.

The trust fund case dragged out for almost a year, long after Palin had resigned. It was handed over to a new investigator, the man who had exonerated her in the personnel board's Troopergate inquiry: Tim Petumenos. Palin critic McLeod was quick to question his objectivity, since others in his law firm did a fair amount of business with the state of Alaska, whose CEO was Sarah Palin.

Petumenos started from scratch but came to a similar conclusion as the departed Tom Daniel. On June 25, 2010, the *Anchorage Daily News* reported,

> An investigator has determined former Gov. Sarah Palin's legal defense fund broke state ethics law and said Palin has agreed to settle the matter by having the trust return more than $386,000 to donors.
>
> Tim Petumenos, an Anchorage attorney hired by the state Personnel Board to investigate, said Thursday the legal defense fund violated state

law because it "constituted using public office to obtain private benefit." He said the fund, which was set up while Palin was still governor, inappropriately announced it was the "official website" of Palin.

Petumenos found that "the terms of the trust showed that its benefits to Palin weren't limited to legal fees, and that her family, and other members of the executive branch, could also tap into the fund," according to the *Daily News* report.

Palin had ignored the advice of her personal attorney to check with the state attorney general's office and make sure the trust fund complied with Alaska's ethics law. She instead relied on the advice of out-of-state attorneys who had advised other Republicans on ethics questions, according to Petumenos's report. For that reason, she did not "knowingly" break the law, he concluded.

Palin and her supporters immediately began raising replacement money through a new legal defense fund. By then a private citizen, she was legally free to do so.

In his investigation of the trust fund, Daniel had shown some sympathy for Palin, saying the case raised a legitimate policy question: how is an Alaska public official supposed to handle the potentially huge expense of a legal defense for official actions and not violate the ethics law? He recommended changing the law so that the attorney general can provide free legal defense to the official in question.

With Palin gone, that question was never really engaged in the legislature, which had a bad case of Palin fatigue. In 2010 and 2011, Democratic representative Max Gruenberg pushed bills to repay an official's legal expenses if exonerated in an ethics case, but the measures never made it to a vote of the full house, which was controlled by Republicans. (In 2010, a bipartisan majority in the state senate voted to prevent a governor from living at home and collecting state per diem payments, as Palin had done, but the Republican-run state house did not follow suit.)

Palin's record disappointed some key supporters who had helped launch her early ethics reforms. Wev Shea, the Republican who had been a U.S. attorney for Alaska and coauthored a white paper for incoming Governor Palin on ethics reform, told the *Juneau Empire*, "She has used the ethics process to protect herself from obvious wrongdoing. . . . If these ethics complaints are so frivolous, why are they so worried about them?"[11]

Shea's coauthor on the ethics project for Palin, Democrat Ethan Berkowitz, was even more harsh. He told the *Juneau Empire*, "The administration has been bullying people who lodge complaints. That's a completely unacceptable use of the government's power."

It's ironic that Palin was beleaguered by publicity about complaints that were dismissed and should have remained confidential under the ethics law. She might have been better off if the legislature had passed the controversial ethics bill that it rejected before she took office. In that bill, Republican senator Ralph Seekins had inserted a poison pill that helped sink the ethics reform effort. He insisted on stiff penalties for violating the confidentiality that is supposed to apply to ethics complaints.[12] If his proposal had passed, many of those dismissed ethics complaints against Palin might never have been filed, or might have remained forever locked out of sight.

RESIGNING DIDN'T END THE CONTROVERSIES

After Palin left office, critics did some digging into her property tax records and found an embarrassing omission from her time as governor. She, her husband, and a friend owned remote recreation land that had been undeveloped for a while. But after they built two cabins on it, they did not report the improvement to the local taxing authority. (Prominent anti-Palin blogger Jeanne Devon documented the incident thoroughly on her website, The Mudflats).[13]

The taxing authority, the Matanuska-Susitna Borough, does not require building permits and has no way of tracking when something is built on a property. Owners are on the honor system—and the Palins did not report their new structures, which the tax assessor later determined were worth $99,700. The Palins owed no back taxes for failing to report their new cabin. But it was another blemish on the record of the woman struggling to maintain her image as a crusading ethics reformer.

Palin suffered another blemish on her ethics record in 2011 when disillusioned aide Frank Bailey began shopping the memoir of his career working for her. Looking back at an incident from her gubernatorial campaign, Bailey charged that Palin illegally cooperated with the Republican Governor's Association (RGA) to help the group get good video footage of her in action.[14]

The RGA was shooting the footage for ads that would advocate her election as governor. According to applicable campaign financing laws, the RGA ads were supposed to be completely independent of Palin's own campaign. But there she was, Bailey wrote, at an event in Anchorage's Hotel Captain Cook, repeatedly walking in front of the RGA's camera crew, making sure they got the footage they wanted.[15] It wasn't the most blatant and underhanded violation of campaign laws ever reported, but if Bailey is to be believed, it was a case where Palin did not apply the highest possible standards to her own conduct.

Palin unfailingly portrayed herself as innocent victim besieged by unfair, unfounded ethics cases. And certainly, there was an element of harassment to many of the formally filed ethics complaints against her. But as Juneau state senator Dennis Egan, whom Palin appointed to his seat, told the *Juneau Empire*, "Some of them were frivolous, but dog-gone-it, not all of them were."[16]

13

Personnel (Mis)Management

As an insurgent who rose outside of the Republican power structure, Palin didn't have a deep talent pool for filling the ranks of her administration. Two terms as mayor of a town with 7,000 people didn't give her that many potential recruits for helping run the multibillion-dollar enterprise known as the state of Alaska. Team Palin had a few solid performers, especially in oil and gas policy, but in other areas, it was amateur hour. She relied heavily on people she knew from her hometown, some of them from her school days.

Her disorganized management style tended to burn out those working closely with her. Palin had more press aides than Liz Taylor had husbands. Almost nobody had ever heard of the small-town lawyer she picked to be her first attorney general. Palin picked a public safety commissioner named Kopp (no joke), but her fellow religious conservative lasted only two weeks before a past scandal did him in. The one person she trusted and relied on, above all others, was her husband, Todd, who literally set up shop inside the governor's office.

■ ■ ■

In his memoir, Frank Bailey described working for Palin as a tumultuous, emotionally volatile world. He referred to "Sarah's chaotic management style, the frantic phone calls, and the knee-jerk reactionary stuff that filled our days and nights." Bailey said her husband, Todd, wasn't much help focusing Sarah on what really mattered. His passions, Bailey wrote, "tended to run from overheated to scalding."[1] That could explain why Palin had trouble keeping those who worked closely with her.

Just after Palin had become famous as John McCain's surprise pick for vice president, the *Juneau Empire* reported, "Palin's gubernatorial office has been plagued by turnover. She just appointed a new chief of staff this week, she's on her third legislative director in 21 months, and her press office has had numerous staff coming and going."[2]

Frank Bailey was himself a good example of the limited network Palin could tap for expertise. When she ran for governor, he was so impressed with her religious values and reformist agenda that he walked in off the street to volunteer. A middle manager for Alaska Airlines, Bailey at first handled yard signs. He soon worked his way into her inner circle by devoting some eighty-plus hours a week to her cause. Bailey knew they were amateurs—his nickname for their part of the campaign was the Rag Tags.

After Palin became governor, Bailey eventually landed a state job handling her boards and commissions appointments. In that job, Alaskans paid him to be part of her rapid response team, assailing her critics every time they said an unflattering word. Bailey made himself so valuable, Palin refused to sack him when he was caught on tape in Troopergate, trying to get her ex-brother-in-law fired.

When Palin won her Republican primary, she realized her general election campaign needed more professional help. She brought aboard two veterans who had worked for a candidate she'd just defeated, Johne Binkley. Binkley was a likeable former state legislator and well-connected member of the Republican establishment, but he didn't get much traction against the anticorruption crusader Palin. Toward the end, Binkley's campaign launched some harsh attacks on her, citing unfavorable headlines from her time as Wasilla mayor. Palin reacted angrily to the attacks, but that didn't stop her from picking up two of Binkley's key aides, Mike Tibbles and John Bitney. They did such good work in helping her win the general election that she hired them for key positions in her administration. Tibbles became her chief of staff. Bitney was her lobbyist for dealing with the legislature.

Pondering Tibbles's powerful role in her administration, Frank Bailey in his memoir asked a question many of Palin's supporters might have posed: "This former Binkley advisor attacked our campaign viciously one day then joined up for position and money the next. Wasn't he the type of professional we had promised to replace once in office?"[3]

The problem for Palin was that her pool of supporters and key staff was short on people who knew how government worked. In making appointments, she didn't have a big universe to draw from, one of her early political advisers told me, because "she demonized all the insiders she had to work with" as governor.[4]

For her attorney general, she turned to a lawyer from the town of Palmer, the next town over from Palin's hometown of Wasilla. She thought Talis Colberg could help her clean up after the scandals that had erupted, because he had no political or ethical baggage. Colberg also had no experience running a large organization and was totally unprepared for the hyperpolitical environment created by Troopergate and Palin's run for national office. In early 2009, after legislators grilled him for helping resist legislative subpoenas in Troopergate, Colberg left for the quieter life back in Palmer.

The man Palin appointed to replace him, Wayne Anthony Ross, was unimpressed with his predecessor. According to Frank Bailey's memoir, Ross said, "With a friend like Talis, who needs enemies? He makes Pontius Pilate look decisive."[5] State representative Mike Doogan (D-Anchorage), an early ally of Palin's on several of her legislative victories, told the *Anchorage Daily News* that Colberg "seemed to be a guy that was not very well suited to his position in the first place."[6]

Bitney was well suited to help Palin learn her way in Juneau. Though he was one of several key appointees she'd known from school days back home in Wasilla, he did have political skills. Bitney led her legislative lobbying effort during her hugely successful first year, when she pushed through ethics reform and a totally new way of pursuing the state's thirty-year dream of getting a North Slope gas pipeline.

But performance wasn't all that mattered to Palin. Personal values counted as well. Bitney made the mistake of wooing a woman who was married to a close personal friend of the Palins, Scott Richter. Upon learning of Bitney's affair, Palin fired him. He was quickly hired by House Speaker John Harris, who would emerge as a significant opponent to her oil tax and gas line proposals.

Some critics faulted Palin for letting her personal values affect her personnel decisions, especially since Bitney eventually married the woman in question, Deborah Richter. I had no problem with Palin deciding she didn't want to work closely with someone involved in causing serious pain to one of her close friends. But, to use a sports metaphor, she didn't have a good replacement for Bitney on her bench, so she paid a serious price for dumping him. Her legislative operation never recovered. Republican speaker John Harris would later say on the house floor that firing Bitney was one of the biggest mistakes Palin made.[7]

AN EXCEPTION: THE OIL AND GAS TEAM

Her last two big victories (on oil taxes and her gas pipeline contract) drew heavily on great work by her very capable oil and gas team, more so than her legislative lobbyists. Her legislative allies (liberal Democrats and reformist Republicans) also played a much bigger role in pushing through those later initiatives. Hollis French, a Democratic senator who helped Palin win both fights, told me he didn't get much help from Bitney's replacements.

Palin could rely so heavily on her oil and gas team because it was so strong. Her predecessor, Frank Murkowski, did her a favor by making solid appointments in those areas and then losing them because of fundamental policy differences. The departed staff, Natural Resources Commissioner Tom Irwin and key aides Marty Rutherford and Mark Myers, thought the multibillion-dollar concessions Murkowski offered Exxon, Conoco, and BP for getting a gas pipeline were both too generous and ineffective. Palin brought the three of them back and elevated Pat Galvin to the top spot at the department of revenue. Picking Galvin was a somewhat riskier move, since he'd never handled such a prominent job. But he was an integral part of the team that delivered Palin's victories on the gas pipeline and oil tax battles.

I dealt frequently with her oil and gas team on those big issues, and I found them to be capable, well informed, highly professional, and deeply committed to doing what was right for Alaska, despite strong pressure from the oil industry and its allies. Palin had the good sense to rely on her team's expertise and not to micro-manage them.

Marty Rutherford told me, "For us, she was very supportive, very good to work with. We could access her relatively easily. She was attuned to what we worked on. She wanted regular briefings. She asked good questions and gave good feedback."

But Rutherford also said, "Her relations with us were very different from a lot of other departments. . . . She gave us more latitude than is the norm—more than I experienced with other governors. . . . She was rarely involved in the day to day politics of getting the [gas pipeline] bill through or getting the [gas pipeline] license approved. But when bigger questions came up, she was key in making those decisions."

Rutherford describes a "team of rivals" type environment on oil and gas issues. She said one aide, Kurt Gibson, described their intense internal arguments as "steel against steel. We beat the hell out of each other coming up with the right decisions," Rutherford said. Usually they'd try to work out their differences before going to Palin, but couldn't always do it. Palin "would engage, help make decisions. . . . We learned to value and involve her," Rutherford told me. "We got comfortable doing that where we were not in alignment. She liked it. She encouraged us."[8]

Beyond Palin's oil and gas team, though, it was a different story. In a detailed look at Palin's appointments and management style, the *New York Times* found that Palin drew heavily on hometown connections and schoolmates for significant positions. Describing Palin's high school classmate, Franci Havemeister, whom she appointed to a high-ranking post, the *Times* article said, "A former real estate agent, Ms. Havemeister cited her childhood love of cows as a qualification."[9] Palin picked another high school classmate, Joe Austerman, to run the state-owned Matanuska Maid dairy in its final money-losing days.

COMMISSIONER "KOPP-A-FEEL"

Palin's biggest personnel blunder was the two-week term served by her public safety commissioner, Charles Kopp. Kopp was her choice to replace Walt Monegan, the commissioner who wouldn't fire Palin's ex-brother-in-law, the hot-headed trooper Mike Wooten.

At first, Kopp sounded like a good choice. He was police chief in the city of Kenai, a small town of 7,000, but still one of the largest in Alaska. He had nineteen years service on the Kenai force. He'd served on Palin's public safety transition team. And though Palin didn't mention it publicly, it surely didn't hurt that Kopp was "a rising star in Alaska's Christian conservative movement," as *Anchorage Daily News* columnist Alan Boraas later described him.[10] In the press release announcing his appointment, Palin lauded Kopp's record and called him a "person of great integrity."[11]

Oops. Slight problem: Even as he was being announced, Alaskans learned that Kopp had a sexual harassment incident during his time as a cop in Kenai. He'd received a letter of reprimand and was removed from supervising the woman, but the incident was expunged from his official record after he went two years with no further problems. As Palin prepared to announce Kopp's appointment, the woman in question alerted the press to that chapter of his history.

Kopp at first denied there had been any problem. "There's no job action ever taken against me," he said at his first press conference. His theory was that the letter had been expunged, so it never existed. In his mind, its removal meant the original charges against him were not valid. Even after he admitted being disciplined, Kopp told the *Anchorage Daily News*, "The allegation was not substantiated. . . . The letter of reprimand was removed and my record is clean."[12]

Palin at first stood by Kopp. Her spokeswoman, Sharon Leighow, said Palin was "concerned" and "disappointed" but wanted to sort through the "misinformation" circulating about him.[13] Leighow said Palin had known about the complaint against Kopp, but thought it had not been substantiated and did not know about the letter of reprimand. In a July 24 e-mail to key staff, Palin complained that "many emails pertaining to 'Kopp/Sexual Harassment' were evidently sent over the past week, but not one was forwarded to me."

Kopp characterized his behavior toward the woman as "friend-to-friend" hugs. The woman told the *Anchorage Daily News* that she felt Kopp was trying to establish an "icky closeness" with her.[14] Jokes began circulating about how his name might be "Commissioner Kopp-A-Feel." More important, his hairsplitting distinctions about the legal status of his sexual harassment record were just not acceptable from someone serving as the state's highest-ranking law enforcement officer.

The next day, Kopp resigned. In his memoir, Frank Bailey described the hurried, informal way Kopp had been chosen: "No interview of superiors or co-workers, no review of personnel files, and not even an updated resume had been reviewed ahead of his appointment."[15]

In Palin's fiasco with Kopp, there's an eerie parallel to the impulsive way John McCain did so little vetting of his little-known vice-presidential candidate from Alaska.

THE ONE CONSTANT

Amid all the staff turnover and turmoil in the Palin administration, there was one constant in her inner circle: husband Todd. He wasn't your typical governor's spouse: Oil field worker, member of a union, a hands-dirty kind of guy, a commercial fisherman, and renowned long-distance snowmachine racer. Alaskans knew him by the nickname, First Dude. To political observers, he was also known as the shadow governor. Though his resume made him an unlikely candidate for handing out political advice, in any discussion about who was on Palin's list of advisers, again and again Todd's name would come up.

Soon after she entered the vice-presidential race, the *New York Times* reported on the "widely held understanding among lawmakers, state employees and lobbyists about Mr. Palin's heavy engagement in state government."[16] In his book, Palin confidant Frank Bailey described how he was constantly dealing with Todd about Trooper Mike Wooten and many other issues. One e-mail Bailey got from Todd dealt with whether a deputy transportation commissioner was sufficiently concerned about aviation safety.[17]

The head of security for Governor Palin, Gary Wheeler, told the legislature's Troopergate investigator that Todd was in the governor's office about 50 percent of the time, often working from a conference table with a phone.[18] Senate president Lyda Green reported being surprised to see Todd sitting in the governor's office during meetings with Palin, though he didn't speak up. Green said other visitors to the office had the same experience.

"The First Dude" routinely sent or was copied on e-mails dealing with state business of all kinds. When an activist requested copies of those e-mails under public records law, the Palin administration withheld them, saying correspondence on state business with Todd was protected under the "deliberative process privilege" because he was a "trusted advisor" to the governor. So far, the courts have upheld Palin's position, in effect confirming Todd's role as adviser.

At least one formerly close Palin adviser believes that her combative streak comes from Todd. Early in her career, the adviser told me, Palin struck him as coachable, perfectly willing to consider less-than-flattering feedback. Todd, he indicated, was the one who reacted with the hostile passion of a mama grizzly defending the brood. The adviser described Todd as a "blue collar guy, very competitive," someone who has a chip on his shoulder toward those who might have more expertise in the matter at hand.[19]

This sounds like the Palin the world now knows: sarcastically criticizing those she perceives as "elites" and never admitting a mistake.

AN ACCUMULATION OF FRACTURED RELATIONSHIPS

In his memoir, Palin-aide-turned-critic Frank Bailey admitted that a certain amount of personality conflict is inevitable in high-pressure environments. "But in the distance of time," he wrote, "what became enlightening was the accumulation of Sarah's fractured relationships."[20] *Vanity Fair*'s look at Palin's political future after her vice-presidential race found that "many people who have worked closely with Palin have found themselves disillusioned."[21]

Lobbyist Paul Fuhs, a Palin campaign volunteer and advisor, was one of them. After reading *Going Rogue*, he wrote a stinging op-ed, saying, "It wasn't that Palin had the wrong advisers with too much experience as 'insiders.' It was that she wouldn't listen to them."[22]

Palin's issues with staff continued even after she quit as governor. In November 2010, a long, and not particularly critical, profile in the *New York Times* noted, "It's a curious feature of Palin World that none of its charter members knew her before 2008. (Her two longtime Alaska aides, Kris Perry and Meghan Stapleton, left amicably but wearied by the demands involved with working for an overnight celebrity.)"[23]

In that story, *Times* reporter Robert Draper said, "Palin confessed to me a tendency to avoid longtime political operatives—'these unprincipled people who are in it for power, money and job titles.'"[24] He didn't ask her why as governor she had given such critically important positions to Mike Tibbles and John Bitney, two political operatives who immediately joined her campaign after she beat the man they had been working to elect. Nor did Draper ask why her choice to succeed Tibbles as chief of staff was Mike Nizich, a career bureaucrat who had served several Democratic and Republican governors.

Filmmaker John Ziegler is among those who once worshipped Palin and now see fatal flaws. He made the movie *Media Malpractice: How Obama Got Elected and Palin Was Targeted* and volunteered much of his time defending her against unfavorable mainstream media coverage. But Ziegler thought she killed her chances at the presidency by resigning as governor, and told her so. She didn't want to hear it, and that was the beginning of the end for him.

"My loyalty meant very little to them. I was done," Ziegler wrote in June 2011 for the *Daily Caller* website. "Even those most loyal to her get tossed under the bus. . . . If people like me who would once have taken a bullet for Sarah (and at least figuratively I did many times) can't get behind her any more, what the hell happened?"[25]

■ ■ ■

Politics is a strange sport, in which the superstar has to build and run her own team. To be an effective leader, the star politician has to be player, coach, and general manager. Palin has figured out the superstar player role—it's building the rest of the team where she had trouble. As Ziegler, Bailey, and so many others discovered, Palin's political ambitions can make her difficult to work for. She hasn't retained an experienced crew that is willing to do whatever it takes to further her political career.

What she does have is Todd. Draper's report in the *New York Times* confirmed Palin's reliance on her husband. Longtime Palin friend, former state legislator Rick Halford, told Draper that Todd is "the one person she trusts." She gave Todd special recognition in the concession speech she wanted to deliver on the night she and McCain lost: *"Along the way in this campaign,"* the draft read, "it was Todd, as always, who helped with the children, gave me advice, and kept me strong."

I asked State Sen. Hollis French about Palin's trouble retaining staff and whom she relied on for advice. French, a Democrat who was one of her strongest allies on oil and gas issues, said, "We always wondered who the inner circle was. It was a *very* small group that had her trust. Was it Todd? It didn't seem plausible . . . but in retrospect . . ." He trailed off, as if to say, "Now we know it was."

14

This May Sound Familiar from High School

Before John McCain picked Sarah Palin, Alaskans had not seen the hyperpartisan conservative who whipped up huge, adoring crowds in a losing cause. Palin had been a people-before-party reformer on the outs with her party's establishment, and she worked well with Democrats in the legislature. But Alaskans did see signs of the political pettiness that would go on display in her memoir and her postings on Facebook and Twitter. As governor, she let personal considerations drive political decisions, treated political differences as a personal insult, and made a point of settling scores.

■ ■ ■

Less than a month before Palin was elected governor, she made a campaign stop in her hometown of Wasilla, in the heart of the area known as the Mat-Su Valley. She surprised many people by saying she would show a hometown bias as governor. "Certainly, people will assume I'm biased toward the valley in the decisions I make," she told the crowd. "So be it, because I will be."[1]

Her supporters downplayed the remark, suggesting she merely got carried away in showing affection for her home community. But that comment drew renewed scrutiny after she hacked $230 million from the capital budget passed by the legislature during her first year in office.[2]

A story in the *Anchorage Daily News* noted, "Palin cut funds for 40 sports-related projects around Alaska, saying sports was not an essential government service. . . . So why was there still money [$630,000] for a kitchen for the Wasilla Sports Complex—not to mention funds for several other Mat-Su sports projects, including new lights at the Houston High School field and new bleachers at Palmer High?"[3]

Palin defended the apparent hometown bias by saying that the Mat-Su Valley items were higher priorities for their local communities than the projects she vetoed. She told the paper that the Mat-Su got 8.5 percent of the capital project funding, while Anchorage got 22.8 percent. However, Anchorage had 3.6 times as many people as Palin's home area, while getting only 2.7 times as much money after her vetoes.

Palin's attempt to rescue the money-losing state-owned dairy was another example of hometown bias. The at-least $600,000 she spent trying to save the four remaining dairy farmers in her home region, along with about fifty jobs at the dairy, contradicted her supposedly free-market philosophy of government. Many observers, myself included, wonder if she would have made the same decision if the failing government-run business had been in a different part of the state.

With Governor Palin, the personal was political, and the political was personal. To put it in terms familiar to anyone who survived high school, the governor was a former beauty queen and popular athlete who presided over a powerful clique. If you were in her clique, she could be charming and all would go well. If you got on her bad side, woe unto you.

Early on, she was gracious to her supporters in the legislature. Democratic state representative Mike Doogan, writing about Palin in the *Washington Post*, mentioned that she hosted an event where she gave him cupcakes, blazing with candles, for his sixtieth birthday.

Another ally on Palin's early victories in the legislature, Anchorage Democratic senator Hollis French, told me about how Palin and husband Todd accepted a routine invitation to come to a constituent pizza party in his district during her first year in office. It was quite unusual for any governor to attend such a mundane function, let alone one held by the opposite political party. Palin and Todd didn't just parachute in and out, French said—they stayed an hour and had a good time.

And yet, both legislators would come to know what it was like to feel her wrath. Doogan told the *Washington Post* readers that after he criticized her plan to give each Alaskan $1,200 worth of extra cash for high energy bills, "the next time we met she lit into me like I was a pork chop and she was a starving wolf."[4]

Senator French got on Palin's bad side by supervising the legislature's Troopergate investigation. After John McCain picked her, French became a target of intense partisan attack. That wasn't such a surprise. But in writing her memoir, when she might have been more reflective and balanced, she let her juvenile side show. In *Going Rogue*, she mocked French by using the nickname "Gunny," referring to a trumped-up controversy over whether he had overstated his military service on his senate campaign resume.[5]

French's experiences with Palin left him puzzled. Several times, he had met with Palin and key aides during the big battles on the gas pipeline and oil taxes. "I wondered what I didn't see or recognize at the time," French told me in an interview. "She seemed like a pleasant person, not the Sarah Palin we've seen since the Republican nominating convention."

A CURIOUS FEUD

In the early days of her term, French hadn't seen the side of her that others already knew. Coming in as governor, Palin already had a bitter feud with fellow Wasilla Republican Lyda Green, president of the state senate, despite sharing the same stands on many big issues. "If you had looked at our résumés, as far as being pro-life, pro-N.R.A., pro-family, pro-parental control, saving taxpayer dollars, keeping government out of our lives, we would have been identical," Green told the *New Yorker* during Palin's vice-presidential campaign.[6] She and Palin had been allies for twelve and a half years, Green told MSNBC's Rachel Maddow on *The Rachel Maddow Show*, broadcast on September 22, 2008.

Until Green made her big mistake, that is. During Palin's run for governor, Green stayed neutral in the Republican primary, since she was still a sitting senator dealing with an incumbent Republican governor with power over pending issues that Green cared about. That was enough to get Green a permanent spot on Palin's enemies list.

In early 2008, the public got a good look at how low Palin would go in that feud. She had called into a morning radio talk show hosted by Bob and Mark, two shock-jocks who were among her favorite media supporters. (It was a bit odd that Alaska's governor would revel in the approval of two deejays who regularly pushed the boundaries of good taste.) As co-host Bob Lester condemned Green, a long-serving state senator, as a "bitch" and a "cancer" on Alaska, Palin merely giggled. Green, who had survived breast cancer a decade earlier, wasn't the only one stunned by Palin's reaction.

Green told the *New Yorker*, "Sarah can be heard in the background tittering, hee-heeing, never saying, 'That's not appropriate, let's not talk like that, let's change the subject,' or anything. I had breast cancer in '97 and had a radical mastectomy," Green said. "Sarah certainly knew I had breast cancer, because she sent me flowers when I was ill."

Palin was even more dismissive of Green in private. Political aide Frank Bailey, in his memoir, quoted an e-mail from Palin saying, "The only way (her staff) can work with Lyda is to just keep remembering she's 'Mean, Mean Lyda Green.'"[7] Bailey said Palin plotted against Green, whose senate seat was up in the 2008 election, suggesting in another e-mail, "Hey- Ivy [Frye, a key Palin aide] even lives in [her] district come to think of it! Never hurts to rumormonger."[8]

Palin's relations weren't much better with the Republican speaker of the Alaska state house, John Harris. It was bad enough, in her mind, that he was part of the Republican old guard that resisted her agenda on ethics, the gas pipeline and oil taxes. After her first round of ethics reforms passed, Harris disagreed with her that further changes were needed in state ethics laws. "I don't know what the hell they've been smoking" if they think more reforms are needed, Harris said at the time.[9]

In internal e-mails that came out long after her run for vice president, Palin said, "Sheeeeesh, Harris is saying some very foolish things in there," and called his reaction "the most stupid comment I've heard all year." "Nice talk, Mr. Speaker," she said in another internal e-mail. "Reflects well on your commitment to ethical leadership,"[10]

Harris also had the audacity to hire John Bitney, the legislative director she'd fired for having an affair with the wife of a Palin family friend. That move earned Harris a less-than-friendly call from Palin's husband, Todd. "I understood from the call that Todd wasn't happy with me hiring John and he'd like to see him not there," Harris told the *New York Times* shortly after John McCain made Palin famous to the nation. "The Palin family gets upset at personal issues. And at our level, they want to strike back."[11]

The feud with Harris was just one instance, the *Times* reported, of the Palin's administration's "siege-like atmosphere. Top aides keep score, demean enemies and gloat over successes." Troopergate was another instance of Palin's penchant for getting personal when dealing with controversy. Palin mocked Public Safety Commissioner Walt Monegan's claim he felt "pressured" to fire Palin's ex-brother-in-law, suggesting that if what Monegan experienced was "pressure," how did he handle all the real pressure that cops face? In so many words, she basically called her former public safety commissioner a wimp.

THE ANTAGONISTS

Frank Bailey's memoir documented the huge amount of time Palin and her political staff spent responding to critics. "Her fragile emotional makeup was unnerving," he wrote. "To stay in her good graces, counter-attacking anyone opposing her became the top priority. . . . Minor slights, many of which would have withered under their inconsequentiality, became magnified obsessions that made governing the state of Alaska a lesser priority."[12]

Chief among Palin's antagonists were right-wing talk show host Dan Fagan, blogger and defeated gubernatorial candidate Andrew Halcro, serial ethics complaint filer Andree McLeod, and a fundamentalist conservative blogger, Sherry Whitstine. Palin's critics, and her obsession with them, sounded much like what goes on in high school.

Halcro, the former Republican legislator who'd won respect for questioning conventional wisdom in his party, was the smartest kid in the class, the guy who just never got over losing the class presidency to the wildly popular and pretty, but not all that smart, female jock. Dan Fagan, a man with the body type of William Howard Taft, was the class clown, vying for attention with his increasingly strident blasts at the most popular girl in the class. Andree McLeod was the outcast, the misfit rejected by the clique, determined to wreak vengeance on those who tormented her. Sherry Whitstine filled the role as leader of a rival clique, trying to draw away those who might normally have followed Palin.

Some people around Palin tried to steer her in a more productive direction. According to Frank Bailey's memoir, the man Palin picked as her second attorney general, Wayne Anthony Ross, said at one point, "As somebody in (Governor Palin's) cabinet said the other day, 'You can't kick every dog that barks at you, . . .' I'm trying to convince her that she ought not get treed by the Chihuahuas."[13]

Palin had tried to stop paying so much attention to critical comments posted on media Internet sites. In June 2008, though, she was back at it, reacting to a story about how she and her kids had sighted a bear in the heart of Juneau. She e-mailed a complaint to her press staff on June 9: "OK—I had to finally read a blog (yuck!). . . . Sheesh—nothing's changed since I stopped reading that ADN [*Anchorage Daily News*] blog nearly two months ago. . . . I didn't put my kids in any danger, as the idiot blog comments claim. Now, remind me to not peek in again at that ridiculous media forum—it's the most unhealthy and idiotic forum imaginable." Press aide Rosanne Hughes e-mailed back, "It's the snotty comments of all five people in town who have nothing better to do that snipe at you."[14]

Nonetheless, Palin continued to pay close attention to what her critics were saying.

CHEAP SHOTS

Palin took a cheap rhetorical shot at one of her former Democratic allies when he left the state senate for a job in the Obama administration. Juneau senator Kim Elton had helped Palin win her early battles on ethics, the gas pipeline, and oil taxes. But in Palin's mind, by going to work as Obama's special assistant handling the U.S. Department of Interior's many issues in Alaska, Elton was consorting with the enemy.

In her press release reacting to the appointment, the very first words of her quotation were, "Senator Elton pledged his allegiance to President Obama last summer." It was as if Elton had somehow been disloyal to Alaska by supporting the man who was elected president of the entire country. It was a truly bizarre thing to say in a press release that also said, "We wish him well as he moves on."[15] That was the only diplomatic nicety in her entire statement. Elton had chosen sides and left her clique, and Palin wanted to make sure everyone knew it.

PAYBACK TIME FOR A SUPPORTER-TURNED-CRITIC

With Kim Elton's departure from the senate, Palin started a bitter fight over who would replace him. Under Alaska law, the replacement has to be from the same party as the departed senator. The governor picks a nominee, but that nominee has to be confirmed by the party's remaining members in the senate (or house, if the vacancy is there). By tradition, nominations come from the party organization in the departing legislator's district. Also by tradition, Alaska governors have avoided public fights in replacing a legislator from the opposite party. Not so for Sarah Palin.

Senate Democrats wanted to promote Juneau's Democratic state representative, Beth Kerttula. The house minority leader, and a widely respected legislator, she had also supported Palin on her big, early victories in the legislature. Kerttula was an obvious choice—so obvious that Democrats didn't include any other names on their list to the governor.

Sending only one name to the governor was a break with tradition, and any governor might have blanched at that. But to Palin, the nomination of Kerttula was a special affront. Kerttula had had the audacity to say what many Alaskans thought at the time Palin was selected to run for vice president: "I've worked real well with the governor, but she's not ready for this step. She's not ready to be a heartbeat away from the presidency."[16]

With that remark, Kerttula apparently made sure she'd never get appointed to the senate as long as Sarah Palin was governor. No matter that Kerttula had crossed party lines to defend Palin, toward the end of her vice-presidential race, when the Associated Press ran a piece attacking Palin's integrity in handling the gas pipeline issue. Kerttula had broken from Palin's clique, and she wasn't going to get any political break from Palin.

After refusing to nominate Kerttula, Palin held an open recruitment for applications to the Juneau senate seat. Her first pick was Tim Grussendorf, from a well-known political family. Only one problem: he until quite recently had been registered as a Republican, and the law required replacing a Democrat with a Democrat. Senate Democrats refused to confirm Grussendorf. Palin contended their rejection was illegal, saying it should have been done by open vote in public. Senate Democrats refused to yield on that point, but Juneau Democrats did give Palin a list of four other potential nominees.

Palin still refused to follow tradition and choose from among the party's nominees. Instead, she nominated Joe Nelson, an Alaska Native. He had no political experience, but he had political connections: he was married to an Alaska Native, a Democrat, who had served in the state house.

It was a cynical but politically adept move on Palin's part. She was no particular friend of Alaska Natives—relations with them were strained throughout her time as governor. But Palin knew that the Senate Democrats included two Alaska Natives. With Nelson, Senate Democrats would be boxed in: to keep fighting Palin, they'd have to reject a minority candidate, potentially costing them support in their own caucus and with a key constituency.

Nonetheless, Senate Democrats again refused to confirm Palin's choice, citing Nelson's lack of local support and experience. The standoff continued. Palin then offered Senate Democrats three choices: the two they'd already rejected, plus an obscure businessman who'd applied on his own initiative, Alan Wilson. When Democrats refused to act on any of them, Palin renominated Grussendorf.

As the legislature headed into the last days of the session, the capital city had no representation in the state senate. The fight over the Juneau senate vacancy was producing bad headlines for both sides.

Finally Palin and Senate Democrats agreed on a compromise candidate: former Juneau assemblyman Dennis Egan. After all that sparring, Palin had made sure her nemesis Kerttula didn't get the seat, while Democrats got a replacement who was an unquestioned Democrat with a solid reputation. Palin, however, tried to get in the last word. Even as she welcomed Egan to the Senate, she insisted that the Senate Democrats' confirmation vote should have been held in public session.[17]

PALLING AROUND WITH SECESSIONISTS

One of the stranger things Palin did as governor was sending a warm welcome message to the annual convention of the Alaska Independence Party. The party's official platform contended that Alaska's decision to enter the union was fatally tainted. It demanded that residents should have a chance to vote on seceding from the union, among other options. For several years, her husband, Todd's, voter registration identified him as a member of the Alaska Independence Party.

"I share your party's vision of upholding the constitution of our great state," she told the party in her welcome message. In fact, the fundamental purpose of the Alaskan Independence Party's is to question Alaska's status as a state, rather than being an independent nation.[18] During her vice-presidential race, Palin accused Barack Obama of palling around with terrorists, when she had been palling around with secessionists.

She issued her greeting to the Alaskan Independence Party when she was still immensely popular with Alaskans. Being charitable, one might speculate that she merely wanted to share her love with all members of the Alaska family. You could also speculate that Palin had an unhealthy desire to be liked by everybody—even secessionists.

SETTLING SCORES

In *Going Rogue*, Palin treats readers to more of her high-school mentality and score settling. The popular girl jock let the smartest kid in the class have it, calling her nemesis Andrew Halcro "a wealthy, effete young chap."[19] (It sounded as if she was saying Halcro was not man enough to hold Todd's toolbelt.)

John Bitney, the legislative director whom she fired for having an affair, came in for special abuse. Her break with Bitney is so complete, she doesn't even use his name. She calls him "a BlackBerry games addict" and insults his fashion sense, saying he "couldn't seem to keep his lunch off his tie. . . . The fact that his shirt was buttoned one button off and his shirttail was poking through his open fly didn't exactly inspire confidence."[20] The most popular girl in the class, she of the Naughty Monkey peep-toe pumps and the $150,000 worth of free clothes on the national campaign trail, really handed it to the disheveled nerd whom she had ejected from the clique.

All politicians have egos. You can't get very far in politics without a big one. For some, their egos lead them to flaunt their power and revel in the perks that come their way. But that wasn't the case with Palin—in keeping with her populist, insurgent image, she sold the previous governor's state jet, often traveled without a driver or security detail, and transferred the governor's chef to a different job.

But Palin did have a high opinion of herself. Writing in the August 2009 *Vanity Fair*, Todd Purdum shared a perspective familiar to those of us who'd followed Palin: "More than once in my travels in Alaska, people brought up, without prompting, the question of Palin's extravagant self-regard."[21] Again, there's a parallel to the high school world: the girl who thinks she's great and makes sure you know it.

However, along with her abundant self-regard, Palin had trouble admitting a mistake and learning from it. Paul Fuhs, a former adviser to Palin and campaign volunteer, put it this way in an op-ed after her book came out:

> Every one of us knows someone like this: They always find someone else to blame for their own mistakes or shortcomings and never take responsibility for their own actions. Sarah Palin's new book is a classic study in this form of self-delusion.
>
> Her attacks on John Bitney and others in her administration and the John McCain campaign are petty and mean-spirited. . . . She had a chance in this book to say something significant . . . . Instead, she chose the politics of persecution and blaming others.[22]

In his memoir, Frank Bailey shared this e-mail Sarah Palin sent to talk show host Dan Fagan during her run for governor in 2006: "I've gone through life never holding grudges because life is too short and that's why I have a good disposition. God's blessed me with that—in fact it's not me but Him in me that has always allowed me to walk in forgiveness and peace."[23]

Sarah Palin has many qualities, but forgiveness—and accurate self-awareness—are not among them.

15

The Truth Can Be So Inconvenient

In spring 2011, journalist Geoffrey Dunn published a book entitled *The Lies of Sarah Palin*.[1] It provoked many jokes about how he could fit all of Palin's lies into just one book.

Dunn's book is 400 pages of critique, but not an archive of lies. Most of it lacks the hyperventilated tone suggested by the attention-grabbing title. Dunn has written a strongly critical account, but he is a journalist and documents his criticism in a fairly typical journalistic fashion. Its prologue, focusing on the "lies" theme, reads as if it had been tacked on to support the title the publisher's marketing department wanted.

Some of the "lies" that Dunn and blogger Andrew Sullivan and others accuse Palin of making were cases where she went back on her word and flip-flopped for transparently political reasons. Others were cases in which she took a shred of truth and twisted it to create an impression grossly at odds with reality. So, unlike author Dunn, I hesitate to say Sarah Palin has dished enough lies to fill a book.

Instead, let's look at how Sarah Palin displayed, shall we say, a conveniently casual disregard for the truth.

TROOPERGATE

The most astonishing example was her claim that she was vindicated by the legislature's Troopergate report. She said that it found "no unlawful or unethical activity on my part" and that it indicated "there was no abuse of authority at all in trying to get Officer Wooten fired."[2] She made those claims more than once.

Talking to Alaska reporters on the phone, Palin said she was "very, very pleased to be cleared of any legal wrongdoing . . . any hint of any kind of unethical activity there."[3] On the campaign trail in Pennsylvania, Palin said, "I'm thankful that the report has shown that, that there was no illegal or unethical activity there in my choice to replace our commissioner."[4]

Yet the very first finding of the report by investigator Steve Branchflower, on page 8, says: "I find that Governor Sarah Palin abused her power by violating Alaska Statute 39.52.110(a) of the Alaska Executive Branch Ethics Act." Palin's claim of vindication was patently false, blatantly obvious, and she was immediately called on it. She nonetheless continued to assert that the report found no wrongdoing. It was the Mother of All Mistruths that emanated from Palin's mouth. The fact checkers at Politifact.com, a nonpartisan organization, gave it their "Pants on Fire" rating—essentially saying it was an outright lie.[5] What she said was the equivalent of standing in the middle of a raging hurricane and telling reporters, "Wind? What wind? The weather's fine!"

THE GAS PIPELINE

Almost as blatant was what she told the nation about her work promoting an Alaska natural gas pipeline. In her acceptance speech on September 3 2008, she said, "I fought to bring about the largest private-sector infrastructure project in North American history. And when that deal was struck, we began a nearly $40 billion natural gas pipeline."

Using the words "bring about" and "began" made it sound to the average listener that construction was under way. In the one debate between the vice-presidential candidates, Palin went even further, claiming, "We're building a nearly $40-billion natural gas pipeline."

In fact, Palin's work had not produced any construction on that pipeline, or any commitment from anybody to build it. What she got, thanks to a state pledge of $500 million in matching funds, was nothing more than a commitment to do the preliminary planning for a pipeline and to recruit customers. At the time, the fact-checkers at PolitiFact.com said Palin's statement was flat-out false.

In the years since, not a spade of dirt had been turned to build that pipeline. It was still stuck in the customer-recruitment stage. No one had committed to ship gas on it, or to build it or any part of it. The way she described it in her acceptance speech would make the average listener think the project was, in fact, being built. That wasn't true then, and it isn't true now.

TODD PALIN, SECESSIONIST?

Palin told another whopper when talking to the McCain campaign about her husband, Todd's, past membership in the Alaskan Independence Party (AIP), which advocates secession from the United States.

According to a CBS news account, based on campaign e-mails, Palin had complained about a "ridiculous issue that's cropped up . . . claiming Todd's involvement in an anti-American political party." "It's bull," Palin's e-mail said. "Pls have statement given on this so it's put to bed."[6]

But it wasn't bull, and the McCain campaign wasn't going to take her advice and lie to the nation about it. McCain campaign manager Steve Schmidt e-mailed back, "He was a member of the aip? My understanding is yes. That [i.e., secession] is part of their platform. Do not engage the protestors. If a reporter asks say it is ridiculous. Todd loves america."

Palin wouldn't let it go. She e-mailed back a ridiculous—and false—cover story: "That's not part of their platform and he was only a 'member' bc independent alaskans too often check that 'Alaska Independent' box on voter registrations thinking it just means non partisan. He caught his error when changing our address and checked the right box. I still want it fixed."[7]

In the *Lies of Sarah Palin*, Dunn documents how Todd registered with the Alaska Independence Party three different times.[8] Contrary to what Palin claimed, on Alaska's voter registration rolls, there is no "Alaska Independent" box to mistakenly check. The AIP is clearly listed as "Alaskan Independence Party." Alaskans who don't want to align with a political party sign up as "nonpartisan." Only an astoundingly ignorant voter would see "Alaska Independence Party" and think that is the box to check for someone wishing to be a registered "independent."

Schmidt was having none of Palin's bogus explanation. His e-mail said:

Secession. It is their [party's] entire reason for existence. A cursory examination of the website shows that the party exists for the purpose of seceding from the union. That is the stated goal on the front page of the web site. Our records indicate that todd was a member for seven years. If this is incorrect then we need to understand the discrepancy. The statement you are suggesting be released would be inaccurate. The inaccuracy would bring greater media attention to this matter and be a distraction.[9]

The McCain campaign could not trust what their own vice-presidential candidate was saying about her husband's political affiliations.

TODD'S HEALTH INSURANCE

Nor could the McCain campaign trust what she said about her husband's past health insurance coverage. Writing for *Vanity Fair*, Todd Purdum provides this summary of Palin's truth-stretching in that incident:

At one point, trying out a debating point that she believed showed she could empathize with uninsured Americans, Palin told McCain aides that she and Todd in the early years of their marriage had been unable to afford health insurance of any kind, and had gone without it until he got his union card and went to work for British Petroleum on the North Slope of Alaska. Checking with Todd Palin himself revealed that, no, they had had catastrophic coverage all along. She insisted that catastrophic insurance didn't really count and need not be revealed.[10]

DIVESTITURE FROM SUDAN

During her vice-presidential campaign, Palin also gave the nation a slippery account of her stand on divesting state of Alaska funds from companies doing business in Sudan, because of its genocidal campaign in Darfur. In the vice-presidential debate, she said, "When I and others in the legislature found out we had some millions of dollars in Sudan, we called for divestment through legislation." She made it sound like she had sprung into action when she first learned that the state's investments included tainted money in Sudan.

Not so. She had been asked in a letter dated November 2006, before she even took office, to support divestment. In December 2007, divestment advocates had sought a meeting with her on the issue. In early February 2008, her deputy revenue commissioner Brian Andrews told a state house committee that the Palin administration opposed divestment from Darfur.

It wasn't until later in March, fifteen months after first exposure to the issue, that Palin relented and agreed to have her revenue commissioner support a senate version of divestment legislation. By then it was too late in the legislature's ninety-day session, and the divestment bill died—a point Palin, of course, failed to mention in the vice-presidential debate.[11]

THOSE ETHICS COMPLAINTS

Palin's claims about all the ethics charges filed against her had a significant fudge factor. In 2009, she boasted that she'd "won" all fifteen complaints that had been filed against her. In a strictly legal sense, that was true—none of them, at that point, had produced findings of "probable cause" that she or her administration had violated state ethics law.

However, in one case—involving changes to state hiring specifications so a Palin supporter could get a state job—the investigator found cause for concern. The final finding recommended that one of her top aides, Frank Bailey, get training on the ethics law. She may have "won" that case, but the referee basically called a foul on the play.

In another ethics complaint, she in effect settled out of court. She preempted any official finding of wrongdoing by agreeing to repay the state for ten trips her children had taken at state expense. As is often the case in out-of-court settlements, it was accompanied by a legalistic disclaimer from Palin that no wrongdoing had been established. Only a Palin-esque definition of "winning" or "victory" would allow her to claim she "won" in a case where she had to repay thousands of dollars in questionable state payments.

The Associated Press later reported that Palin had altered some of the official state travel forms to improve the odds the trips would qualify as official state business.[12] It was the kind of news that might easily have produced an investigation into whether any of the added information was false or fraudulent and broke any laws. But in Alaska, state prosecutors report to a cabinet official appointed by the governor. If there ever were an investigation, it was never disclosed to the public. Altering the forms was another example of where the simple truth did not serve Sarah Palin's interests.

"SPLITTING HAIRS"

In spring of 2009, during her last months as governor, Alaskans saw two notorious incidents where Palin peddled high-profile falsehoods.

On April 2, 2009, the *Fairbanks Daily News-Miner* ran this story by reporter Rena Delbridge:

> JUNEAU—Gov. Sarah Palin on Thursday echoed a call from the Alaska Republican Party for U.S. Sen. Mark Begich to resign after the Justice Department asked a judge to toss out corruption charges against former Sen. Ted Stevens.
>
> "I absolutely agree," Palin responded in an e-mail Thursday to the Daily News-Miner.
>
> She said Begich should step down and a special election should be held to fill the seat.

Delbridge had explicitly asked her by e-mail to confirm that she was agreeing with the Republican Party press release and asking Begich to step down. That's when Palin wrote, "I absolutely agree."

But before the news cycle was even complete, Palin denied she had called on Begich to resign. Reporters Scott Conroy and Shusannah Walshe, in their book *Sarah from Alaska*, documented Delbridge's work and Palin's backpedaling on the question. At a news conference, Palin was asked about it and said, "I didn't call for Begich to step down either. I said I absolutely agree that Alaskans deserve a fair, untainted election for the United States Senate seat."[13]

Of course, there is no way to have a special election for a Senate seat unless it is vacant, and that requires the person holding it to die or resign. Since Begich was alive, the only way to have the special election Palin wanted was for Begich to resign.

The same day of the *News-Miner*'s report, the *Anchorage Daily News* ran this account of what Palin was saying:

> Alaskans deserve to have a fair election not tainted by some announcement that one of the candidates was convicted fairly of seven felonies, when in fact it wasn't a fair conviction, Palin said in a Thursday interview with the Daily News.
>
> The governor said she does not want to "split hairs" on whether Begich should resign or not but agrees with the Republican Party's call for a special election.[14]

To Palin, whether or not she was telling the truth about calling on Begich to resign was "splitting hairs."

Walshe and Conroy wrote, "Palin also knew there was evidence, in the form of an e-mail exchange with a reporter, that she had called on Begich to resign. . . . It was another example of her tendency to refuse to acknowledge any error in judgment and to offer instead a version of events that could easily be proved false."

SEARCHING FOR (NONEXISTENT) STRINGS

Palin's second high-profile assault on the truth in spring 2009 came during her unsuccessful effort to reject some of the federal economic recovery money offered to states. She wanted to burnish her credentials as a Tea Party conservative and desperately looked for plausible reasons to turn down any of the federal aid.

At first, Palin said she would reject about one-third of the $900-plus million the federal government was offering Alaska. That didn't sit well with Alaskans. As I clearly saw during my thirty years there, Alaskans love to gripe about the heavy hand of the federal government, but that doesn't stop them from eagerly taking federal money. Federal spending supports about one-third of Alaska's economy.

Palin relented and agreed to take the vast majority of the federal aid money, but she continued to look for excuses to turn down some significant chunk of it.

Looking at some federal energy conservation funding, she thought she'd found a place to take her stand against an overbearing federal government. This $28.6 million "bucket" of money, as she called it, would require "universal energy building codes for Alaska, kind of a one-size-fits-all building code that isn't going to work up there in Alaska." The feds' demands weren't just onerous strings on the money, she said, they were "ropes."[15]

It was just not true. When asked, the federal energy department showed great flexibility in what states would have to do to qualify for that pot of money. Politifact.com described the federal response:

Steven G. Chalk of the DOE (Department of Energy) said the stimulus provision recognizes that not every state has statewide building codes, and that the governor does not have the authority to force local governments to implement building codes. In those cases, Chalk wrote, it's sufficient for the governor to simply "promote" the codes. It is enough, he wrote, for the state to work with local governments to create model energy efficiency standards.

Politifact.com noted, "A strict reading of the requirements for the energy-efficiency money might give credence to Palin's concerns. But the experience of Missouri and the explicit letter from the Department of Energy to Palin's office made clear the feds are not imposing a 'one-size-fits-all' building code." Their conclusion: "Palin sounds like someone looking for a fight when there isn't one. We find her statement to be False."[16]

Facing that kind of scrutiny, Palin eventually changed her complaints. She wrote in the *Anchorage Daily News*: "The Department of Energy finally admitted section 410 and their previous statements were 'inappropriate' for some states but still wanted an agreement to push model codes on all Alaskan communities. I said no. Beware of Washington, D.C., trying to cajole local community leaders to eliminate the choices Alaskans have when building or renovating homes and businesses."[17]

Now instead of saying "the federal money has onerous strings attached," she was saying something more like "the money has unwelcome suggestions attached."

That wasn't a good enough reason for the legislature to reject the money, not at a time when Alaskans in remote villages were dealing with heating oil and gasoline prices of $6 or $7 a gallon and spending up to 40 percent of their income on energy bills.

The legislature overrode her veto, even though it took forty-five of sixty legislators to do so, and Palin's fellow Republicans held a majority of seats. On the day of the vote, a key legislative aide who'd researched Palin's dubious claims noted that her credibility with legislators was shot. "They view her as an irrational, factually inaccurate, emotional, self-serving, self-aggrandizing personality," said Larry Persily, aide to Republican house finance co-chair Mike Hawker, according to Geoffrey Dunn's account in his book.[18]

Having been defeated on the stimulus money, Palin struck back in *Going Rogue*. She resurrected the canard she'd used to attack the federal home energy conservation aid: "The documents clearly stated that acceptance of the funds required the adoption and enforcement of energy building codes. Universal building codes—in Alaska! . . . A state so geographically diverse that one-size-fits-all codes simply wouldn't work."[19]

Her book also made a demonstrably false statement about the final outcome. She wrote, "After Sean Parnell took over as governor, the Democrat-controlled legislature overrode my veto."[20] In 2009, Democrats had only twenty-eight of the legislature's sixty seats. If Democrats "controlled" the legislature, it would have been news to them—both the senate president and the speaker of the house were Republicans.

In any event, overriding an appropriations veto takes forty-five of Alaska's sixty legislators. Eighteen Republicans—more than half their ranks in the legislature—voted to override. If all Palin's Republican colleagues had supported her, her veto would have easily stood. If there's any partisan blame to be meted out, it's on the Republicans who didn't support their governor. Maybe Palin thought the Democrats exercised mind control over those eighteen wayward Republicans and made them override her veto.

The battle over taking the federal economic aid was a case in which Palin insisted on having the last word—and as was often the case with Palin, that word was false.

During that fight, Palin had served up another falsehood. The Republican president of the Alaska Senate basically charged Palin with lying—not about the "strings" tied to the aid, but about her willingness to meet with legislators.

On March 27, 2009, the *Juneau Empire* reported,

> Top legislative leaders and Gov. Sarah Palin clashed Thursday in a battle of press conferences and press releases. Both sides are accusing the other of canceling a meeting to discuss accepting federal stimulus money.
>
> Senate President Gary Stevens, R-Kodiak, called Palin's statements "absolutely false" that legislators would not meet with her to discuss accepting funds.

The *Empire* story noted, "It is rare for the easygoing Stevens to clash with anyone."[21] Palin had been called for telling a lie by a genial politician in her own party, someone who was hardly looking for a fight.

POLITICIZED SCIENCE?

Palin's lawsuit against the federal listing of the polar bear as a threatened species was another case in which she played fast and loose with the truth. At the time she filed the suit, Palin attacked the scientific case for the listing with words like "uncertain," "unproven," "arbitrary," and "speculation." She claimed the suit was based on a "comprehensive review" of the federal science. In an op-ed for the *Washington Post* after she quit as governor, she said the suit was a case in which she "took a stand against politicized science."[22]

In fact, Palin's op-ed was a classic example of an important propaganda technique: accuse your opponents of doing exactly what you are doing.

Palin had refused to release the state's supposed "comprehensive review" of the federal science. She refused to release any of the correspondence from the state's own biologists familiar with the subject—even though she had pledged to run an "open and transparent" administration. As we pointed out in an *Anchorage Daily News* editorial, "When it comes to polar bear 'science,' the Palin administration is hardly 'open and transparent.'" The reason? Openness and transparency would have showed Palin was using politics to override science.

A disclosure made under the federal Freedom of Information Act showed that the state's own experts agreed with the federal scientists' analysis. The federal scientists had received an e-mail from the state's marine mammal expert at the Department of Fish and Game saying, "Overall, we believe that the methods and analytical approaches used to examine the currently available information supports the primary conclusions and inferences stated in these 9 [federal] reports."[23]

University of Alaska professor Rick Steiner helped pry loose that e-mail and wrote about the incident in an op-ed for the *Seattle Post-Intelligencer*. "Contrary to Palin's assertions," he noted, "the state of Alaska's marine mammal scientists agreed with the federal conclusions that the polar bears are in serious trouble because of global warming and loss of their sea ice habitat, and that they would be gone from Alaska by 2050."[24]

It was Palin whose decision on polar bears was based on "politicized science."

BLAMING DEMOCRATS

Palin also tries, in *Going Rogue*, to blame the Troopergate scandal on Democrats. Of firing her public safety commissioner Walt Monegan, she writes, "Democrat legislators and the [state troopers] union spun up a false story that Walt had been fired for personal reasons" and suggests she was being hounded by "the Democrat lawmaker pushing the ginned-up scandal."[25]

It was an amazing exercise in revisionist history. The Troopergate episode is so well known, having been covered extensively by national media during the McCain campaign, you wonder why she would bother to mislead readers with such petty mistruths.

The fact is the Troopergate investigation was launched by unanimous vote of the legislature's interim governing body, the legislative council, which had eight

Republicans and four Democrats. Alaska press accounts had plenty of quotes from Republicans wondering why she fired Monegan and saying Alaskans needed a look at what really happened.

EARLY WARNING SIGNS

Even before she was elected governor, Palin displayed a disturbing ability to go back on her word. During the 2006 governor's race, in a September 27 editorial, we at the *Anchorage Daily News* compared what she told us in May with what she said in later meetings, and asked, "Was she for or against the cruise ship tax initiative? Is she for or against the natural gas reserves tax initiative? How about the billion-dollar Knik Arm bridge, the proposed bridge to the Ketchikan airport or the 50-mile road extension to bring Juneau closer to a highway link out of town?"

On all those issues, she had given different answers at different times. "On May 30, at a meeting with the Daily News editorial board," we wrote, "Ms. Palin said of the cruise ship tax initiative: 'If it were today . . . I'd be a yes.' Then, at a second meeting, just two weeks before the August primary, she said she hadn't made up her mind."

Palin also told us at the May 30 meeting she would vote yes on the natural gas reserves tax initiative. At a meeting three and a half months later, she had changed her mind, saying of the reserves tax, "I still don't like it."

In May, Palin told our editorial board that one spending cut she'd make was the expensive and controversial road connecting Juneau, the state capital, to a new ferry terminal. But in Juneau on September 16, speaking to a group of Republican Women, she said she fully supported the Juneau project.

Of the controversial "Bridge to Nowhere" in Ketchikan, she told our editorial board in May that it was hard to believe the bridge was the best use for all the money it would cost. By our next meeting with her, on August 8, we noted in our editorial, "She said she would love to see the Ketchikan bridge constructed, though she also acknowledged Alaskans need to be realistic about where the money would come from."

We also reported in that editorial that she'd said yes to the Alaska Family Council survey question about whether she supported state-funded school vouchers for religious and private schools. Questioned about it later, Palin told the *Daily News* she knew those vouchers would violate the Alaska Constitution and her answer on the questionnaire was just a mistake—she'd checked the wrong box.

It's true, Palin was an inexperienced candidate, working her way up a steep learning curve as she discovered how some very big issues were playing in her race. Early on, she hadn't done enough homework to decide, once and for all, where she was going to stand on some very controversial issues in the campaign.

But in retrospect, the flip-flops and political wiggling we discussed in that editorial were a sign that Palin's word was not to be trusted.

■ ■ ■

One of Palin's opponents in the Republican primary for governor hit her hard on the "trust" theme. Former legislator Johne Binkley sent a flier reprinting a scathing editorial from her local paper about Palin's early performance as Wasilla mayor.

The editorial, from a February 1997 edition of the *Frontiersman*, is worth quoting at length:

> Palin seems to have assumed her election was instead a coronation. Welcome to Kingdom Palin, the land of no accountability. . . .
>
> Wasilla residents have been subjected to attempts to unlawfully appoint council members, statements that have been shown to be patently untrue, unrepentant backpedaling, and incessant whining that her only enemies are the press and a few disgruntled supports of former Mayor John Stein. . . .
>
> Mayor Palin fails to have a firm grasp of something very simple: the truth. For example compare her statements about NOT firing police chief Irl Stambaugh and library director Marry Ellen Emmons Jan. 30 with the text of the letters she wrote to each. They cannot be reconciled.

Palin managed to get past those early controversies in Wasilla, avoid the recall election that some were seeking at the time, and later easily win reelection as mayor. She had a smooth first nineteen months as governor, with popularity ratings pushing 90 percent.

But when the Troopergate scandal broke, the truth-challenged, accountability-evading Palin reemerged. Under political stress, she resorted to old habits. There's a saying in journalism that truth is the first casualty in war. For Palin, truth is the first casualty when facing political criticism.

"GOING ROGUE" WITH THE TRUTH

Palin's habit of dancing around the truth continued after she quit Alaska's governor's office and focused on being a national conservative celebrity. She continued to display a knack for hanging a statement on a shred of truth and twisting it to produce a totally distorted, self-serving picture for her audience.

In *Going Rogue*, she writes this about her big tax increase on the oil industry: "Of course, I took the political hits as the oil companies launched a smear campaign that we were raising taxes on industry."[26]

A smear campaign is when you are being attacked with false or irrelevant charges that are highly inflammatory. Palin had in fact raised taxes on the oil industry and the industry used its First Amendment rights to criticize her for doing so.

To call the industry's true statement about her a "smear" is not technically a lie, since opinions can vary about what constitutes a "smear," but Palin's claim is remarkably brazen. She grossly twisted the meaning of the word "smear." To her, any criticism of her, even if true, is by definition a "smear." By using that emotionally charged word, she clearly intended to demonize her opponents and cast herself as victim, when in fact she had done exactly what she was accused of doing. It's Propaganda 101: make people think you are the victim of unfair attacks, even when what your opponents say is true.

She had done the same thing during her governor's race, responding to an incident uncovered by conservative journalist Paul Jenkins, with the *Voice of the Times* in Anchorage. Jenkins wrote about how Palin used her mayor's office in Wasilla to campaign for lieutenant governor in 2002. Palin accused Jenkins of a "smear" as well—even though what he'd said was true, fully documented in records he obtained from city files and later corroborated in other media coverage.[27]

Palin's memoir had more revisionist history about her oil tax increase. "A year later," she wrote in *Going Rogue*, "vindication came when industry officials admitted that the legislation was working and had even significantly increased their profits while spurring them to invest more."[28]

That would be news to the big companies like Exxon, BP, Conoco, and Chevron, which pay the vast majority of the state's oil taxes. The extra billions raised by ACES came straight off their bottom line. The oil tax increase had been the right thing to do, in my humble opinion. But it's just false for Palin to say a multibillion-dollar tax increase on Alaska's oil companies "increased their profits."

Palin's claim might have been true if she had said she was talking about only a couple of small newcomers to Alaska like Eni and Pioneer. They got new state tax breaks for exploration drilling they'd already committed to do, while not yet having any oil production subject to the new tax. Their profits probably did go up. But her claim in *Going Rogue* was deliberately worded to make it sound like all "industry officials" liked the tax change—a gross distortion of the truth.

In *Going Rogue*, Palin writes, "I loved every part of my job" as governor.[29] That is the politically correct thing to say, of course. Contrast that statement with what she said when millions of readers were not looking. Frank Bailey's memoir about working for Palin reports that he got a message from her in 2009 in which she said, "I hate this damn job." In that e-mail, she mentioned "quitting in a heartbeat if we have the right message for Alaskans to be able to understand that

I can affect change outside the system better than inside this flippin' kangaroo court joke of a job."

When you are dealing with politicians, you have to watch what they do, not what they say. And what Palin did was quit her job as governor. She was not being pressured to resign because of scandal. She simply quit—which is what you do when you don't love your job. What she e-mailed to Frank Bailey fits the behavior we saw. Her claim in *Going Rogue* does not. Did she lie in her book or just tell a polite, politically correct fib? Either way, it just was not true.

Palin's problems with truth telling about her tenure as governor continued long after her book came out. In an interview with the *New York Times* in the fall of 2010, Palin took credit as governor for "getting things out of the government's hands, like the state-owned dairy creamery in Alaska."[30]

That slippery bit of political spin made her sound like a hard-line, privatizing, less-government Republican, in spite of the state money she had poured into the failing dairy operation. She got the dairy creamery "out of the government's hands" only after trying and failing to save it.

■ ■ ■

To parents who have survived guiding children through adolescence, Palin's unreliable behavior and truth-stretching in the face of criticism feel very familiar. An adolescent will routinely do the same. He will say, "Sure, I'll be home by the 1 a.m. curfew," and at the time, he really, sincerely means it. Then 1 a.m. comes and goes, and the adolescent is still out having a good time.

To the parent, it looks like the adolescent went back on his word. To the adolescent, he has merely made a different decision based on new information—all of a sudden, here are wonderful good times that are just too much fun to pass up by going home as promised.

Going back on his word may cause some grief with the parents, but he will deal with that later. Maybe he'll get lucky and the parents will be asleep when he gets home and not notice his late arrival. If they do notice, he'll try to fast-talk his way out of it.

When trying to fast-talk her way out of trouble, Palin has a couple of techniques. At first, she may respond in a way that defies the plain meaning of words. Her opponents are "smearing" her with truthful criticisms. She "won" on all of the first fifteen ethics charges against her, even as she repaid questionable payments for her children's travel. Let's not argue whether she called on Alaska U.S. senator Mark Begich to resign—that would be "splitting hairs."

In the dictionary that exists only in Sarah Palin's mind, responses like that are not lying or even distorting the truth. Although, if she thinks it's necessary to protect herself, she'll resort to outright falsehoods, hence her remarks on Troopergate, Todd's involvement with the secessionist party and his health insurance, and whom to blame for her political defeats.

When I interviewed Juneau-based journalist Bob Tkacz about his experience covering Palin as part of the capital press corps, I asked him what is the most important thing people should know about her, based on his firsthand experience. His reply: "She is not an honest person."

Palin has repeatedly shown she can manipulate language in a way worthy of the best propagandists and hired-gun lawyers. While the public puts lawyers and political spinners in the same loathsome class as used car salesmen, Palin has never suffered the politician's usual fate for regularly serving up falsehoods, distortions and, yes, even lies.

On her last day in office, as she officially handed power over to her lieutenant governor, Palin launched this famous jab, aimed at "some in the media": "How about, in honor of the American soldier, ya' quit makin' things up?"[31]

She would have done better as governor if she'd taken her own advice.

16

"Where's Sarah?"

When John McCain made Sarah Palin internationally famous, the world was suddenly eager to learn about her record as governor. At the *Anchorage Daily News*, we addressed that curiosity in a series of editorials. In the one about Palin's leadership, we said she had, up to that point, "been very effective, surprisingly so, considering her previous leadership experience was as mayor of a town with about 6,000 people."[1] (Her lack of experience was a big reason we at the *Daily News* had not endorsed her for governor. Her extreme socially conservative views were the other big factor.)

Palin's successes were all the more remarkable given her lack of skill at the inside game of politics. In our editorial, we noted:

> Palin dislikes the give-and-take that usually helps smooth the way for political decisions. She states her case and expects legislators to base their actions on the merits of the issue."
>
> Palin racked up her legislative victories even though her allies in the Legislature criticized her lobbying effort. Here at the *Daily News*, we repeatedly heard the complaint: The governor is missing in action; her staffers aren't working the halls the way they should be.[2]

Staying off the front lines of legislative work was probably a good thing for Palin. She wasn't very good at it.

One example came during her push to pass ethics reform. She wanted some amendments to the bill that had emerged from a senate committee. Instead of looking for a sponsor in the bipartisan majority coalition, where she had allies like Democratic ethics reform advocate Hollis French, she had a member of the senate's all-Republican minority introduce her amendments. All but one of her proposals were defeated. She apparently didn't realize that it's standard legislative practice for the majority to vote down floor amendments from the minority, especially if it is a potentially complicated issue that would ordinarily receive careful review in committee.

Palin responded with a press release blasting the senate for failing to make her changes in the ethics bill. Senator French had to go to Palin, explain her mistake, and suggest how they could work together as the ethics reform bills moved ahead.

Another awkward incident came in dealing with the powerful House Finance co-chair, fellow Republican Mike Chenault. Near the end of her first legislative session, when she learned he was holding up one of her priority bills, she decided to march down to Chenault's office, unannounced, with reporters tagging along. Chenault refused to see her and kept the bill bottled up. It was quite the spectacle for those who saw it.

Sabra Ayres of the *Anchorage Daily News* was there. She told me that the press corps

> can't believe this is happening. This troop of us shows up with Palin in front. . . . His office assistant's jaw is agape. . . . It was *very* awkward. . . . We're sure this is *not* good legislative protocol. Later, I was talking to legislative aides and they were really insulted. They took it pretty seriously. It stung pretty bad. They saw it as an ambush. They saw it as unprofessional, especially dragging all the press along.[3]

■ ■ ■

During Palin's first legislative session, oil prices spiked upward, giving Alaska's oil-dependent state treasury lots of money for legislators to think about spending. It was a chance to stuff more than the usual amount of special projects into the annual capital budget, and legislators took advantage of it.

Palin announced that "there needs to be an adult in the house" and vetoed $230 million of projects. Some level of vetoes was warranted—legislators had gone overboard, as we said in a *Daily News* editorial. But legislators complained she gave them no warning such huge cuts were coming and no chance to pare back their spending plan on their own. It was as if she didn't mind them passing a bloated capital budget, because it would let her look good at their expense by vetoing so many items.

Writing in the *Juneau Empire*, Republican representative Bill Thomas and Democratic senator Albert Kookesh offered a bipartisan complaint:

We provided backup information with our project requests and followed up with the legislative Finance committees and the governor's budget staff. . . . We were never contacted by the governor, her chief of staff or her legislative director on her capital project agenda. There was no communication regarding the budget between the executive branch and the legislators—Republican or Democrat.[4]

Contrast that with her boast from her speech to the Republican National Convention: "I came to office promising to control spending, by request if possible, but by veto, if necessary." Once in office, she skipped the request part and went straight to the veto.

Many others, including the *Anchorage Daily News*, noted that Palin seemed to show a hometown bias in the list of projects she vetoed and those she approved. That caused even more ill will with the affected legislators.

Palin's lobbying touch got a little better that fall, during the special session that produced a multibillion-dollar oil tax reform. In the archive of her e-mails released by the state in June 2011, Palin writes about frequent meetings with legislators, as she works with her legislative staff and oil and gas team to round up votes for her oil tax plan. She mentions having to deal with claims by her opponents that she was "threatening" legislators on the oil tax issue. (The e-mails the state released show no evidence of any threats. However, such e-mails, if they existed, might have been among the hundreds withheld under the state's interpretation of the state law that exempts internal deliberations involving the governor from disclosure.)

During the oil tax fight in the autumn of 2007, Palin was still dealing with fallout from her "adult in the house" remark. In a November 3 e-mail, she noted this report from her legislative lobbyist Russ Kelly: "Russ says in walking the halls the universal msg he receives re: why legislators have chips on their shoulders, mad at us (even republicans who like us) is based on one msg they heard me say through the budget process when I made my cuts: 'We need an adult in the house.'"

She blamed that remark on her previous legislative director, John Bitney, the man she fired for having an affair with the wife of a family friend. By then Bitney worked for her fellow Republican, House Speaker John Harris. Palin's November 3 e-mail said, "Ironically, when Russ asks, he's told it's Bitney perpetuating that msg, rubbing it in and reminding legislators I said it. The irony is it was Bitney who gave me that line." (Bitney later told the *Anchorage Daily News* he may have tossed that line off during a discussion with her, but he did not suggest she use it in public.)

In the high-stakes fight on oil taxes, Palin managed to overcome the resentment she'd created among legislators. An insider told me that Palin was the one who cut the final deal with Democrats to limit deductions on the state's largest oil fields. That deal, made on her own, cleared the way for the final package of oil tax changes to pass.

The following year, when it was time for the legislature to approve awarding the state's gas pipeline development incentives to TransCanada, Palin had to be prompted to come to Juneau so she could lobby legislators. One of her key oil and gas aides, Marty Rutherford, e-mailed Palin on July 26: "I do want to reiterate the message Tom [Irwin, resources commissioner] sent to you last night, that we do need you here in Juneau early next week to start working Legislators before the AGIA vote."

At the same time, Palin's e-mail archive shows her busy dealing with Trooper-gate and the emerging sexual harassment scandal that would soon sink her new public safety commissioner, Charles Kopp. In one of her e-mails, she complained that with "Walt [Monegan's] stirred-up controversy, the whole AGIA issue was overshadowed."[5]

Once in Juneau, Palin did reach out to legislators. The e-mail archive shows her arranging to talk to a couple of wavering Democratic senators who eventually voted to approve the TransCanada deal (Donny Olson and Bill Wielechowski). She also hosted a breakfast for the members of the senate minority. The out-of-power senators in the minority were conservative Republicans, and all of them eventually supported her on the vote. Palin offered to meet three of the hard-core Republican opponents of the deal, but they remained unpersuaded and voted no.

■ ■ ■

When Governor Palin first came to Juneau, one of her early advisers told me, "She was totally unprepared for what that's like. . . . I don't think she knew the first thing about how to work with the legislative leadership." He told how one member of the leadership, a fellow Republican, an easy-going guy, was already on the outs with Palin after just a month or two. "They call me the enemy," the Republican leader told him. "They've written me off."[6]

Palin's distaste for wheeling and dealing comes through in e-mails the state released to news organizations in June 2011. On February 24, 2008, as the legislature worked over her budget, she wrote to her chief of staff, "Im [*sic*] just appalled at them trying to drag us into deal-making. Who has the time for such nonsense?" The next day she wrote her attorney general, "It's political—it's to get us to have to strike deals with leggies on capital budget items, and we're not playing those games."

How, then, was Palin so successful in passing ethics reform, her gas pipeline legislation, and a multibillion-dollar oil tax reform?

One key was that she had the good fortune to present herself as a let's-clean-house reformer just as corruption scandals involving legislators and the state's oil industry were erupting. Palin jokingly referred to her good fortune in an e-mail on July 11, 2008. She thanked her media staff for "excellent work" and "your amazing ability to mandate another indictment at just the right time. . . . :)"

Thanks to her good timing, there was a strong vein of popular outrage she could tap, and tapping it was the kind of political work she was good at. In an *Anchorage Daily News* editorial we said, "She uses her charisma and a simple, clear vision to mobilize mass support for her agenda, then leaves the details and heavy lifting to others."[7]

One of Palin's key aides in passing her gas pipeline legislation, Marty Rutherford, told me Palin "had a good sense of how people would react, of how to talk about it with the public."[8] When trying to persuade reluctant legislators about the details of gas line legislation, though, Palin had to rely on her team of experts to handle the job. That worked well for those highly complex issues.

On other issues, we said in our editorial at the *Anchorage Daily News*, "The limitations of Gov. Palin's leadership style begin to show. She delegates much of the detail work and spends little time on second tier subjects." Larry Persily, a former journalist who worked for Palin on federal issues in Washington D.C., told me, "People couldn't get her attention on things beyond oil and gas." Working on issues, he said, "required more knowledge and more depth than she was willing to put into it."[9]

Palin heard criticism like that from her public safety commissioner, Walt Monegan, shortly after she fired him. In her defense, she worked up this response by e-mail with her staff (July 21, 2008): "The time spent on AGIA [her gas line inducement act] over the last year and a half has not been to the detriment of ANY department or its missions." She admitted spending a good deal of time on the issue—which is one reason she had "high expectations" for cabinet members, whom she expected to be "self-starters and results-oriented."

"She just wanted to do the fun stuff, not the work stuff," Persily said. "She liked dealing with the public. She got her energy from it. . . . Working on policy or with legislators was like Kryptonite to her. It sapped her strength."[10]

As her term continued, relations with the legislature continued to deteriorate. Shortly after her vice-presidential nomination, the *New Yorker* magazine reported this from a conversation with Republican senate president Lyda Green:

Green says, Palin, unlike her predecessors—Democrats and Republicans—has ignored leaders in the legislature and turned every policy disagreement, whether a dispute over a tax on studded tires or a recent debate on rebate checks, into a personal vendetta.

"That became her style: in the media implying a negative picture of the legislature," Green said.[11]

In *Going Rogue*, Palin put the blame on others, notably her fired legislative director, John Bitney. Paul Fuhs, a lobbyist and disaffected former adviser to Palin, defended his friend Bitney in his newspaper op-ed about Palin's memoir:

> Her attacks on Bitney in her book are just plain false and show her basic misunderstanding of how government works. She castigated him for saying he was "friends" with some legislators and so because of that she had to wonder "whose side he was on."
> Well, to start with, the Legislature is not the enemy. They are an equal, elected, constitutional branch of government.[12]

THE BLACKBERRY GOVERNOR

When dealing with people one-on-one, Palin could be quite charming. David Finkelstein, a former Democratic state representative known for his work on ethics and campaign finance reform, met Palin when she was a candidate for governor. "She called me by my first name, put her hand on my arm in a very warm manner, and thanked me for my work on an ethics reform bill," he told me. "Her good looks and warm style created a very winning effect on me. . . . If our politics weren't so opposite, she might have won me over."

You would think a woman with that kind of charisma would make it a top priority to talk directly to people and use her charm to get her way. Odd then, that she conducted so much of her business as governor by BlackBerry.

Palin used her BlackBerry extensively, in part because she was basically the state's first tele-commuting governor, trying to maintain her home in Wasilla (some six-hundred miles from the state capital in Juneau) and keep her family there as much as possible. But Revenue Commissioner Pat Galvin told me she was well known for BlackBerrying during face-to-face meetings. She would convene a cabinet meeting, Galvin said, make some introductory remarks, then proceed to spend the rest of the time working two different BlackBerrys. In *The Lies of Sarah Palin*, Geoffrey Dunn quotes a member of Palin's security detail, Gary Wheeler, saying, "She often seemed more interested in her two BlackBerrys when talking to other people, to the point of being rude at times."[13]

Her aide, Larry Persily, told me that "her BlackBerry addiction was legendary." He'd heard about one meeting where she'd been made to let go of her BlackBerrys so she would not be distracted. "When another staff member's BlackBerry went off, she twitched," Persily said.

During one early cabinet meeting about the state-owned dairy, Palin banged out a 163-word e-mail to her brother. He had suggested she convene a task force on the problem. She wrote back:

> From: <gov.sarah@yahoo.com> [gov.sarah@yahoo.com]
> Sent: Friday, June 15, 2007 7:33 PM
> To: Annette Kreitzer; John Katz; Larry Persily; Emil R Notti; Joseph D Schmidt; Lawrence L Hartig; Tom Irwin; Leo Von Scheben; Walt C Monegan; Roger L Sampson; Denby S Lloyd; Joseph R Balash; John W Bitney; Karen J Rehfeld; Kristina Y Perry; Meghan N Stapleton; Michael A Nizich; Michael A Tibbles; Sharon W Leighow; Sean Parnell; Karleen K Jackson; Clark C Bishop; Talis J Colberg; Patrick S Galvin; Craig Campbell; chckheath; Todd Palin; Franci Havemeister
> Subject: Re: mat maid
> Chuck: Yes—we need this task force. We're in a cabinet mtg right now discussing the topic. Have Joe Austerman get thinking on this—I just cleared his participation with Commissioner Notti. Mike Tibbles will be in charge. Let him talk to you about it and some of the other plans we have for revitalization/changes within Ag. (And MatMaid.). This will be awesome!
> Stand by for Tibbles and Kris Perry to contact you with directives.
> You have my blessing and THANKS for being concerned and energized and excited about finding solutions. . . .

Sitting in a meeting with her cabinet members, she didn't speak up and say, "I just told my brother we're moving ahead with a task force on this"—she notified them by e-mail. "I'm ccing Cabinet members bc [because] their areas are also affected by the MatMaid issue and just wanted to let them know we're off and running with the task force idea," she wrote in that e-mail to her brother.

If she could type forty words per minute on a BlackBerry, a pretty fast rate, this message took at least four minutes—right in the middle of meeting on the same subject she was writing about.

Palin's oil and gas aide, Marty Rutherford, told me Palin would sometimes BlackBerry during their meetings. Occasionally Rutherford got frustrated at that, but Palin showed "she could listen and be BlackBerrying at the same time." Rutherford said there were times when she thought Palin wasn't listening and asked her to focus in. Palin consistently surprised her by picking up the thread of the conversation right away, showing she had been following along. "She can double-task," Rutherford told me.

Was that constant BlackBerrying a good use of her time? In *The 7 Habits of Highly Effective People*, Stephen Covey distinguishes between matters that are "urgent but not important" and "important but not urgent."[14] To Palin, whatever was on her BlackBerry was urgent and got attention, regardless of how important it might have been.

Her aide, Frank Bailey, reported in his book that much of what Palin was doing on her BlackBerry was defending herself against her critics, what her second attorney general called the "Chihuahuas" nipping away at her. Palin's addiction to BlackBerry work had carried over from her campaign for governor. Seeing how she operated during the campaign, Bailey wrote, "She had a lot to learn about time management as she spent countless hours on details that likely deserved delegation." One example he gives is this e-mail lament from her during the campaign:

5/15/2006 4:52:39 PM
    ok—i have to clone myself or something. . . or i'm going to have a nervous breakdown. . . . i just returned home (to pick up kids and cook dinner) and I see a dozen more email questions i have to add to my list of 81 other emails needing answers. we have to have a different system. . . or i must concentrate on only this task and forget many other things that are piling up.

Todd Palin knew his wife needed help dealing with her time-management issues. Bailey's book included this e-mail from him, after she won the primary: "We need to stop, shield and intercept any e-mails from supporter's [*sic*] who have fallen through the cracks and are mad, from getting to Sarah. When she receives these e-mail [*sic*] she feels obligated to respond, taking valuable time away from her preparation for the next day's events."

Todd's plan for shielding his overstressed wife didn't work, according to Bailey. Palin would inevitably discover the screened-out complaints and launch a tirade about how they'd been withheld from her. In the campaign, and her time as governor, her BlackBerry gave her a steady supply of information she wanted, regardless of how important it might have seemed to others around her.

Bailey's account is confirmed in the 24,199 pages of Palin's e-mails the state released in June 2011. The *Anchorage Daily News* reported that the e-mails "show a chief executive who was engrossed with countering her critics and increasingly upset at news coverage as she vaulted into international celebrity."[15]

Palin closely followed reader comments on the *Anchorage Daily News* politics blog. In one e-mail, she wrote, "i need folks to really help ramp up accurate counter comments to the misinformation that's being spread out there." She even took it upon herself to recruit responses that others could submit in her defense. In late July 2007, she wrote, "I'm looking for someone to correct the letter writer's goofy comments, but don't want the letter to the ADN [*Anchorage Daily News*] in response to come from me."

At one point, Palin complained she didn't have enough time to monitor how she was being talked about. She wrote that she "will try to carve out time in the day to more fully scan news clippings and try to catch some of the talk shows via internet, but so far I haven't even found an extra minute to be able to tune into the shows unless I'm . . . driving in my car."

Governor Palin was juggling heavy family responsibilities, with school-aged children and a husband who commuted to week-long shifts on a job in Alaska's North Slope oil fields, a thousand miles away from the state capital. She preferred to work from her home base in Wasilla when the legislature was not in session. By the time she ran for vice president, state travel records showed that she'd spent 312 nights at home in Wasilla—almost half her term up to that point.

As much as she used her BlackBerry and e-mail, Palin was not always able to keep up with state business from a distance. On August 9, 2007, she wrote to key aides to "please give me MORE info on ALL issues as opposed to less. please send that direction to all staff. I am too far out of the loop on too many issues and then things get in panic-mode. . . . My email is always on."

The e-mails the state released show her struggling to balance work and the family life she wanted to have. Several indicate she was looking for opportunities to have her children travel with her at state expense.[16]

E-mails to Erika Fagerstrom, manager of the governor's mansion, show Palin reluctant to accept her help arranging meals for the Palin children, since reassigning the previous governor's chef was one of the popular changes she'd made. "I can't afford to have the perception be that I'm using staff as full-time chefs," Palin wrote in one. "I'm happy to cook, and Willow is expected to do so also."[17]

Palin also got help looking after her girls from Ivy Frye, one of her key political aides. At 6:23 p.m. on Friday, May 24, 2007, Frye wrote this e-mail to Palin, "Just went tanning with Bri (Bristol). I told her I would stop by later to see how things were going. I told Willow I'd take her to rent some movies. I have both my phones if you need anything. Hope you had a good trip!"[18]

After Palin won big battles on ethics and oil taxes in her first year, legislators took out some frustration with her by resisting lower-profile bills she wanted. On April 11, 2008, she e-mailed her key legislative and media staff, "Seems a lot of actions have been one-way negotiations where they're winning their projects and bills, but we're still not getting the few and far-between requests I've had." Palin asked, "Are we not pushing hard enough, but instead seeming to cave to their wants?"[19]

Eventually, Palin decided on an outside-game tactic to help pass her bill reducing business license fees. It had been stalled in Senate Finance Committee for almost a year. On April 10, she sent an e-mail blast to 22,940 names gathered from the state's business license office, asking them to call their senators about the bill, HB111.

Her use of state business records to pressure the legislature drew some criticism. But within two days, senate finance passed the license fee reduction and the full senate approved it, in the hectic last few hours before adjournment.

Shortly after Palin started her vice-presidential campaign, a story in the *New York Times* gave this review on her work as governor: "Democrats and Republicans alike describe her as often missing in action. . . . During the last legislative session, some lawmakers became so frustrated with her absences that they took to wearing 'Where's Sarah?' pins."[20]

The *Times'* report echoed a story in the *Juneau Empire*, which noted, "Palin has spent little time in Juneau, rarely coming to the state capital except when the legislature was in session, and sometimes not even then. During a recent [summer 2008] special session called by Palin herself, she faced criticism from several legislators for not showing up personally to push for her agenda." Andrea Doll, a Juneau Democrat in the state house, told the *Empire*, "At a time when her leadership was truly needed, we didn't know where she was."[21]

One of Palin's aides, Tara Jolie, sent her an e-mail on August 2, explaining "why we (Commerce) got reamed by House Finance [Committee]." Jolie reported that she was told by a key legislative aide: "There is frustration with the governor's office because they expect more legislation (or ideas) from the Governor because she is our elected leader. This nasty hearing was an expression of their frustration."

Legislators wanted more initiative from Palin administration commissioners, the legislative aide told Jolie. That led Jolie to write, "My question is—who is on first? Do you need to ask us for ideas and solutions that we process through our Commissioner? . . . DCRA [Division of Community and Regional Affairs] is sitting on a boatload of data and information especially on rural issues."

The *New York Times* story reported, "Many politicians say they typically learn of her initiatives—and vetoes—from news releases."[22] Palin's e-mail archives includes a report on one such complaint. Aide Ivy Frye e-mailed Palin about a meeting with Ketchikan Republican Kyle Johansen, after the governor cancelled his community's controversial "Bridge to Nowhere." "He was caught off guard and found out via the press release," Frye reported to Palin on September 22, 2007.

Palin's penchant for government-by-press-release foreshadowed her enthusiasm for the safe one-way communication of Facebook and Twitter. Reporters who got press releases had a pesky habit of asking questions that might challenge the wisdom or accuracy of what she said. Facebook and Twitter offered an impenetrable wall against follow-up scrutiny from the "lamestream" media.

Palin wasn't distant just from the media and her fellow state lawmakers. According to the *New York Times* story, "At an Alaska Municipal League gathering in Juneau in January [2008], mayors across the political spectrum swapped stories of the governor's remoteness. How many of you, someone asked, have tried to meet with her? Every hand went up, recalled Mayor Fred Shields of Haines Borough. And how many met with her? Just a few hands rose."[23]

Paul Fuhs, the lobbyist who had been an enthusiastic Palin volunteer and adviser, wrote this in his op-ed about her: "It was well known that she wouldn't even meet with her own commissioners, much less, say, members of the public or the business community."[24]

Palin became even more disengaged during her vice-presidential campaign—no surprise there. But what was surprising, and even offensive to Alaskans, was the way the McCain campaign took over key aspects of her job as governor. We Alaska-based journalists found it was almost impossible to get an answer from the Palin administration about anything having to do with running the state of Alaska. Every query had to be run through the McCain campaign.

In 2008, I contributed to an *Anchorage Daily News* editorial about the situation:

> Gov. Sarah Palin has surrendered important gubernatorial duties to the Republican presidential campaign. McCain staff are handling public and press questions about actions she has taken as governor. . . . Residents of any state would be offended to see their governor cede such a fundamental, day-to-day governmental responsibility to a partisan politician from another state. It's especially offensive to Alaskans.
>
> Official state business—like Troopergate—should be handled by the governor of the state, not by McCain presidential campaign operatives.[25]

After she lost, Palin didn't realize it at the time, but she came back to a very different state, with a very different political climate, from the one she left in August.

17

Palin Returns to Her Day Job

After losing the vice-presidential race, Sarah Palin returned to her day job. The small-town girl had gotten a taste of the big wide world and—surprise!—had trouble adjusting after being forced to come back home. At the *Anchorage Daily News*, we wrote an editorial asking:

> Which Sarah Palin is coming back to finish her term as governor of Alaska?
>
> The pragmatic centrist who built effective coalitions with Democrats and reform-minded Republicans and declined to legislate her socially conservative values?
>
> Or the highly partisan Sarah Palin who tried to tar her political opponent with terms like "socialist" and "terrorist," while touting her stands on divisive issues like abortion and same-sex marriage? . . .
>
> The former approach is what made her such a wildly popular governor here in Alaska. . . Alaskans chose her because she promised a different way of doing business, not more of the same mindless partisan warfare.
>
> Her obligations as governor point her in one direction. Her national ambitions point her in another.[1]

At first, Palin did not realize that her partisan-pitbull work for John McCain had shattered her governing coalition back home. Her former Democratic allies were no longer eager to help her. Establishment Republicans, who had dutifully supported the national ticket, did not rally to her side. Many of her fellow Republican legislators grew even more alienated.

Her national ambitions required her to play up her conservative, less-government credentials, but Alaskans wanted and needed an activist government in their oil-rich but underdeveloped state. Her desire to keep getting national attention clearly distracted her from the mundane duties of the job Alaskans had elected her to do.

Palin was clueless about how her behavior on the campaign trail had changed the climate she would face back home as governor. She had actually expected Alaska Democrats and "the left" to be bipartisan and support her run for vice-president.[2] A November 8, 2008, *New York Times* story said, "Ms. Palin suggested in the interview that how she ran for vice president would not shape how she governs Alaska. . . . If anybody wants to try to criticize and say, 'Oh, all of a sudden she's an obsessive partisan,' they're wrong, she said."[3] Alaska filmmaker Dennis Zaki caught Palin's return to Alaska. When questioned about her partisan attacks for the McCain campaign, she said, "Nobody should have hurt feelings. . . . This is politics, and politics is rough and tumble."[4]

That was not the people-before-politics attitude that candidate Sarah Palin promised to Alaska voters when she ran for governor. In a campaign flier issued after winning the Republican nomination, she had told Alaskans, "We need the energy and courage to throw 'politics as usual' out the window."

Gubernatorial candidate Palin had sent a letter, dated October 27, 2006, courting nonpartisan registered voters like me, saying, "I am also concerned about the extreme partisanship that has come to dominate our public affairs lately." That critique of "extreme partisanship" might have described her own behavior two years later in the vice-presidential race.

Democratic state representative Les Gara, a supporter of Governor Palin on several of her early initiatives, noted the toll her partisan attacks had taken. He told the *New York Times* after the election, "She's coming back to a divided state, where Democrats had supported her but they watched her for two months call the president-elect of the United States a terrorist sympathizer."[5]

Palin was "chagrined" to learn she'd lost the support of her former Democratic allies in Juneau, according to an interview she gave Robert Draper of the *New York Times* in late 2010. Draper wrote,

> I brought up her past efforts at bipartisanship to Palin. "I was so innocent and naïve to believe that I would be able to govern for four years and if I ever moved on beyond the governorship I could carry that with me nationally," Palin said. "And it was proven when John McCain chose me for the nomination for vice president; what it showed me about the left: they go home. It doesn't matter what you do. It was the left that came out attacking me. They showed me their hypocrisy; they showed me they weren't willing to work in a bipartisan way."[6]

Upon her return as governor, her fellow Republican legislators were not clear how Palin would conduct herself and what she wanted to do. Just days after she and McCain lost, the *New York Times* quoted a Republican house member, former speaker John Harris, saying, "We were just trying to figure out what kind of policy things the governor may want to address and we were kind of scratching our heads, because we don't know."[7]

The *Times* also quoted another influential house Republican leader, Rep. John Coghill, saying, "She's coming back to a whole different world from when she left. If she comes back with a puffed up ego there's going to be problems. But if she comes back ready to work, that will be better."[8]

BACK AT WORK

Legislators and Alaskans soon found out what kind of governor they were dealing with: ambitious, distracted, inaccessible, difficult to work with.

During what would prove to be Palin's last legislative session, House Finance Committee co-chair Mike Hawker, a Republican, complained, "I've had a lot of friction with the governor this year on her lack of connection, frankly the appearance that she's more concerned about her national ambitions than what's going on in the state."[9]

Republican Alan Austerman of Kodiak had the same complaint. "Nobody from the [Palin] administration has been to my office at all. . . . I see a number of different legislators all shaking their heads, same thing, nobody's been in their office," he said.[10]

When legislators did try to deal with Palin that session, they got more frustrated. The *Juneau Empire* reported that Republican senator Gary Stevens "has been among a growing number of legislators who have complained that they can't find out from Palin's staff what her goals for the [federal] stimulus money are. . . . She left Juneau in the midst of the stimulus debate Thursday" to announce her pick for attorney general in Anchorage. "We really need to have a face-to-face with the person who is the chief of government," Stevens said, according to the *Empire's* story. Palin's staff, he said, "often have trouble answering questions or making decisions or letting us know the intentions of the administration."[11]

Bob Tkacz, an independent journalist who covers fisheries and business issues in Juneau and followed Palin closely, told me: "I've never seen a person change that much. . . . The kind of person she was up to when she was nominated and the person she was when she came back—except for her personal appearance, it was almost two different people."

INVINCIBLE NO MORE

Palin was no longer the conquering heroine, cleaning up Alaska politics, and putting the people's interests above all else. She was a celebrity worrying about how the outside world was watching her. Because Alaskans could see that, her popularity in her home state began to wane. The many legislators she had alienated felt emboldened to stand up to her, and that's what they did when she nominated a controversial Anchorage lawyer to replace her Troopergate-tainted attorney general, Talis Colberg.

Wayne Anthony Ross was one of Alaska's most flamboyant and best-known conservative lawyers. A former board member of the National Rifle Association, and probably Alaska's most famous defender of Second Amendment gun rights, Ross drove a Hummer with a vanity plate sporting his initials, "WAR." Ross had once defended a man who threw water on peace protesters in the dead of Alaska's winter, claiming that what his client did was not assault, but simply an exercise of his free speech rights.[12]

Personally genial, Ross wasn't afraid to say what was on his mind, insulting though it might be. In one notorious incident from 1993, he had opposed a gay rights ordinance, writing a commentary that called gays "degenerates . . . whose beliefs are certainly immoral in the eyes of anyone with some semblance of intelligence and moral character."[13]

Ross was bitterly unpopular with Alaska's rural legislators, because he was a high-profile defender of urban sportsmen in disputes over who got priority hunting and fishing rights in Alaska. Alaska Natives overwhelmingly took the other side from Ross in those disputes. To them, Ross, with his unyielding opposition to their cause and unsympathetic rhetoric, was seen as anti-Native. It was another case where Palin wrote off the concerns of Alaska's substantial Native population, even though she liked to boast about her husband's Native heritage.

Ross probably could have withstood all the controversy and won confirmation despite his boss's alienation from so many legislators—but for one notorious incident after Palin named him. Governor Palin was in the middle of a prolonged fight with senate Democrats about filling a vacant seat in Juneau. The dispute had kept the capital city unrepresented in the senate for weeks.

As is the case in Alaska, Ross was serving in office temporarily, pending legislative confirmation. The *Anchorage Daily News* summarized the infamous incident with Ross this way:

> Ross signed off on Palin forwarding three names to the Senate Democrats to consider for the single seat (two of whom the Senate Democrats had already rejected). The Legislature's legal division declared that an illegal move. In response, Ross told a reporter Wednesday, "it seems to me the most important thing that can be done by the Senate is not argue with legal or illegal but to appoint somebody to represent Juneau."[14]

It was really not the best idea for the nominee to the state's top law enforcement job to recommend doing the politically expedient thing even though it might be illegal.

It also wasn't a good idea for Palin to leave the state just before Ross's confirmation vote. The *Anchorage Daily News* account noted that Palin had left to speak in Indiana at a Right to Life event.[15] She went on that trip even though there were only a few days left in the legislative session and lawmakers' work was, as usual, coming to a climax on multiple fronts.

Without Palin around to shore up support for her choice for attorney general, legislators easily rejected Ross, 23 to 35. It was the first time in Alaska history that the legislature rejected a governor's cabinet nominee. Among the "no" votes were nine Republicans, including the speaker of the house and senate president.[16] It was as if legislators in both parties were saying, "Take that, Ms. Former-Vice-Presidential nominee." And Palin, by her absence at such a key time, seemed to be saying, "I don't really care that much about the job I'm supposed to be doing in Alaska. I'd rather be in the Lower 48, talking to adoring crowds."

NATIONAL AMBITIONS VS. ALASKA REALITIES

In early June 2009, another notorious incident suggested Palin was gearing up to leave Alaska behind for greater things in the Lower 48.

She gave an interview to Fox TV personality Sean Hannity in which she asserted that the recent rebound in oil prices was a bad thing for Alaska. In Alaska, this is heresy, since oil taxes and royalties fund about 90 percent of routine state operations, making it possible to live without a state sales tax or personal income tax. Alaska's abundant oil money also built a $30-plus billion savings account that pays each Alaskan an annual dividend of over $1,000.

Speaking as the price of oil pushed $70 a barrel, up from the $30 level that would have blown a multibillion-dollar hole in Alaska's budget, Palin said, "I thank God it's not at $140." She told Hannity that people ask her, "Aren't you glad the price of oil is going up?" Palin said she tells them no: "The fewer dollars the state of Alaska government has, the fewer dollars we spend, and that's good for our families and the private sector."[17]

At the *Anchorage Daily News*, we wrote an editorial saying that her remark was "astounding." This, we said, was "the governor who used the revenue from $140-a-barrel oil to pay every bona fide Alaska resident—man woman and child—an extra $1,200 straight from the state treasury."[18]

Palin also perplexed Alaskans with her stubborn insistence on refusing significant parts of the economic recovery money the federal government offered states to help pull the economy out of the worst downturn since the Great Depression.

The feds were offering Alaska $930 million—big money in a state where one-third of the economy depends on federal spending. Palin, though, knew that the federal recovery money was hugely unpopular with the national Republican right-wing base she'd courted in the presidential race.

So she cast about for reasons to turn down substantial parts of the federal money. At first, she said she'd reject half the federal aid—the part that funds ongoing government services—while keeping money for one-time-only construction projects. But her math was bad in saying she'd reject one-half, since it included extra Medicaid money that she planned to take. Even Palin knew the Medicaid money was welcome, given the strain the costly joint federal-state program inflicts on state budgets.

Correctly counting the Medicaid money, Palin amended her claim to say she would turn down about a third of the federal money, a total of $288 million for schools and other public services. "In essence we say no to operating funds for more positions in government," she said.[19]

Early on, Palin had some political support for her approach. Asking, as she and others did, "What happens in two years when the extra money runs out?" was a valid question. But even some Republicans wondered early on about the wisdom of turning down $171 million for education. They were reassured to hear school leaders say they would not build up staff that would later have to be laid off.

Anchorage school superintendent Carol Comeau, a popular, nonpartisan community leader, said, "We clearly, clearly recognize that it's going away in two years. . . . We go through this every time we get a grant, or a special program starts."[20]

An outcry was already starting to build, complaining that Palin was hurting Alaska by turning down money to further her national ambitions. Within a day, Palin was scrambling to put out the word that taking the federal money was still an option—she had made no final decision to refuse it.

The more legislators looked at it, the more comfortable they became taking the federal aid money for education and other existing programs. But Palin kept complaining that the money came with burdensome strings.

The legislature thoroughly investigated and found that the strings Palin talked about just didn't exist. Lawmakers got explicit reassurance from the feds that there were no binding strings, only guidelines, on the one last piece Palin complained about, $28.6 million for energy conservation.

House Finance Committee co-chair Mike Hawker, a fiscally conservative Republican, had shared some of Palin's concerns about the federal stimulus money—at first. He led the legislature's search for the strings Palin warned about. Hawker told the *Anchorage Daily News*, "Over that time, I've sometimes begrudgingly and sometimes, quite frankly, slowly and reluctantly, acknowledged that the facts as they bore out did not support those earlier anxieties."[21]

By the time the legislature finished its work, it voted overwhelmingly to take all the federal recovery money. The house voted twice, 40–0, to take all the funding Palin had objected to. In the senate, only four of twenty senators voted no on the bill to take the disputed federal money. It was another big defeat for the small-state governor who'd enjoyed international fame as a vice-presidential candidate.

In an *Anchorage Daily News* editorial covering both her complaints about taking federal recovery money and her remarks to Sean Hannity about oil prices, we said, "Gov. Palin is trying to have it both ways—presiding over an oil state whose economy depends heavily on state oil dollars and on huge amounts of federal spending, while trying to run for national office as a small-government conservative who is tough on spending and taxes. Memo to Gov. Palin: It isn't working."[22]

Palin was so disengaged in the spring of 2009 that she was MIA for work on what the nationally famed antiabortion advocate claimed was one of her top personal priorities—requiring parental consent or notification for a minor to get an abortion.

Republican representative Bill Stoltze brought an abortion consent bill up for a hearing in his committee, but no one from the Palin administration was there to testify about it. "I can't explain their not even being in the room; that baffles me," Stoltze told the *Juneau Empire*. "This is supposedly a top administration priority."[23]

Palin could travel across the continent to speak to a Right to Life convention in Indiana, just days before her state's legislature adjourned, but somehow she couldn't manage to have one of her staff testify on a right-to-life issue, right there in the same building as her Alaska governor's office. It was becoming clearer where Sarah Palin's priorities lay.

While Sarah Palin was missing in action in Juneau, she had a growing presence on Twitter and Facebook. The social media outlets were a way to get her message out, unfiltered, without pesky follow-up questions from the media. Begun in April, her official state Twitter account served up as many as a dozen tweets a day.

Many of Palin's messages were blurbs about her travels across the state to bill-signing ceremonies, her trip to Kosovo to visit Alaska National Guard troops, and the state response to spring floods and summer wildfires. She tweeted a few tidbits of family news and the occasional conservative platitude.

Palin also tweeted prolifically on subjects in the news that journalists would have been happy to ask her more about. She often tweeted about the ethics complaints against her, how well her gas pipeline strategy and oil tax increase were working, her efforts to help ease the economic and energy crises in Alaska's remote villages, the national need for Alaska's energy, pending judicial appointments, and federal court rulings. With Twitter, she could skim the surface of a given subject and zip on to the next topic, without having to prepare for follow-up questions. It was the perfect medium for a governor with a wide popular following and a short attention span.

MOVING ON

At 4:15 p.m. on July 3, Palin's Twitter account served up this message:

"We'll soon attach info on decision to not seek re-election . . . this is in Alaska's best interest, my family's happy . . . it is good, stay tuned." By then, the word was already out across the nation: Palin had announced she would resign. The news had even reached me on my vacation, sitting in the lodge at Alaska's largest national park, Wrangell-St. Elias, some sixty miles from the nearest paved road.

I was as stunned as the rest of the world. I figured she probably wouldn't run for reelection. But to quit in the middle of her term? I didn't believe it when I first heard people at the lodge talking about it, but the publisher of the *Fairbanks Daily News-Miner* was also there and she quickly confirmed the news with her office.

Palin's resignation speech, as with much of her time as governor, was a slap-dash event, hurriedly thrown together, delivered lakeside at her home in Wasilla. She had rounded up available staff and cabinet commissioners, some of whom had been summoned without being told why.[24]

She framed her resignation as a decision not to run for reelection—something everybody would have understood—and went on say she would leave shortly, so as not to be a lame duck governor. "Many just accept that lame duck status and they hit the road, they draw a paycheck. They kind of milk it. And I'm not going to put Alaskans through that."[25]

In her resignation speech, she spun the act of quitting into the opposite of quitting, suggesting that to finish her term was to "appease those who demand: 'Sit down and shut up'" and would actually be "a quitter's way out." But she isn't "wired that way." "Only dead fish go with the flow," she said, in one of the more famous lines Palin would toss off. Apparently referring to ethics complaints and controversies, Palin said, "My staff and I spend most of our day dealing with this instead of progressing our state now."

If that was a problem, it was one of her own making. Facing a new complaint, she could have chosen to issue one quick press release, then let the state screening process play out from there, reviewing the complaint for probable cause. If the complaints were indeed frivolous, she didn't have to waste any significant time or legal fees on them.

Family considerations played a role, too. She said her children supported her decision with "four 'yes's' and one 'hell yeah!' The 'hell yeah' sealed it." She continued, "I think much of it for the kids had to do with recently seeing their baby brother Trig mocked by some pretty mean-spirited adults recently."

This was a classic Palin-as-victim overreaction. The incident that really set her off was a photo mocking her and her adoring talk show host supporter, Eddie Burke. A picture of her holding Trig had been doctored to replace her infant son with the face of her talk show pal. Somehow she twisted that satirical jab into an attack on Trig.

She closed with a famous quote she attributed, as many mistakenly do, to Gen. Douglas MacArthur, rather than one of his generals: "We are not retreating. We are advancing in another direction." [*Time* magazine coverage of the original quote, in 1950, attributed it to one of MacArthur's underlings, Maj. Gen. Oliver Prince Smith.]

Palin certainly was advancing—to national prominence, a large book contract, big speaking fees, a Fox TV contract, a reality TV show. If the "we" who were advancing included Alaska, it was not clear how the state would be "advancing" with her.

Unlike General MacArthur's army, driven from contested Korean territory by the overwhelming force of an invading Chinese army, Palin was driven from office by a rag-tag band of critics filing ethics complaints and being mean to her children.

Palin's decision to quit was widely panned in Alaska. "The reaction to her resignation among Alaskans has been strangely contradictory," veteran Juneau journalist Gregg Erickson wrote later that month. "People criticize her for being a quitter, yet in the next breath say, 'good riddance,' and, 'glad to see her go.'"[26]

Conventional wisdom was that she'd just killed her national political career. (In the following two years, that prediction hadn't exactly panned out.) A few sympathetic national conservatives put a positive spin on her decision to quit. Mary Matalin called it "brilliant." Palin's early booster, founder and editor of the *Weekly Standard* Bill Kristol, suggested she was "crazy like a fox."[27]

Palin did not take questions after delivering her resignation speech. She soon posted more thoughts on Facebook. This message was clearly aimed at her national audience, rather than the Alaskans she'd addressed from Wasilla. "It's about country," she wrote. "I am now looking ahead and how we can advance this country together."

She suggested in a backhanded way that she was just another politician moving up—a fish going with the flow, you might say. Her Facebook message read: "And though it's honorable for countless others to leave their positions for a higher calling and without finishing a term, of course we know by now, for some reason a different standard applies for the decisions I make."

Palin's resignation came so far out of left field (or in her case, right field), it led to speculation that some scandal was brewing and she was leaving office before it broke. Rumors had been swirling about whether her rather large house in Wasilla had been built with materials or labor illegitimately obtained when Wasilla built its multimillion-dollar city sports complex. The rumors led the FBI to issue a public statement saying Palin was *not* under investigation.[28] The rumors and the FBI announcement gave Palin another chance to do what she often did—play the victim of unfounded attacks. In this case, she was—after she left office, there was no news of any scandal that would have explained her decision to quit.

In her resignation speech, Palin had said, "I thought about how much fun some governors have as lame ducks . . . travel around the state, to the Lower 48 (maybe), overseas on international trade—as so many politicians do. And then I thought—that's what's wrong."

However, during her last two months in office, Palin's description applied to what Palin herself did. She took what in retrospect looked like the typical junkets of a lame duck politician. She went to Kosovo and West Germany, met the Lithuanian minister of defense, and went on expensive trips to remote Alaska communities like Kotzebue, Unalakleet, and McGrath to sign bills.

It's true, some of those trips occurred before she announced her resignation. But she said in that speech, "This decision has been in the works for a while." If she didn't want to be a typical lame duck politician, enjoying free travel at taxpayer expense, she would have canceled those trips and saved Alaskans some of those "millions of dollars" she said were being wasted by her staying in office.

In her farewell speech on the day she left office, Palin did no better at convincing the world she'd made a rational, selfless decision to quit. Mostly she spoke of her love for Alaska, recapped her accomplishments and thanked her family and others who'd helped her. She thanked by name her personal attorney, Thomas Van Flein; her media pitbull, Meg Stapleton; and her "right-hand man Kris Perry." She didn't mention anybody from the oil and gas team that spent two years, often working seven days a week, to deliver her biggest victories—on her gas line promotion plan and her multibillion-dollar oil tax increase.

Responding to a heckler, Palin again touched on the I-won't-be-a-lame-duck theme, saying, "With this decision now, I will be able to fight even harder for you, for what is right, for truth. And I have never felt like you need a title to do that."[29] No specifics beyond that.

She took aim at two of her favorite targets, the media and the federal government. "And one other thing for the media: Our new governor has a very nice family too. So leave his kids alone," she said.[30] The *Anchorage Daily News* account followed that quote with the print equivalent of an arched eyebrow, noting that her daughters were right there in the public eye: "Palin daughters Piper, Willow and Bristol, who embarked on a media tour this spring to promote abstinence as an alternative, watched the ceremony. Piper was holding Palin's baby son, Trig."[31]

Palin also warned about "enslavement to big central government" and the dangers of taking "largess" from the government: "It doesn't come free, and often accepting it takes away everything that is free. Melting into Washington's powerful, caretaking arms will just suck incentive to work hard and chart our own course right out of us."

That warning was certainly ironic, coming from the governor who handed Alaska's 660,000 residents "largess" amounting to more than $700 million when she pushed through the $1,200-a-person payment to help offset high energy costs.

Gregg Erickson, in his commentary for the *Anchorage Daily News*, wrote, "In terms of shaping policy, Palin's work as governor was finished, regardless of whether she stayed or resigned."[32] A poll in May showed Palin's favorability rating with Alaskans had dropped by 33 percentage points. "That dramatic drop emboldened her Republican legislative opponents," Erickson said. She wouldn't be able to accomplish much.

Conservative columnist Paul Jenkins was even more harsh. One of the most vociferous, and colorful, of Palin's Alaska critics, Jenkins wrote after Palin's hand-over of power in Fairbanks:

> She came home with a taste for life bigger than Alaska. There are things, she discovered, more important than being governor of some hick state up north.
>
> Imagine what Sarah Palin could have done with her stratospheric approval ratings and people around her who knew what they were do-ing. She was invincible. Who could have told her no? With the tiniest flash of vision she could have transformed this state. Instead, she settled for platitudes and jingoistic drivel and flights of paranoia and egoism spurred by self-aggrandizement.
>
> In many quarters nowadays she's little more than a joke, a Twitter queen, quitting her job because people are mean to her.[33]

ALASKANS MOVE ON

With Palin gone, her uncharismatic lieutenant governor took the helm, and calmed the stormy partisan seas Palin left behind. Sean Parnell settled down to work and got good reviews—in no small part because he actually wanted the job.

Palin's disillusioned former supporter and informal adviser, Paul Fuhs, wrote in an op-ed five months after her departure, "Alaskans seem relieved to be rid of the constant drama and to now have Gov. Parnell, who actually does understand how government operates. This shows in his recent 81 percent positive rating as reported by pollster Dave Dittman."[34]

In making way for Sean Parnell, Palin botched the process of filling the new vacancy as lieutenant governor. She announced that the new lieutenant governor would be Craig Campbell, who was her commissioner of military and veterans affairs. Only one problem: as provided by statute, Palin had earlier designated a different cabinet commissioner, Joe Schmidt, as next in the line of succession.

To straighten out the confusion Palin created by not following the state's succession law, the legislature had to hold a special summer session to confirm Campbell as lieutenant governor. Piqued by being summoned to clean up Palin's parting mess, legislators also used the occasion to override her token veto of $28.6 million in federal stimulus money for energy conservation.

In February 2010, some of Palin's e-mails as governor had been released. They included unflattering remarks about her fellow Republican, House Speaker John Harris. Asked for his reaction by the *Juneau Empire*, Harris said, "I want to forget that Sarah Palin ever existed. We have a governor who wants to work with us. Sarah Palin is off making money. Let her be."[35]

■ ■ ■

So why did Sarah Palin resign?

Was it because she spent so much time and personal money fighting ethics charges? Did being in the spotlight bring too much harsh scrutiny of her kids? Was it the chance to make real money, not her piddling $125,000-a-year salary as governor? Was it because she had accomplished the big things she'd set out to do? Was it her fading popularity? Her loss of political support in the legislature? The prospect of being stuck doing the boring work of passing a budget and other routine matters of state governance? Was it so she could have more time to burnish her national image? Did she think that being in office forced her to be "politically correct"? Was being the mom of a special needs kid too much while maintaining a full-time job based far from her home? Did she simply hate the job?

In my humble opinion, the answer is all of the above.

Palin gave many of the above answers in public, and some of them in private. Here's what she told her *Going Rogue* ghost writer, Lynn Vincent:

Created: 7/11/2009 7:36:23 AM
    Subject: Re: Important dot-connecting.

    [By leaving I'm] "sending the message that 1) I'm not a professional politician; 2) I've accomplished the goals as Governor that I promised: ethics reform; mandated new clear and equitable share of Alaska's resource development for Alaskans; built vehicle to get gasline built;

slowed the rate of growth of govt; eliminated personal luxuries the state used to fund for governors so we could set the example. . . So handing the reins to Sean is just sensible and fair and efficient instead of suffering Alaskans through a lame duck session!"[Her emphasis.]

Palin added another reason in a Twitter message a few days later: "Everyone elected is replaceable; Ak WILL progress! + side benefit—10 days til less politically correct twitters fly frm my fingertips outside State site."

Some of the best insight on her decision to quit came in *New York Times* reporter Robert Draper's piece in November 2010. He recounted an interview with Fred Malek, a sympathetic political adviser she'd met during the McCain campaign, about the advice he gave Palin in June 2009:

> "Focus on amassing a good record as governor," [Malek] advised her. "Run for a second term. Develop some policy expertise. Do some extensive overseas travel. Generate some good will by campaigning for fellow Republicans."
>
> Malek told me that he could tell that this wasn't what Palin wanted to hear. Here's the problem, she replied impatiently: I've got a long commute from my house to my office. I don't have the funds to pay for my family to travel with me, and the state won't pay for it, either. I can't afford to have security at my home—anybody can come up to my door, and they do. Under the laws of Alaska, anybody can file suit or an ethics charge against me, and I have to defend it on my own. I'm going into debt.[36]

As is often the case with Palin, her complaints included exaggerations and problems of her own making. Instead of commuting from Wasilla, she could have chosen to spend her term living in state-paid housing—the governor's mansion in Juneau—just a couple of blocks from her office in the state capital. She actually reduced her state trooper security detail, as documented in the Troopergate investigation. She could have had state-paid security at her home if needed—but it would have undercut her populist image as an ordinary Alaskan forgoing perks, accessible to the people.

The vast majority of Palin's legal fees were to defend herself in Troopergate, after she filed a formal ethics complaint against herself. It's unclear why she needed to pay her lawyer hundreds of dollars an hour, for example, to attack an ethics complaint filed under the pseudonym of a British TV character.

Palin complained that media scrutiny of her kids was growing intolerable, even though her status as a mother—a family-values hockey mom with a special needs kid—was an integral part of her political "brand," and she routinely displayed her children at political events.

It's true, Palin had already accomplished a lot, as she mentioned in her e-mail to her ghost writer. It's also true she had destroyed her governing coalition and realized she wouldn't accomplish much if she served out her term. She would be stuck working on the boring nuts-and-bolts aspect of the job, like compiling the annual budget and getting it passed by the legislature.

Leaving also gave her more time with her family, and family is genuinely important to her. Quitting let her keep a schedule of her own choosing and not worry about meeting the expectations others have for a public office holder. She would have been the rare case in which a politician said, "I'm leaving in part because I want to spend more time with my family"—and it would have been true.

While she professed in public that she "loved her job," she had e-mailed her aide, Frank Bailey, safe from public sight, saying, "I hate this damn job."

Only two explanations offered at the time for Palin's quitting can be ruled out. She was not fleeing ahead of a breaking scandal. And she wasn't quitting because she and Todd were getting a divorce.

She probably did do Alaska a favor by stepping aside, although not for exactly the reasons Palin tried to express. Alaska was better off having a governor who actually wanted the job, rather than one who had grown bored and frustrated and was ready to move up and move out. Parnell kept her cabinet intact and did a reasonable job continuing her legacy until he won election on his own. With his own mandate, he felt free to begin rolling back parts of her agenda, especially on oil taxes.

"PROGRESSING ALASKA"?

In the years after Palin's departure, there were no obvious examples of how she worked to "progress" Alaska—unless you count the publicity the state's tourism industry may have gotten from the state-subsidized episodes of her reality TV show.

She had done nothing to help shore up political support in Alaska for her signature initiative—the effort to bring Alaska a $40 billion natural gas pipeline. Her preferred version of the project was still stuck in the planning and permitting process, while Conoco and BP dropped their competing project.

However, the state-subsidized venture Palin launched still doesn't have any committed customers—a huge source of frustration to Alaskans. Opponents in the legislature constantly talk about trying to withdraw the $500 million commitment the state made to Palin's gas line effort. She had become so unpopular in Alaska, though, she wouldn't have been much help warding off those attacks.

With her other major accomplishment, the record-breaking oil tax increase, Palin was somewhat more active. Her successor, Sean Parnell, the man she said would keep Alaska in good hands, has pushed legislators to give back about $1.5

billion a year of the extra money Palin's new tax system raised. She defended the tax, known as ACES (Alaska's Clear and Equitable Share) in her memoir and on Facebook. She did not, however, go to the front lines of the fight in Juneau.

And that was probably just as well. As unpopular as she had become at home, showing up to defend her oil tax probably wouldn't have helped. It's certainly ironic: The governor who was once so popular probably made the right call by not making highly public efforts in Alaska to defend her accomplishments.

When resigning, Palin said she'd "fight for all our children's future from outside the governor's office." If she has done much fighting, it was hard to find evidence of it. There was no sign that she had used any of her new-found millions to start a foundation for special needs children. If she had done so, Palin surely would have let her supporters know. It would be totally out of character for her to do good works without seeking the limelight.

Some of her "fighting" for children was apparently done as a mercenary, getting paid to help raise money for them. In spring 2011, she headlined an event for a start-up charity called the Exceptional Foundation, being founded in the small Alabama coastal town of Point Clear, to help special needs children. Tickets were $600 a person minimum, with some spaces going for $1,500. Press reports indicated about 200 people attended, suggesting the event grossed at least $120,000.

A local media report noted that "Foundation officials have not released the speaking fee charged by Palin."[37] However, her fee must have been substantial, because organizer Bob Callahan, Sr. told Guy Busby of the *Press-Register*, "I think we're going to end up in the black, not in the red. I'm not concerned, but we need to get in all the bills before we know what the final totals are."[38]

If an event that grossed at least $120,000 was anywhere close to losing money, that suggests Palin's fee was in fact close to the $100,000 that blogger Malia Litman reported, after a conversation she had with organizer Callahan.[39]

■ ■ ■

My long-time colleague at the *Anchorage Daily News*, Michael Carey, wrote about Palin, "Not once did she provide a convincing explanation of why she is leaving office. We are left to guess. The only thing we can be absolutely sure of is this: Palin did not tell the truth when she said she is leaving for the good of Alaskans. She is leaving for her own good. With Sarah Palin, 'me' always comes first."[40]

Twice, Sarah Palin held high-level jobs in Alaska state government. Twice, she quit before her term was up. (She lasted less than a year at the Alaska Oil and Gas Conservation Commission.) The only political jobs Palin held for a full term were in her hometown of Wasilla, population about 7,000—but she is still considered a serious contender to be elected leader of the free world.

In researching this book, I talked about this part of her record with someone who had worked closely with Palin on her major victories as governor. "Do you think she has a political version of A.D.D. [attention deficit disorder]?" I asked. The source, who obviously doesn't want to be named, said, "*Political* A.D.D.?" Think about her incessant use of BlackBerrys, I was told, and her disinclination to master the details of issues she handled.

The point: A.D.D. wasn't just a metaphor for her track record in holding jobs. It might be a real phenomenon that explains much more about Sarah Palin.

■ ■ ■

By 2011, Palin's popularity rating in Alaska had sunk to new lows. A poll by Dave Dittman, a Republican pollster, showed her approval rating among Alaskans had hit the mid-30s. In Alaska, there was little sign of popular adulation for Sarah Palin, the quitting-governor-turned-national-celebrity.

Jeanne Devon, author of the widely read blog, Mudflats, and one of Palin's most prominent Alaska critics, explained Alaskans' attitude this way:

> One cause of the 49th state's newly icy relationship with our ex-governor that cannot be overestimated is simply this—she quit. Quitters don't make it far in the frontier, and Alaskans lose respect quickly for those that flee when the going gets tough. Surviving discomfort and hardship and risk is a badge of honor here. It's practically the price of admission. . . . Alaskans don't like a whiner, and we don't like a quitter. Case closed.[41]

In all her explanations for quitting as governor, Palin never mentioned the $1.25 million advance she got for *Going Rogue*. The ex-governor soon had a lucrative contract as Fox TV commentator and began giving speeches at a price that could reach $100,000 for each appearance. Palin made even more money doing a reality TV show that drew millions of viewers.

Her path beyond the governor's office contrasted sharply with remarks she made to the *Anchorage Daily News* after her triumphant first legislative session, with her popularity still high. "If you want to be in public service, it is being willing to serve Alaskans for the right reasons," she told the paper. Using a term with special meaning to her religious supporters, she said, "It is having to have a servant's heart when you come into these positions. It's not to get rich."[42]

18

Legacy and Prospects: A Republican Geraldine Ferraro or a Modern-Day Aimee Semple McPherson?

Sarah Palin and John McCain had a chance to transform the national political climate with the "brand" they had established in Arizona and Alaska—a pair of people-before-party mavericks who would clean up government on behalf of ordinary citizens. But John McCain decided that running as a nonpartisan maverick reformer would not hold the Republican Party base. He turned Palin loose as a partisan pitbull. She relished the role and won the adulation of hard-core Republican audiences.

It was not the Sarah Palin Alaskans had seen as their governor, when her approval ratings approached 90 percent. Making such an abrupt and fundamental change in her political style, along with the unfolding Troopergate scandal, started to erode her popularity in Alaska, even as she thrilled adoring crowds in the rest of the country.

Republican-leaning Alaskans were skeptical about her return to more familiar policies and themes: lower taxes, cut government, be nice to business. They knew that much of her work as governor had contradicted Republican orthodoxy, especially her oil tax increase and refusal to give Alaska's oil companies the concessions they wanted for (maybe someday) building a $30 or $40 billion natural gas pipeline.

Democratic-leaning Alaskans, previously won over by her ethics reform work, challenges to Big Oil, and her willingness to work across party lines, questioned her sudden transformation.

Across the political spectrum, Alaskans began to wonder, "Which is the real Sarah Palin? At her core, what does she stand for? Is it just all about Sarah?"

By the time she resigned, her approval rating had plummeted. Alaskans knew that her mind and ambitions were elsewhere. There was a sense of relief that she had moved on.

ALASKA LEGACY

Regardless of what she does in 2012 and beyond, history will remember Sarah Palin as the Republican Party's first female candidate for vice president. Her tenure in Alaska will be noted for three things: She was the state's first female governor; she was the first Alaska governor to resign; and she was a reformer who reined in the political power of the state's oil industry, at least temporarily.

The most lasting difference she made in Alaska was pushing a drastically increased tax on oil production. With the change, Alaska rolled up multibillion-dollar surpluses even as most other states had to slash spending during the worst economic crisis since the Great Depression.

All that extra oil tax money piled up in state savings accounts as insurance against inevitable declines in future oil revenue. Alaska's oil production has dropped by two-thirds since the late 1980s, and every $1 drop in the price of oil costs the state treasury tens of millions of dollars. Having billions of ready spending money in the bank protects against the economic fallout that would occur if the state had to make deep budget cuts or (perish the thought) start charging ordinary Alaskans a sales or income tax.

As if to emphasize the liberal bent of Palin's signature accomplishment, her Republican successor as governor tried repeatedly to undo it. Sean Parnell, who'd once been government relations director for Conoco, one of Alaska's big three oil companies, wanted to give the oil industry back roughly $1.5 billion a year through new tax concessions, with no guarantee the multinational companies would reinvest their tax savings in Alaska.

With Palin gone, the Republican majority in the state house reunited on oil issues, and agreed to a huge oil tax rollback. The measure stalled in the state senate where Democrats shared power in a bipartisan coalition with a handful of Republicans, including some who remained skeptical of oil industry claims.

Palin was not able to do what might have truly transformed Alaska's future—induce the private sector to build the $30–$40 billion natural gas pipeline that Alaskans had dreamed about for more than thirty years. Her innovative incentive package was probably the best hope for getting the gas line built, but the project faced too many obstacles, including its enormous cost and competition from the phenomenal growth of natural gas production from shale deposits all across the Lower 48.

After leaving office, Palin was not interested in the "wise elder" role Alaska governors typically play. She moved on from Alaska, politically speaking, if not in her legal residency.

A REPUBLICAN GERALDINE FERRARO?

Based on Palin's resume so far, she may well occupy a similar place in national history to the only other woman picked for vice president on a major party ticket,

Geraldine Ferraro. It took Republicans twenty-four years to match the gender landmark Democrats set with Walter Mondale's choice of Ferraro in 1984.

Both women were relatively obscure figures before they were selected, with little international experience. Both owed their nomination to being the right gender at the time a male presidential candidate needed a game-changing gambit. Both Palin and Ferraro inspired women to think, "If she can do that, then I can do more with my life, too."

Though Ferraro was the first woman to ascend so high in American politics, she never achieved the kind of national star power that Palin gained from her time on the national ticket. Ferraro was a ground breaker whose strongest appeal was to women and to fathers who wanted to encourage their daughters to dream big.

Ferraro didn't help Democrats carry the women's vote in 1984. As with John McCain's selection of Palin, some analysts thought Ferraro may have hurt the ticket more than she helped. Her *New York Times* obituary noted "a barrage of questions about the Ferraro family finances—often carrying insinuations about ties to organized crime."[1] With the economy roaring back from a deep recession, President Reagan was enjoying strong popularity and won in a landslide.

Palin didn't help her ticket carry the women's vote in 2008, either. Her shaky performances when operating away from a prepared script led many voters to doubt her readiness to take over the presidency—and to question McCain's judgment in picking her.[2]

However, McCain's goal was not to woo female voters but to energize the Republican Party's conservative base. And in that, he and she succeeded. Her popularity came more from her populist, antielitist appeal than from being a gender trailblazer. Palin's appeal reached further across gender lines than Ferraro's.

Many people of both sexes looked at Palin and saw someone like themselves. She seemed like an ordinary person who had ascended to a powerful position, someone who shared their perspective and would make sure it was heard. That populist appeal gave her much more stature in defeat than Ferraro had. There was no serious talk that Ferraro would run for president. She waited eight years to run for the U.S. Senate in her home state of New York. Both times she ran for Senate, she failed to make it through the Democratic primary.

Sarah Palin's postelection popularity owed a lot to changes in the media landscape since the 1980s. Internet and social media technology made it possible for Palin to reach a mass audience without waiting for coverage in what she called the "lamestream" media. The rise of the bluntly partisan, pro-Republican Fox TV network gave her a paid platform for staying in the national conversation among conservatives.

Like Palin, Ferraro wrote books and eventually landed a job in the media, as host of the cable TV public affairs show *Crossfire*, but that came a decade after her run for national office and lasted only two years. Ferraro also served as ambassador to the United Nations Human Rights Commission for President Bill Clinton.[3]

It's hard to imagine Palin accepting a government job like that, a second-tier post involving nitty-gritty detail work, far from headlines and the levers of power. She showed little interest in running for Congress, which would require her to work as part of a large group, rather than be the person in charge. In the 2010 congressional election, she stayed on the sidelines, cheering on Republican candidates as the party took back control of the U.S. House and nearly took the Senate as well.

A MODERN-DAY AIMEE SEMPLE McPHERSON?

Anchorage Daily News columnist Michael Carey has suggested Palin's place in history would be similar to the early-twentieth-century evangelist Aimee Semple McPherson.[4] During the 1920s and 1930s, McPherson was the religious equivalent of today's rock stars, drawing huge crowds with her Pentecostal revival meetings, complete with speaking in tongues and dispensing miracle cures. Like Palin, McPherson used the new media technology of her day—then it was radio—to expand her audience and influence.

McPherson and Palin were both unconventional figures for their times. Divorced twice during her lifetime, McPherson prompted frequent gossip that she was having affairs. In 1926, she disappeared in broad daylight while swimming at a Southern California beach. Search parties found no trace of her. Thirty-two days later, she emerged from the Arizona desert, saying she'd walked thirteen hours to freedom after being kidnapped and held in Mexico. Her shoes showed no signs of heavy wear and she was fully dressed. Rumors swirled that she'd disappeared to have an abortion or plastic surgery or was trysting with a lover. Authorities prosecuted her for allegedly lying about her disappearance, but she was not convicted. The bizarre incident didn't hurt McPherson's popularity on the revival circuit, much as Palin's supporters easily accepted her decision to resign as governor, along with her rambling and unfocused explanation.[5]

Compared to McPherson and her tumultuous personal life—she eventually died of an overdose of barbituates—Palin is the picture of religious rectitude. Palin, though, has yet to match McPherson in good works and building an institution that might outlive her. McPherson's popularity helped raise the $1.5 million her congregation needed to build a 5,000-seat church, Angelus Temple, in 1923. It still operates today as Foursquare Church, which boasts about McPherson's role in the church's history and claims a global membership of two million. The church's publicity materials credit McPherson with helping feed 1.5 million people during the Great Depression.[6]

If Palin is doing comparable good works, she is uncharacteristically silent about them. Her public response to difficult economic times has been to hector Democrats and President Obama about cutting taxes and government spending—even though government cutbacks would kill more jobs and worsen the nation's economic woes. Palin hasn't built a legacy remotely like the charismatic McPherson's.

■ ■ ■

Social historians, when they look back at gender roles in America during Palin's rise to prominence, may find her experience worthy of note. At first, Palin was cited as a glorious example of the opportunity open to modern American women. She could have it all—be governor of a state and run for the second most powerful political office in the nation while still having children at home, including a special needs baby and a husband who had his own work life. It was considered sexist to even question a woman's ability to handle all the responsibilities Palin was juggling.

But in both her decision to resign as governor and later to skip running for president, Palin cited family issues. Announcing her resignation, Palin said, "This decision comes after much consideration, and finally polling the most important people in my life—my children (where the count was unanimous . . .)."

On October 5, 2011, she wrote in an e-mail distributed by SarahPAC, "I have decided that I will not be seeking the 2012 GOP nomination for President of the United States. As always, my family comes first and obviously Todd and I put great consideration into family life before making this decision."

In announcing that decision, she created one last ethical controversy, involving whether she had been misleading potential donors to her political action committee, SarahPAC. The issue was brought to light by political satirist Jon Stewart on the Comedy Central program, the *Daily Show*, October 6, 2011.[7] As summarized by David Ferguson, blogger at the website RawStory, the *Daily Show* explored

the notion that Palin may have known all along that she's not running, but has continued to bilk donors out of their money by dangling the possibility that she might. He [Jon Stewart] produces what we'll call Exhibit A, a letter from "SarahPac" dated September 20 that specifically asks donors to give money to show their support for the ex-Alaska governor should she decide to run. And yet as far back as June, in what we will call Exhibit B, Bristol Palin appeared on Fox saying that her mother had made her decision, but was keeping the answer "in the family."[8]

If her daughter is to be believed, for almost three months Palin continued raising money through her political action committee by holding out the prospect she'd run for president, when, in fact, she had already decided not to run.

NOT IDEAL TEA PARTY TRAINING GROUND

Unfortunately for Palin, Alaska is not the best launching ground for a conservative aiming to tap Tea Party resentment with government. Alaskans might say they don't like big government, but they enjoy getting an expansive list of services from state government, basically for free. Oil taxes and royalties pay for most everything Alaskans want from their state government; there is no state sales or personal income tax; and the state hands every resident a check every year—typically more than $1,000—as a way of sharing the wealth produced by oil, most of which is produced from state-owned land.

Palin's early work as governor was much more in tune with Alaska's unique political climate. Compare her record to traditional Republican themes, and you see significant gaps and contradictions.

Small government? Alaska has the biggest state government, per capita, in the country and Palin did nothing to shrink it. She could only claim that she "slowed the growth of government."

Low taxes? As governor, Palin passed the biggest tax increase in the state's history. As mayor of Wasilla, she pushed for a sales tax to support what is hardly a core function of a limited government—a sports arena. Sarah Palin ran governments that redistributed wealth—as governor, taking money from oil companies through higher taxes; as Wasilla mayor, collecting sales tax from the many shoppers who live in residential areas outside official city limits—and used those other people's money to deliver benefits to her constituents.

Free markets and less regulation? Palin boasted about improving regulation of the oil industry after a series of costly and damaging pipeline leaks on Alaska's North Slope. She restored the habitat-protecting agency her predecessor had emasculated because he thought it was an obstacle to resource development.

Personal responsibility instead of government intervention? There was that extra $1,200, taken from oil companies, to help cover their energy bills. Palin pushed through an admittedly very popular ethics reform, a series of "thou shalt" and "thou shalt not" rules for politicians. Those rules contravene the more common Republican view that you can't legislate good behavior, you just need to elect ethical people to office.

Strong on defending the nation? Palin likes guns, but as viewers of her reality TV show saw, she is not a particularly good shot. She has killed a caribou, but that animal was no threat to any human, much less the nation. Palin's chief claim to fame on the national defense front is that she has a son who served in the infantry in Iraq. Having a son who served is an honorable thing, and few who voted to authorize that war can make the same claim.

Alaska was far from the front lines of the domestic fight against terrorism, and she has no particular expertise or credibility in that field. During the vice-presidential race, she made the now-notorious claims that one of her qualifications was Alaska's proximity to Russia—as if living next to a bank qualifies you to be a hedge fund manager.

Palin tried to burnish her limited experience by claiming Alaska is a "microcosm" of America—a patently ridiculous claim. Alaska swims proudly out of the national mainstream. The unofficial Alaska state motto is, "We don't give a damn how they do it Outside," which is how Alaskans refer to the other forty-nine states. It's a state that once formed an official statehood commission to reevaluate Alaska's relationship with the United States government. It's a state where an avowedly secessionist party, the Alaskan Independence Party, routinely has candidates on the ballot. A state that has barely more than one person per square mile, boasts the nation's only arctic territory, and collects about $14,500 per resident in state government revenue without a sales or personal income tax is hardly a "microcosm" of America.

SHE'S NO RONALD REAGAN

Like many aspiring national Republican leaders, Palin tried to claim the mantle of Ronald Reagan, especially in her memoir, *Going Rogue*. Writing after her defeat in the vice-presidential race, she tries to present herself as something noteworthy, a "Commonsense Conservative," but her views are standard-issue Republican fare.

What is unusual about her is not what she stands for, but the packaging. She is the frontier woman from Alaska, hauling in fish and shooting caribou, while also being the hockey mom who juggles working with raising kids, including a Down syndrome child.

Like Reagan, Palin is charismatic, lacks intellectual curiosity, and doesn't speak well off-the-cuff, but can really read a great speech. However, Reagan was first and foremost an economic conservative. He was indifferent to the issues that loomed so large with social conservatives. Palin is first and foremost a social conservative. To the economic elites that dominate the upper echelons of the Republican Party, Palin has an unreliable record on their issues. The tough stance she took against Alaska's oil industry won her plaudits in her home state, but it made pro-business Republicans in the rest of the country wonder if her establishment Republican critics in Alaska were right when they called her antibusiness.

Reagan was promoted, mentored, and supported by economic royalists who wanted to rein in the federal government so they could avoid regulation, make more money, and get lower taxes. Reagan, a divorced, non-church-going actor from Hollywood, mostly paid lip service to socially conservative issues, like opposing abortion. He governed effectively because he surrounded himself with capable people who knew how to get things done—unlike Palin, whose closest staff fed her obsession with maintaining her public image instead of focusing on more substantive work. Reagan came to fame in the entertainment field and moved to prominence in politics. Palin did the opposite, turning her political prominence into entertainment riches. She's more personally insecure than Reagan was, and less worldly, so she has trouble assembling a core team that compensates for her weaknesses.

In November 2010, Robert Draper of the *New York Times* pointed out another key difference: "Like many Republicans, Palin hails Reagan as her political guiding light. But she has yet to channel the Gipper's soothing sunniness. Instead she seems haloed in static electricity."[9] Reagan the leader sold Americans on an upbeat, optimistic vision of the country. It was "morning in America" again. We were the Shining City on the Hill.

As a national figure, Palin paints a much darker picture. She has perfected the politics of grievance. She assails elites, the mainstream media, liberals, and the left. She divides the country into "them" and "us." She appeals to the darker vein of the American character.

Obama tapped the Reaganesque vein in the American psyche during the 2008 campaign. McCain-Palin resorted to fear mongering, invoking the specter of the "other," suggesting Barack Obama was a "socialist" and palled around with "terrorists" like William Ayers.

Palin has a national following, but unlike Reagan, she does not herald the emergence of a significant new movement among Republicans or conservatives. While adored by Tea Party conservatives, she is one of many politicians running to be at the head of that parade. She isn't part of the Republican economic elites and power brokers who are funding the Tea Party and advising it behind the scenes.

What Palin leads is more like a cult of personality. In Alaska, her supporters were called Palinistas or Palinbots. They accuse her critics of suffering from "PDS," shorthand for "Palin Derangement Syndrome" and defend her against all criticism, no matter how justified it might be in a particular case. Palin is a political celebrity, not a transformational leader.

When I interviewed a key Democratic ally of Palin in her early legislative victories, State Sen. Hollis French, he raised the same question Joshua Green raised in his June 2011 essay in *The Atlantic* about Sarah Palin: What if she had tried to do for the nation what she had done in her early time as Alaska governor, when she was a bipartisan reformer, not a partisan pitbull?[10]

The best answer to that question came from noted Alaska Palin-watcher Jeanne Devon, author of The Mudflats blog:

The real question [Green]'s asking is—What could Palin have achieved if she had a different personality, if she were not a political opportunist and had actual integrity, if she were qualified, if she knew her stuff, if she were an effective leader, if she knew how to manage people, if she were intellectually curious, if she didn't quit? The question Green asks is really what Sarah Palin might have achieved if she hadn't been Sarah Palin.[11]

THE USUAL RULES DON'T APPLY

Everywhere you look in Palin's career, you find a recurring theme: the usual rules do not apply to me.

Sometimes, that was a good thing. She could be a conservative Republican who was open-minded enough to work with Democrats to do what was good for Alaska. She broke the stranglehold the oil industry had over Alaska politics. She rejected the notion, common in her party, that Alaska's oil industry automatically gets what it wants, because what's good for Big Oil is by definition good for Alaska.

She raised taxes on the industry, replacing a tax regime tainted by corruption. She didn't give the state's big oil companies multibillion-dollar concessions in return for a mere promise to build a gas pipeline some day. She pushed through a system of competitive bidding for state financial incentives and brought in an independent pipeline company to pursue the project.

But Palin's fundamental political mode of operating—the usual rules don't apply to me—has produced a morass of contradictions and controversies that would have sunk ordinary politicians:

- She can be a small government, Tea Party conservative even though she passed the biggest tax increase in Alaska state history.

- She can attack Barack Obama for wanting to "share the wealth," when she raised taxes on Alaska's oil industry and shared the wealth with every Alaskan.

- She can complain that the nation is headed toward socialism while governing the most socialist state in the union and doing nothing to shrink the size of its government.

- She can quit with seventeen months to go in her term, for fame and fortune in the private sector—and complain that people call her a quitter.

- She can work with Democrats to pass major initiatives, then be shocked when they're shocked that she bitterly attacked their party's presidential candidate and all the party stands for.

- Palin the crusading ethical reformer can endure her own ethical controversies by blaming jealous critics, not her own poor judgment.

- She can win a nonpartisan race for mayor of Wasilla with partisan help from the Republican Party—and still claim to be a politician who rejects "politics as usual."

- She can run for a local government office that has nothing to do with hot-button issues like abortion and guns by bringing abortion and guns into the race—and still claim to be a politician who rejects politics as usual.

- She can conduct politics as usual in a presidential race with bitter partisan attacks on her opponents—then be surprised that people are surprised at her politics-as-usual behavior.

Palin expects to be spared any and all criticism because, in her mind, she is a good person with good intentions. Whatever she says about critics is righteous and true, even when it's not, and whatever they say is wrong, even if it's true. If she does in fact break any rules, like maybe not doing enough homework on national and international issues, it's because they're dumb rules that deserve to be broken, and only she is courageous enough to break them. As she put it, "Only dead fish go with the flow."

It is true, the usual rules do not apply to Sarah Palin. Because if they did, she'd be a footnote to history already, not someone seriously discussed as a potential candidate for president.

"NOT WIRED THAT WAY"

Palin repeatedly said she didn't do what typical politicians do, because she was "not wired that way." One of the things she was "not wired" to do was anything that requires critical self-reflection, self-sacrifice, or self-improvement.

Nationally syndicated conservative columnist Jonah Goldberg noted that problem with Palin when he came to Anchorage two months after she resigned. During an interview at the local university radio station, he said, "I love her for her enemies," but "her star is fading on the right," and he personally had "soured on Sarah Palin." Her resignation speech was "lousy," Goldberg said. "She never gave a good explanation." She needs to "get a couple of interns and a subscription to the *Economist*. . . . She refused to do that." She's guilty of "a huge squandering of political talent," something he called "unforgiveable."[12]

Almost two years later, Palin's long-time booster, Bill Kristol, had grown disillusioned, too. Speaking at Vanderbilt University in March 2011, he said, "She probably shouldn't be the nominee for president." He continued, "She has a very shrewd judgment about politics and policy and very good instincts—but she hasn't done what Reagan . . . did, which is really educate himself over a number of years."[13]

Kristol's disillusionment was shared by the Democrat-turned-Independent who helped coach her during her vice-presidential race. Asked for his thoughts in late 2010 by Robert Draper of the *New York Times*, Connecticut senator Joe Lieberman said, "My impression is that she and Todd are the kind of people I'd like to have as my next-door neighbors. That's a separate question from whether she's capable of being president."

Many people question whether Palin is smart enough to do the necessary homework and develop the command of issues that a presidential candidate should have. One of her key oil and gas aides, Marty Rutherford, told me Palin was perfectly capable of applying herself as needed.

According to Rutherford, "She's *very* smart. Most people don't give her credit for it." She said even though the "complexity of issues was daunting," Palin was engaged. In key sessions, "There were times when we told her 'this is gonna be tough.' She'd put down the BlackBerry. She wouldn't say much. She wouldn't ask much . . . but then we'd hear her turn around and succinctly explain it" to someone else, like a press aide. "We were shocked over and over again at this," Rutherford said.[14]

I did not see this side of Palin in my dealings with her. She came to several *Anchorage Daily News* editorial board meetings as candidate and governor. After she was elected, the meetings were mostly about oil and gas issues, and she let Rutherford and others on her capable team carry the presentation and handle the questions.

During her campaign visits to the editorial board, I expected her to have a pretty superficial command of issues, and she was somewhat better than that. Palin could carry on a discussion at one level deeper than soundbites, but she did not show any notable expertise or knowledge in any subject. She was not the sharpest of any statewide candidate I encountered in my Alaska journalism career, nor was she the dimmest. She was neither dangerously dumb nor especially smart.

Three weeks after John McCain picked her, conservative columnist David Brooks wrote, "Sarah Palin has many virtues. If you wanted someone to destroy a corrupt establishment, she'd be your woman. But the constructive act of governance is another matter. She has not been engaged in national issues . . . like President Bush, she seems to compensate for her lack of experience with brashness and excessive decisiveness."[15] Brooks had seen what eight years of George W. Bush looked like and he was in no mood for a repeat.

Like George W. Bush, Palin is personally likeable. Like Bush, she is inarticulate and intellectually shallow. Unlike Bush, she doesn't have a Karl Rove to help her overcome her weaknesses and get elected, and her father isn't a former president who can supply a talent pool to help her govern.

The aide who once worshipped Palin and all she stood for, conservative Frank Bailey, concluded in *Blind Allegiance*, "I am convinced her priorities and personality are not only ill-suited to head a political party or occupy national office, but would lead to disaster of, well, Biblical proportions."[16]

Bottom line: Until the Troopergate scandal erupted, Sarah Palin was a much more effective governor than progressives and establishment Republicans expected. That controversy, along with the brutal pressure and microscopic attention that comes with running for national office, exposed her fundamental weaknesses. Returning to work as governor, she faced so much turmoil and frustration, much of her own making, that she decided to resign.

Palin stayed in the national limelight, but she didn't do the homework needed to show that she is a competent and credible figure who could serve in higher office. After keeping her supporters guessing about her presidential decision for more than a year, she did what fellow fundamentalist conservative and possible presidential candidate Mike Huckabee did: take a pass and keep taking a big paycheck for being a commentator on Fox TV.

When announcing she wouldn't run, Palin might have said that it's easier to balance family life and political celebrity as TV commentator, speech maker, Twitter tweeter, and Facebook poster, than to take on the grueling work of running for president.

When John McCain picked her, she lacked the experience, judgment, and temperament to serve as either vice president or president.

She still does.

Notes

Preface

1. Alaska Press Club, "Alaska Press Club 2008 Prize Winning Entries," April 2009, alaskapressclub.org.
2. Dennis Cauchon, "At State Level, GOP, Dems Learn to Get Along," *USA Today*, June 21, 2007.

Chapter 1. Highlights and Lowlights: From Bipartisan Maverick to "Pitbull with Lipstick" to Former Governor

1. Sen. Hollis French, "When State Drew ACES, Success Ensued," *Anchorage Daily News*, November 21, 2009.
2. Tax Foundation, "State Spending Per Capita, Fiscal Year 2007," February 5, 2009.
3. See www.legis.state.ak.us/basis, 24th Legislature (2005–2006), history of HB4001, vetoed 12-28-06.
4. Lisa Demer, "Palin Bucks Pressure in Supreme Court Appointment," *Anchorage Daily News*, March 4, 2009.
5. Dan Joling, "Palin Unveils State Energy Goals," *Associated Press*, January 16, 2009. See also Renewable Energy Alaska Project, "In Alaska" (www.renewable energy.org): "2008 was a landmark year for renewable energy and energy efficiency in Alaska. . . . the State Legislature appropriated $360 million for home weatherization and rebate programs. The year 2008 also saw the passage of H.B. 152, which established the Renewable Energy Grant Program administered by the Alaska Energy Authority. In the Fund's first two years the Legislature has appropriated $125 million for grants."
6. "Ethics probe: Palin Defense Fund Illegal," cbsnews.com, June 24, 2010.
7. "Bailey's Return," editorial, *Anchorage Daily News*, October 1, 2008.
8. "The Branchflower Report," posted by Alaska Politics blog, adn.com, *Anchorage Daily News*, October 10, 2008.
9. See Sec. 1(b) of HB4001, signed by Palin on September 15, 2008.

10. Sean Cockerham, "Stalled Gas Line Project May Need Another Boost from State," *Anchorage Daily News*, October 24, 2011.

11. Official results for all elections mentioned in the book can be found at the Alaska Division of Elections website, http://www.elections.alaska.gov/ei_return.php.

12. See, for example, Politifact.com, "Palin Exaggerates Status, Cost of Pipeline," undated posting.

13. Scott Goldsmith, "Oil Pumps Alaska's Economy to Twice the Size—But What's Ahead?," UA Research Summary no. 17, February 2011, Institute of Social and Economic Research, University of Alaska Anchorage.

14. Tax Foundation, "State Spending."

15. See Alaska Permanent Fund Corporation website, www.apfc.org.

16. Permanent Fund dividend amounts can be found at the website of the Alaska Department of Revenue, Permanent Fund Division, http://www.pfd.state.ak.us /dividendamounts/index.aspx.

17. Elstun Lauesen, "Palin Enthusiastically Practices Socialism, Alaska-style," *Anchorage Daily News*, November 7, 2008.

18. Timothy J. Petumenos, "Report of Findings and Recommendations," October 15, 2008, prepared for Alaska Personnel Board (cited as "Petumenos Report").

19. Sean Cockerham, "Ross Confirmation Shot Down," *Anchorage Daily News*, April 17, 2009.

20. "Oil Prices: Palin's View is Surprising," editorial, *Anchorage Daily News*, June 15, 2009.

21. See the summary at Politifact.com, "Sarah Palin Says She Vetoed Stimulus Money for Energy Efficiency Because It Required Tougher Building Codes," undated.

22. "Palin Resigns from AOGCC," *Petroleum News*, January 16, 2004.

23. "Palin Reports $1.25M So Far from Book Deal," *CBS News*, October 27, 2009.

Chapter 2. The Key to Palin's Popularity as Governor: Meet Her Predecessor

1. Eric Morrison, "Seniors Want Longevity Checks Back," *Juneau Empire*, October 29, 2006.

2. Timothy Inklebarger, "Ruedrich's Last Effort on Oil and Gas Commission was to Try to Kill It," *Juneau Empire*, November 16, 2003.

3. Sean Cockerham, "Ruedrich Resigns Post as Regulator on State Oil and Gas Commission," *Anchorage Daily News*, November 9, 2003.

4. "State Enters Settlement with Randy Ruedrich on Ethics Charges," State of Alaska, Department of Law, press release, June 22, 2004.

5. Paula Dobbyn, "Search is On for Missing Renkes E-mail," *Anchorage Daily News*, February 10, 2005.

6. Matt Volz, "Governor Twits Renkes for Not Seeking Ruling," Associated Press, published in *Juneau Empire*, January 30, 2005.

7. Sean Cockerham and Paula Dobbyn, "Governor Has Renkes Delay His Departure," *Anchorage Daily News*, February 8, 2005.

8. "Governor Can't Seal Pipe Deal," Associated Press, published in *Anchorage Daily News*, November 10, 2006.

9. Gregg Erickson, "Following Murkowski a Stroke of Luck for Palin," *Anchorage Daily News*, September 14, 2008.

Chapter 3. Fiscal Conservative or Republican Robin Hood?

1. Daniel Larison, americanconservative.com, October 3, 2008.

2. Melissa DeVaughn, "Palin's Way," *Alaska* magazine, February 2008.

3. The Alaska Office of Management and Budget has an extensive online library of budget documents, including those from Gov. Sarah Palin's tenure, at omb.alaska.gov, under the tab "Budget Reports."

4. Sabra Ayers, "Palin's Cuts Leave Operations Intact," *Anchorage Daily News*, July 6, 2007.

5. "Governor Palin Signs Budget Bills," Office of Gov. Sarah Palin, press release no. 09-128, May 21, 2009.

6. Ibid.

7. "Putting Alaska First: A Newsletter from Alaska Governor Sarah Palin," Office of Gov. Sarah Palin, March–April 2009.

8. Emma Schwartz, "Palin's Record on Pork: Less Sizzle than Reported," abcnews.go.com, September 10, 2008.

9. Hal Bernton and David Heath, "Palin's Earmark Requests: More Per Person than Any Other State," *Seattle Times*, September 2, 2008.

10. Paul Volpe, "'Bridge' Going Nowhere Before Palin Killed It," Politifact.com, undated.

11. "She Killed It, But It Was Nearly Dead," Politifact.com, September 3, 2008.

12. "Governor Notes Limits on Stimulus Package Pending in Congress," Office of Gov. Sarah Palin, press release 09–05, January 12, 2009.

13. "Palin Backed 'Bridge to Nowhere,' Then Opposed It," CNN.com, September 9, 2008.

14. Matthew Continetti, "Palin, Personified," *Los Angeles Times*, November 18, 2009.

Chapter 4. Social Conservative, But You Wouldn't Really Notice

1. Lisa Demer, "Abortion Opponents Give Palin High Marks," *Anchorage Daily News*, September 7, 2008.

2. "Palin Took Socially Conservative Stands in 2006 Election," *Anchorage Daily News*, September 4, 2008.

3. "Social Conservative," editorial, *Anchorage Daily News*, September 12, 2008.

4. "Palin Vetoes HB 4001," Alaska Politics blog, *Anchorage Daily News*, December 28, 2006.

5. Ibid.

6. "Palin Wrong on Gay Benefits," Rep. Mike Kelly, Eagle Forum Alaska blog, December 30, 2006.

7. "Palin Vetoes HB 4001," Alaska Politics blog, December 28, 2006.

8. HB4002, signed by Palin December 20, 2006.

9. "Transcript: Palin and McCain Interview," *CBS News*, September 30, 2008.

10. Sean Cockerham, "Senate Panel Takes Turn Pressing Ross on Views," *Anchorage Daily News*, April 14, 2009.

11. Lisa Demer, "Palin Bucks Pressure in Supreme Court Appointment," *Anchorage Daily News*, March 4, 2009.

12. "State Law Gives Palin No Choice but Pro-choice," *Washington Times*, March 15, 2009.

13. Sean Cockerham and Kyle Hopkins, "Former Aide Rips Palin in Leaked Book Manuscript," *Anchorage Daily News*, February 19, 2011.

14. Frank Bailey, Ken Morris, and Jeanne Devon, *Blind Allegiance to Sarah Palin: A Memoir of Our Tumultuous Years* (Brentwood, TN: Howard Books, 2011), iBooks edition, Chapter 36.

15. Cockerham and Hopkins, "Former Aide Rips Palin."

16. Bailey, Morris, and Devon, "Blind Allegiance," Chapter 36.

17. Ibid.

18. Demer, "Palin Bucks Pressure."

19. Pat Forgey, "Palin Rebuffs Call for Abortion Debate," *Juneau Empire*, April 24, 2008.

20. "Palin Responds to Expanded Call Request," Office of Gov. Sarah Palin, press release 08-064, April 23, 2008. Palin's letter to Sen. Lyda Green accompanied the press release.

21. Lisa Demer, "Palin Hasn't Pushed Her Anti-abortion Beliefs as Governor," *Anchorage Daily News*, September 9, 2008.

22. Sean Cockerham, "Abortion Notification Bill Stalls in Senate Health Committee," *Anchorage Daily News*, April 18, 2009.

23. Lisa Demer, "Palin Bucks Pressure in Supreme Court Appointment: Selection Went against Push from Alaska Family Council," *Anchorage Daily News*, March 4, 2009.

24. Lisa Demer, "Palin calls campaign e-mail pitch 'great theater,'" *Anchorage Daily News*, February 11, 2009.

25. Lisa Demer, "Health Director Says She was Forced Out," *Anchorage Daily News*, July 2, 2009.

26. Stephen Braun, "Palin Canny on Religion and Politics," *Los Angeles Times*, September 28, 2008.

27. Bailey, Morris, and Devon, *Blind Allegiance*, Chapter 8.

28. Robert Draper, "The Palin Network," *New York Times Magazine*, November 17, 2010.

29. "Social Conservative," editorial, *Anchorage Daily News*, September 12, 2008.

Chapter 5. Palin Triumphs over Big Oil, Round 1

1. For example, see Daniel S. Sullivan, commissioner, Alaska Department of Natural Resources, letter dated February 28, 2011, to J. Patrick Foley, Pioneer Natural Resources.

2. Matt Volz, "Business Moves to Knowles Camp," Associated Press, published in *Anchorage Daily News*, October 27, 2006.

3. Pat Forgey, "Alaska's Oil Pipeline History Drives Gas Line Fight," *Juneau Empire*, August 3, 2008.

4. Pat Forgey, "Natural Gas Pipeline: State Looks for Lessons in Past Oil Line," *Juneau Empire*, April 22, 2007.

5. Steve Quinn, "Murkowski Adviser Faulted Gas Line Provisions," Associated Press, published in *Anchorage Daily News*, January 26, 2007.

6. Kristen Nelson, "Producers Pan AGIA," *Petroleum News*, April 1, 2007.

7. Ibid.

8. "Palin, Lawmakers: Don't Let Conoco Derail Pipeline Plan," editorial, *Juneau Empire*, January 27, 2008.

Chapter 6. Palin Triumphs over Big Oil, Round 2

1. Kay Cashman and Kristen Nelson, *Sarah Takes on Big Oil* (Anchorage: PNA Publishing, 2008), 10.

2. Sen. Hollis French and Rep. Les Gara, "Senate's Oil Tax Bill Is Far Too Weak," *Anchorage Daily News*, May 25, 2006.

3. Tom Kizzia, "Palin's Oil Agenda Includes Credits as well as Tax," *Anchorage Daily News*, September 3, 2007.

4. Steve Quinn, "Palin Wants Review of Oil Profits Tax; Location Still Undecided," Associated Press, posted on Alaska Politics blog, *Anchorage Daily News*, August 6, 2007.

5. Kizzia, "Palin's Oil Agenda."

6. Gov. Sarah Palin, "It's Time for Oil Tax Reality to Set In," *Anchorage Daily News*, November 2, 2007.

7. "Resource Review," Resource Development Council for Alaska, Fall 2007, www.akrdc.org.

8. Gregg Erickson, "Climate for Tax Hike Was Unexpected," *Anchorage Daily News*, December 2, 2007.

9. "Governor Palin Commends Legislators on Passage of House Bill 2001," Office of Gov. Sarah Palin, press release no. 07-227, November 16, 2007.

10. Sen. Hollis French, "When State Drew ACES, Success Ensued," *Anchorage Daily News*, November 21, 2009.

11. Becky Bohrer, "Is Governor's Oil Tax Plan the Best Direction for Alaska?," Associated Press, published in *Anchorage Daily News*, March 5, 2011.

12. Fred Barnes, "Alaska's Sarah Palin is the GOP's Newest Star," *The Weekly Standard*, July 16, 2007.

13. Erickson, "Climate for Tax Hike."

14. "Tainted tax fixed," editorial, *Anchorage Daily News*, November 18, 2007.

15. Alaska Oil and Gas Association, www.aoga.org/aces.

16. Yereth Rosen, "BP Alaska President Blasts State Business Climate," reuters.com, March 3, 2008.

17. Sarah Palin, *Going Rogue* (New York: HarperCollins, 2009), 164.
18. Tim Bradner, "Slope Operators Pessimistic on Future," *Alaska Journal of Commerce*, January 29, 2010.
19. Sean Parnell, "Time is Now to Unleash Alaska's Economy," *Juneau Empire*, February 14, 2011.
20. Becky Bohrer, "Industry Testifies on Plan to Cut Oil Taxes," Associated Press, published in *Anchorage Daily News*, February 16, 2011.
21. Robert Woolsey, "Hamilton: Legislature Will Cut Oil Taxes Next Session," *KCAW* (posted at kcaw.org), April 14, 2011.
22. Sen. Hollis French, "Oil Companies, State Prosper under ACES," *Anchorage Daily News*, July 21, 2010.
23. Rep. Les Gara, "Orwellian Juneau," *Alaska Dispatch*, February 23, 2011.
24. Rep. Mike Doogan, "Jobs, Oil Revenue Increased under ACES," *Anchorage Daily News*, January 29, 2011.
25. Shannyn Moore, "With Mineral Interests, Alaskans Come First," *Anchorage Daily News*, April 9, 2011.
26. "Palin Sought More Taxes and More Development from Oil Companies," Politifact .com, undated, analyzing a remark she made on August 29, 2008.

Chapter 7. Palin Triumphs over Big Oil, Round 3

1. Primary sources for this chapter are the Palin administration's voluminous research on the natural gas pipeline issue, including the justification for awarding the bid to TransCanada, http://gasline.alaska.gov. The legislation authorizing that bid award was HB3001, and the legislative history on it can be found in the legislature's archive at www.legis.state.ak.us/basis.
2. Pat Forgey, "Palin Responds to Stevens' Criticism of Natural Gas Line," *Juneau Empire*, February 22, 2008.
3. Ibid.
4. SCR22 passed April 6, 2008, just four days after it was introduced.
5. See e-mail by Palin aide Ivy Frye, Tuesday, April 8, 2008, 9:53 a.m., citing an unsourced press account.
6. Wesley Loy, "BP Joins Conoco Phillips in Gas Line Plan," *Anchorage Daily News*, April 8, 2008.
7. "House and Senate Leaders Applaud ConocoPhillips, BP Announcement on Gas Pipeline," House and Senate Majority press release, April 8, 2008.
8. Dan Fagan, "BP, Conoco Make AGIA a Dead Horse," *Anchorage Daily News*, April 13, 2008.
9. Loy, "BP Joins Conoco Phillips."
10. Ibid.
11. "Palin Recommends TransCanada for AGIA," Office of Gov. Sarah Palin, press release no. 08-78, May 22, 2008.
12. Pat Forgey, "Senate Gives Palin Pipeline Victory," *Juneau Empire*, August 3, 2008.
13. Pat Forgey, "TransCanada Winning Over Lawmakers," *Juneau Empire*, June 8, 2008.

14. Ibid.
15. Wesley Loy, "Hickel Ad Threat Riles Palin," *Anchorage Daily News*, July 13, 2008.
16. Eric Lidji, "Former Alaska Governor Asks State to Delay AGIA Vote for Three Months-Plus," *Petroleum News*, July 13, 2008.
17. "Governor Announces Public/Private Gasline Venture To Pursue In-State Gasline for Alaskans," Office of Gov. Sarah Palin, press release no. 08-110, July 7, 2008.
18. Pat Forgey, "House OKs TransCanada plan," *Juneau Empire*, July 23, 2008.
19. From the archive of Governor Palin's e-mails released by the state of Alaska. The archive include some e-mails written by staff, including Balash.
20. E-mail from Sarah Palin to Tom Irwin, Friday August 1, 2008, 10:59 p.m.
21. Forgey, "Senate Gives Palin Pipeline Victory."
22. Pat Forgey, "Democrats Join Defense of Palin, Natural Gas Pipeline," *Juneau Empire,* October 29, 2008.
23. "Misfire at Palin," editorial, *Anchorage Daily News*, November 1, 2008.
24. "Resolution Introduced to Re-evaluate AGIA licensing," press release from Reps. Jay Ramras and Craig Johnson, March 12, 2009.
25. Pat Forgey, "Natural Gas Pipeline Battles May Resume," *Juneau Empire*, March 15, 2009.
26. Joe McGinniss, "Pipe Dreams," *Portfolio*, March 2009.
27. Bill White, Sean Cockerham, and Elizabeth Bluemink, "Exxon Joins TransCanada in Push to Build Gas Pipeline," *Anchorage Daily News*, June 11, 2009.
28. Tim Bradner, "TransCanada-ExxonMobil Deal: A Game-changer?," *Alaska Journal of Commerce*, June 22, 2009.
29. Ibid.
30. Sean Cockerham, "TransCanada Says Bill May Violate License," *Anchorage Daily News*, April 4, 2011.
31. Rep. Beth Kerttula, "AGIA process is Working; Don't Stop It Now," *Anchorage Daily News*, March 3, 2011.
32. "How Much Longer?," editorial, *Anchorage Daily News*, January 31, 2011.

Chapter 8. Palin Triumphs over Big Oil, Round 4

1. A history of the issue through 2005 is summarized in "Denial of the Proposed Plans for Development of the Point Thomson Unit," Findings and Decision of the Director, Alaska Division of Oil and Gas, September 30, 2005.
2. The history of the issue through April 2008 is documented in "State of Alaska Department of Natural Resources Commissioner's Findings and Decision on Remand from Superior Court Point Thomson Unit," Tom Irwin, commissioner, April 22, 2008.
3. "Judge Gleason Rules in Favor of State; Court Affirms DNR Actions on Pt. Thomson," Office of the Governor, press release no. 07-248, December 27, 2007.
4. Irwin, "State of Alaska Natural Resources Commissioner's Findings."
5. "Hanging Tough: State Right to Reject Latest Promises at Point Thomson," editorial, *Anchorage Daily News*, April 27, 2008.

6. Joe Carroll and Sonja Franklin, "Alaska's Palin, Miss Congeniality, Makes Exxon, Conoco Comply," Bloomberg.com, March 3, 2008.
7. "Conditional Interim Decision, Appeal of Exxon Mobil Corporation [et al.]" Office of Commissioner, Alaska Department of Natural Resources, January 27, 2009.
8. Wesley Loy, "Point Thomson Case on Ice," *Petroleum News,* February 21, 2010.
9. Wesley Loy, "Point Thomson Field Remains Stuck in Limbo," *Petroleum News*, published in *Anchorage Daily News*, July 23, 2011.

Chapter 9. This is the Record of a Tea Party Favorite?

1. The *Wall Street Journal* has a useful summary of the issue: Jim Carlton, "Creamery Case Has Palin Critics Taking Aim at Fiscal-Conservative Claim," September 16, 2008.
2. S. J. Komarnitsky, "Governor Gets Cool Reception at Mat Maid plant," *Anchorage Daily News*, June 14, 2007.
3. S. J. Komarnitsky, "Ag Board Saves Mat Maid for Now," *Anchorage Daily News*, June 20, 2007.
4. S. J. Komarnitsky, "Creamery Board Cuts Loose Longtime Chief," *Anchorage Daily News*, July 3, 2007.
5. Red Secoy e-mail to Joe Balash, Monday, June 18, 2007.
6. Jo Becker, Peter S. Goodman, and Michael Powell, "Once Elected, Palin Hired Friends and Lashed Foes," *New York Times*, September 13, 2008.
7. Andrew Halcro, December 22, 2007, post on his blog, andrewhalcro.com.
8. S. J. Komarnitsky, "Mat Maid Ends June with a $62,000 profit," *Anchorage Daily News*, August 7, 2007.
9. S. J. Komarnitsky, "Board Shocked by Dairy's Huge Loss," *Anchorage Daily News*, August 28, 2007.
10. "Palin Criticizes Bailout at GOP Governors Conference," CNN Political Tickler blog, November 13, 2008.
11. Arthur Corliss, e-mail to Gov. Sarah Palin via WebMail@gov.state.ak.us, Friday December 7, 2007. Other e-mails to Palin can be found in the archive released by the State of Alaska in June 2011.
12. "Governor Palin Announces Health Priorities," Office of Gov. Sarah Palin, press release, December 4, 2008.
13. "PalinParnell: Sarah on Issues," Palin for Governor web page, archived at http://web.archive.org/web/20080723181805/http://www.palinforgovernor.com/issues.html.
14. Pat Forgey, "Initiative to Repeal Hospital Certificate of Need Rules Stymied," *Juneau Empire*, April 18, 2008.
15. Ibid.
16. Bailey, Morris, and Devon, *Blind Allegiance*, passim.
17. Sean Cockerham, "Palin Proposes New Funds to Benefit Children: $5 Million in New Money: Denali KidCare, Obesity Prevention and Head Start Would Get Boosts," *Anchorage Daily News*, December 5, 2008.

18. Ibid.
19. Press release, Office of Gov. Sarah Palin, May 15, 2008.
20. Dan Fagan, "Palin is Driven by Desire to Be Popular," *Anchorage Daily News*, May 17, 2008.
21. Testimony to Alaska House State Affairs Committee, February 9, 2008.
22. From Governor Palin's FY2009 budget proposal: http://www.gov.state.ak.us /omb/09_omb/budget/DOC/09crdetail_doc.pdf.
23. "Palin Returns," editorial, *Anchorage Daily News*, November 6, 2008.
24. "Emmonak's Nicolas Tucker Rips Sarah Palin for 'Disrespect,'" alaskareport.com, March 6, 2009. See also Kyle Hopkins, "Letter tells Personal Side of Emmonak Fuel Crisis," *Anchorage Daily News*, January 15, 2009.
25. Video of the encounter is on YouTube, www.youtube.com/watch?v=V-AES-LZeT0.
26. "Emmonak's Tucker Rips Palin," Alaskareport.com.

Chapter 10. Al Gore, She's Not

1. Michael Powell and Jo Becker, "Palin's Hand Seen in Battle over Mine in Alaska," *New York Times*, October 21, 2008.
2. Elizabeth Bluemink, "Mine Settles Water Lawsuit," *Anchorage Daily News*, May 16, 2008.
3. "Palin, Politics and Predator Control," *High Country News*, February 21, 2011.
4. Office of Gov. Sarah Palin, Executive Order 238.
5. "Governor Palin Responds to New Climate and Polar Bear Studies," Office of Gov. Sarah Palin, press release no. 07-209, October 24, 2007.
6. Bryan Walsh, "Palin on the Environment: Far Right," *Time*, September 1, 2008.
7. Sarah Palin, "Sarah Palin on the Politicization of the Copenhagen Climate Conference," op-ed, *Washington Post*, December 9, 2009.
8. Sarah Palin, "Bearing Up," *New York Times*, January 5, 2008.
9. "Governor Palin Responds to New Climate and Polar Bear Studies," Office of Gov. Sarah Palin, press release no. 07-209, October 24, 2007.
10. Draper, "The Palin Network."
11. "Governor Announces Challenge to Beluga Listing Decision; Provides Federal Agencies with Notice of Intent to Sue," Office of Gov. Sarah Palin, press release no. 09-06, January 14, 2009.
12. Ibid.
13. Personal communication, Bob Shavelson, Cook Inlet Keeper, May 15, 2011.
14. Richard Fineberg, "Rogue Star Update, Feb. 8, 2010," FinebergResearch.com.
15. Ibid.
16. Dan Joling, "Palin Unveils State Energy Goals," Associated Press, January 16, 2009.
17. E-mail from Gov. Sarah Palin to Joseph Balash, Sharon Leighow, and Rosanne Hughes, August 4, 2008.
18. "Energetically Wrong," Politifact.com, posted on September 12, 2008, updated on September 17, 2008.

19. "Export Line Does Nothing to Address Immediate Energy Crisis," Fairbanks Pipeline Company press release, May 11, 2011.

20. "Total US Fuel Taxes by State," gasbuddy.com/Tax_Info.aspx.

21. "Legislation Introduced Designed to Restructure Generation and Transmission Assets of the Railbelt Utilities," Office of Gov. Sarah Palin, press release no. 09-47, March 6, 2009.

Chapter 11. From Ethics Crusader to Ethics Target, Part I: Troopergate

1. Kyle Hopkins, "'Out of the Blue,' Top Cop Monegan gets Palin's Axe," *Anchorage Daily News*, July 13, 2008.

2. "Governor Palin Releases Statement," Office of Gov. Sarah Palin, press release no. 08-122, July 17, 2008.

3. Office of Gov. Sarah Palin, press release no. 08-125, July 22, 2008.

4. Megan Holland and Sean Cockerham, "Governor Says Kopp Didn't Tell of Letter," *Anchorage Daily News*, July 28, 2008.

5. Wesley Loy, "Hired Help Will Probe Monegan Dismissal," *Anchorage Daily News*, July 29, 2008.

6. Steve Quinn, "Lawmakers Call for Palin Probe," Associated Press, published in the *Juneau Empire,* July 29, 2008.

7. Loy, "Hired Help."

8. Sean Cockerham, "Palin Staff Pushed to Fire Trooper," *Anchorage Daily News*, August 14, 2008.

9. "Governor to Turn over Findings," Office of Gov. Sarah Palin, press release no. 08-141, August 13, 2008.

10. Bailey, Morris, and Devon, *Blind Allegiance*, Chapter 18.

11. Ibid., Chapter 25.

12. Ibid., Chapter 25.

13. Ibid., Chapter 21 and Chapter 26.

14. Cockerham, "Palin Staff Fire Trooper."

15. Kyle Hopkins and Sean Cockerham, "Palin Says Staff's Calls Were Not Pressure," *Anchorage Daily News*, August 15, 2008.

16. The Alaska Legislature's investigation, known as the Branchflower Report, was submitted to the Alaska Legislature's Legislative Council on October 10, 2008, by Stephen Branchflower.

17. Branchflower Report, 69.

18. Ibid., 67.

19. Ibid., 69.

20. Ibid., 71.

21. Ibid., 70–71.

22. "Report: Palin Abused Power," *Juneau Empire*, October 12, 2008.

23. Lisa Demer, "Palin Says Report Vindicates Her," *Anchorage Daily News*, October 12, 2008.

24. "Palin Vindicated?," editorial, *Anchorage Daily News*, October 14, 2008.

25. Bailey, Morris, and Devon, *Blind Allegiance*, Chapter 24.

26. The State of Alaska Personnel Board report, known as the Petumenos Report, was submitted by Timothy J. Petumenos on October 15, 2008, with the title, "In Re Ethics Complaint Dated August 6, 2008: Report of Findings and Recommendations."

27. "Monegan's Lawyer Re: Petumenos Troopergate Report," Inside Opinion blog, *Anchorage Daily News*, November 11, 2008.

28. Petumenos Report, 20.

29. Ibid., 54.

30. Lisa Demer, "Is Wooten a Good Trooper?," *Anchorage Daily News*, July 27, 2008.

31. Bailey, Morris, and Devon, *Blind Allegiance*, Chapter 21.

32. Sean Cockerham, "Palin Staff Pushed to Have Trooper Fired," *Anchorage Daily News*, August 14, 2008.

33. Petumenos Report, 35.

34. Bailey, Morris, and Devon, *Blind Allegiance*, Chapter 35.

35. "Palin Quits as Alaska Governor," Foxnews.com, July 3, 2009.

36. Bailey, Morris, and Devon, *Blind Allegiance*, Chapter 18.

37. Hollis French, phone interview with author, April 25, 2011.

38. Bailey, Morris, and Devon, *Blind Allegiance*, Chapter 18.

39. "Palin Vindicated?," editorial.

40. Editorial, *Fairbanks Daily News-Miner*, November 9, 2008, reprinted in the *Juneau Empire* as, "Alaska Editorial: Troopergate Reports Still Worth Analysis," November 16, 2008.

41. Ibid.

42. Bailey, Morris, and Devon, *Blind Allegiance*, Chapter 21.

43. Ibid., Chapter 24.

Chapter 12. From Ethics Crusader to Ethics Target, Part II: Oops! Not All Those Ethics Complaints Were Frivolous

1. Tom Kizzia, "Rebel Status Has Fueled Front-Runner's Success," *Anchorage Daily News*, October 24, 2006.

2. The Associated Press summarized the complaints filed against Palin as of June 21, 2009, in "Ethics Complaints Filed against Palin." See also the official reports issued by the Alaska Personnel Board, http://doa.alaska.gov/dop/personnelboard/reports/.

3. "Ethics Complaint on Governor's Apparel Dismissed," Office of Gov. Sarah Palin, press release 09-141, June 3, 2009.

4. Kyle Hopkins, "State Paid Per Diem While Palin Stayed in Wasilla Home," *Anchorage Daily News*, September 10, 2008.

5. Lisa Demer, "Palin to Pay Tax on Past Per Diem," *Anchorage Daily News*, February 18, 2009.

6. Ibid.

7. This passage appears on page 386 of the Microsoft Word version of Frank Bailey's unpublished manuscript, distributed by Joe McGinnis.

8. Demer, "Palin to Pay Tax"; Kyle Hopkins, "9 Trips Gov. Palin Took with Her Children," *Anchorage Daily News*, adn.com, February 24, 2009; and "Governor to Pay for 10th Trip," *Anchorage Daily News*, February 26, 2009.

9. "Governor Palin Comments on Personnel Board Settlement," Office of Gov. Sarah Palin, press release 09-37, February 24, 2009.

10. Sean Cockerham, "Palin Legal Fund May Violate Ethics Law," *Anchorage Daily News*, July 21, 2009.

11. Pat Forgey, "Ethical Dilemma: Palin, Former Ethics Champion, Leaving amid a Storm of Complaints," *Juneau Empire*, July 26, 2009.

12. SB186, 24th Alaska Legislature (2005–06).

13. Devon summarized the story in "Sarah Palin—Tax Cheat? Contents of Mysterious Envelope Revealed," *Huffington Post*, February 3, 2010. The posting includes links to source documents.

14. Sean Cockerham and Kyle Hopkins, "Ex-Aide Rips Palin in Leaked Manuscript," *Anchorage Daily News*, February 18, 2011. See also Bailey, *Blind Allegiance*, Chapter 14.

15. Bailey, Morris, and Devon, *Blind Allegiance*, Chapter 14.

16. Forgey, "Ethical Dilemma."

Chapter 13. Personnel (Mis)Management

1. Bailey, Morris, and Devon, *Blind Allegiance*, Chapter 17.

2. Pat Forgey, "State Leaders Question Palin's Qualifications," *Juneau Empire*, August 31, 2008.

3. Bailey, Morris, and Devon, *Blind Allegiance*, Chapter 17.

4. Interview with Palin adviser. Interview was conducted in confidentiality, and the name of the interviewee is withheld by mutual agreement.

5. Ibid., Chapter 30.

6. Sean Cockerham, "Colberg Resigns amid Legislative Pressure over 'Troopergate,'" *Anchorage Daily News*, February 10, 2009.

7. Paul Fuhs, "Palin Wants to Be a Star in a Democracy," *Anchorage Daily News*, December 4, 2009.

8. Personal phone interview with the author, May 11, 2011.

9. Becker, Goodman, and Powell, "Once Elected."

10. Alan Boraas, "Kopp Hiring Proved Palin's Fundamentalist Street Cred," *Anchorage Daily News*, September 20, 2008.

11. "Palin Names Public Safety Commissioner," Office of Gov. Sarah Palin, press release 08-116, July 14, 2008.

12. Megan Holland, "Kopp Acknowledges Harassment Complaint," *Anchorage Daily News*, July 23, 2008.

13. Megan Holland and Sean Cockerham, "Governor Says Kopp Didn't Tell of Letter," *Anchorage Daily News*, July 25, 2008.

14. Ibid.
15. Bailey, Morris, and Devon, *Blind Allegiance*, Chapter 24.
16. William Yardley, "Active Role for Palin's Husband in Alaska Government," *New York Times*, September 13, 2008.
17. Bailey, Morris, and Devon, *Blind Allegiance*, Chapter 6.
18. Branchflower Report, 45.
19. Interview with Palin adviser. Interview was conducted in confidentiality, and the name of the interviewee is withheld by mutual agreement.
20. Bailey, Morris, and Devon, *Blind Allegiance*, Chapter 12.
21. Todd S. Purdum, "It Came from Wasilla," *Vanity Fair*, August 2009.
22. Fuhs, "Palin Wants to Be a Star."
23. Ibid.
24. Draper, "The Palin Network."
25. John Ziegler, "The Sarah Palin I Know," dailycaller.com, June 12, 2011.

Chapter 14. This May Sound Familiar from High School

1. Tom Kizzia, "Palin Denies Mat-Su Bias in State Budgeting," *Anchorage Daily News*, October 7, 2007.
2. See veto message on SB53 from Gov. Sarah Palin, September 28, 2007, Alaska Legislature, Senate Journal 1394.
3. Kizzia, "Palin Denies Mat-Su Bias."
4. Mike Doogan, "She's Nice—But Not Ready," *Washington Post*, September 3, 2008.
5. Palin, *Going Rogue*, 201.
6. Ryan Lizza, "Naysayer," *New Yorker*, September 15, 2008.
7. Bailey, Morris, and Devon, *Blind Allegiance*, 253.
8. Ibid.
9. Pat Forgey, "Internal E-mails Reveal Early Ethics Efforts, Push Back," *Juneau Empire*, February 7, 2010.
10. Ibid.
11. Becker, Goodman, and Powell, "Once Elected."
12. Bailey, Morris, and Devon, *Blind Allegiance*, prologue.
13. Ibid., Chapter 32.
14. From the archive of Governor Palin's e-mails, released by the state of Alaska.
15. Pat Forgey, "Sen. Kim Elton Resigns for Interior Post," *Juneau Empire*, March 3, 2009.
16. Pat Forgey, "State Leaders Question Palin's Qualifications," *Juneau Empire*, August 31, 2008.
17. The entire dispute is well summarized in Mark Thiessen, "Last Minute Deal Seals Seat for Egan," Associated Press, published in *Juneau Empire*, April 21, 2009.
18. "Palin Had Kind Words for Alaskan Independence Party," *Anchorage Daily News*, September 12, 2008.
19. Palin, *Going Rogue*, 116.
20. Ibid., 144, 151.

21. Purdum, "It Came From Wasilla."
22. Fuhs, "Palin Wants to Be a Star."
23. Bailey, Morris, and Devon, *Blind Allegiance*, Epilogue.

Chapter 15. The Truth Can Be So Inconvenient

1. Geoffrey Dunn, *The Lies of Sarah Palin* (New York: St. Martin's, 2011).
2. Michael M. Grynbaum, "Palin Denies Abuse of Authority in Trooper Case," *New York Times* The Caucus blog, October 11, 2008.
3. Lisa Demer, "Palin: Very Much Appreciating Being Cleared of Any Legal Wrongdoing or Unethical Activity at All," *Anchorage Daily News* Alaska Politics blog, October 11, 2008.
4. Grynbaum, "Palin Denies Abuse."
5. "Report Finds Palin Violated Ethics Law," Politifact.com, October 14, 2008.
6. "Palin E-Mails Show Infighting with Staff," cbsnews.com, July 1, 2009.
7. Scott Conroy and Sushannah Walshe, "Palin Emails Show Infighting with Staff," cbs.com, June 2, 2010. The authors include an account of the controversy in their book, *Sarah from Alaska: The Sudden Rise and Brutal Education of a New Conservative Superstar* (New York: Public Affairs, 2009).
8. Dunn, *The Lies of Sarah Palin*, 26.
9. "Palin Infighting with Staff," cbsnews.com.
10. Purdum, "It Came from Wasilla."
11. Rep. Les Gara, "The Truth About Palin and Darfur," mudflats.wordpress.com, October 6, 2008.
12. Brett J. Blackledge, Adam Coldman, and Matt Apuzzo, "State Charged for Palin Kids' Travel Costs," Associated Press, October 22, 2008.
13. Conroy and Walshe, *Sarah from Alaska.*
14. Erika Bolstad and Sean Cockerham, "Palin, Republicans Call for Special Senate Election," *Anchorage Daily News*, April 2, 2009.
15. Mel Bryant, "Governor Palin's Seward House Address," Conservatives4Palin.com, June 6, 2009, www.c4parchive.com/2009_05_31_archive.html.
16. "Sarah Palin Says She Vetoed Stimulus Money for Energy Efficiency Because It Required Tougher Building Codes," Politifact.com, June 11, 2009.
17. Gov. Sarah Palin, "Stand Blocked Federal Control of Alaskans," *Anchorage Daily News*, May 29, 2009.
18. Dunn, *The Lies of Sarah Palin*, 377.
19. Palin, *Going Rogue*, 361–62.
20. Ibid., 362.
21. Pat Forgey, "Stimulus Battle Getting Personal," *Juneau Empire*, March 27, 2009.
22. Sarah Palin, "Sarah Palin on the Politicization of the Copenhagen Climate Conference," op-ed, *Washington Post*, December 9, 2009.
23. Tom Kizzia, "Palin Misrepresented State's Polar Bear Findings," *Anchorage Daily News*, May 25, 2008.

24. Rick Steiner, "Sarah Palin's Record on Environment is Abysmal," *Seattle Post-Intelligencer*, September 6, 2008.
25. Palin, *Going Rogue*, 215.
26. Ibid., 164.
27. Paul Jenkins, "Palin Trotting Out Her 'Poor Little Me' Campaign Strategy Yet One More Time," *Anchorage Daily News*, July 11, 2009. See also, Tom Kizzia, "Rebel Status has Fueled Front-runner's Success," *Anchorage Daily News*, October 24, 2006.
28. Palin, *Going Rogue*, 164.
29. Ibid., 165.
30. Draper, "The Palin Network."
31. Gov. Sarah Palin, speech on July 23, 2009, Fairbanks, Alaska.

Chapter 16. "Where's Sarah?"
1. "Palin's Leadership," editorial, *Anchorage Daily News*, September 8, 2008.
2. Ibid.
3. Interview with the author, June 3, 2011.
4. Sen. Albert Kookesh and Rep. Bill Thomas, "Palin's Veto Fails Rural District 5," *Juneau Empire*, July 19, 2007.
5. Palin E-mail Archive, e-mail sent July 28, 2008.
6. Interview with Palin adviser. Interview was conducted in confidentiality, and the name of the interviewee is withheld by mutual agreement.
7. "Palin's Leadership," editorial.
8. Interview with the author.
9. Interview with the author.
10. Ibid.
11. Ryan Lizza, "Naysayer," www.newyorker.com/talk/2008/09/15/080915ta_talk_lizza.
12. Fuhs, "Palin Wants to Be a Star."
13. Dunn, *The Lies of Sarah Palin*, 233.
14. Stephen R. Covey, *Seven Habits of Highly Effective People* (New York: Free Press, 2004), 151.
15. Sean Cockerham and Erika Bolstad, "Snapshots of an Era," *Anchorage Daily News*, June 11, 2011.
16. See Palin E-mail Archive, e-mails from January 16, 2008, and from late June 2008.
17. Palin E-mail Archive, e-mail sent January 29, 2008, 2:03 a.m.
18. Ibid., e-mail sent by Ivy Frye, May 24, 2007.
19. Wesley Loy, "Palin E-Mailing Sparks Criticism," *Anchorage Daily News*, April 13, 2008.
20. Becker, Goodman, and Powell, "Once Elected."
21. Pat Forgey, "State Leaders Question Palin's Qualifications," *Juneau Empire,* August 31, 2008.
22. Becker, Goodman, and Powell, "Once Elected."
23. Ibid.

24. Fuhs, "Palin Wants to Be a Star."
25. "Abdication by Palin," editorial, *Anchorage Daily News*, September 20, 2008.

Chapter 17. Palin Returns to Her Day Job

1. "Palin Returns," editorial, *Anchorage Daily News*, November 6, 2008.
2. Draper, "The Palin Network."
3. William Yardley, "Back Home, Palin Finds Landscape has Changed," *New York Times*, November 8, 2008.
4. Dunn, *The Lies of Sarah Palin*, 286.
5. Yardley, "Back Home."
6. Draper, "The Palin Network."
7. Yardley, "Back Home."
8. Ibid.
9. Sean Cockerham, "More Legislature vs. Palin," *Anchorage Daily News*, April 17, 2009.
10. Ibid.
11. Pat Forgey, "Stimulus Battle Getting Personal," *Juneau Empire*, March 27, 2009.
12. Mike Doogan, "Ross' Defense of the Water Thrower Perverts Logic and Patriotism," *Anchorage Daily News*, April 20, 2003.
13. The full quote appears in Frank Bailey's unpublished manuscript, distributed to the media by Joe McGinnis, at page 373. The published version of Bailey's book omits the word "degenerates" (Bailey, Morris and Devon, *Blind Allegiance*, Chapter 32). The "degenerates" part of Ross's quote was noted extensively in media coverage of Ross's confirmation process. See note # 3.
14. Sean Cockerham, "Lawmakers Reject Ross as AG," *Anchorage Daily News*, April 16, 2009.
15. Ibid.
16. Ibid.
17. Pat Forgey, "Palin Objects as Oil Price Increase Bails Out the State," *Juneau Empire*, June 10, 2009.
18. "Oil Prices: Palin's View is Surprising," editorial, *Anchorage Daily News*, June 14, 2009.
19. Sean Cockerham, "Palin Rejects over 30% of Stimulus Money," *Anchorage Daily News,* March 19, 2009.
20. Kyle Hopkins and Megan Holland, "Palin Wants Discussion on Stimulus Funds," *Anchorage Daily News*, March 20, 2009.
21. Anne Sutton, "House Approves Stimulus Funds with 40–0 Vote," Associated Press, April 12, 2009.
22. "Oil Prices: Palin's View is Surprising."
23. Pat Forgey, "Legislators Blame Palin for Deteriorating Relationship," *Juneau Empire*, April 12, 2009.
24. Personal communication to author, by one of her staff who attended the resignation speech. Name of staff member withheld by mutual agreement.

25. Palin's speech can be found at wayback.archive-it.org/1200/20090726070103/
http://www.gov.state.ak.us/exec-column.php.

26. Gregg Erickson, "Stepping Down Gives Palin a Shot at 2012," *Anchorage Daily News*, July 26, 2009.

27. Ruth Marcus, "Bailout, Palin-style," *Washington Post*, July 5, 2009.

28. Sean Cockerham, "FBI Says Palin Not Subject of Inquiry," *Anchorage Daily News*, July 6, 2009.

29. Gov. Sarah Palin, speech on July 26, 2009, http://www.huffingtonpost.com/akmuck
raker/sarah-palins-farewell-add_b_245215.html.

30. Ibid.

31. Sean Cockerham, "Parnell Takes Reins of Government from Palin," *Anchorage Daily News*, July 26, 2009.

32. Erickson, Stepping Down Gives Shot."

33. Paul Jenkins, "Once upon a Time, Palin Was a Cyclone," *Anchorage Daily News*, July 26, 2009.

34. Fuhs, "Palin Wants to Be a Star."

35. Pat Forgey, "Internal E-mails Reveal Early Ethics Efforts, Push Back," *Juneau Empire*, February 7, 2010.

36. Draper, "The Palin Network."

37. Guy Busby, "Exceptional Foundation Pleased with Fundraiser," *Press-Register*, May 9, 2011.

38. Ibid.

39. Malia Litman, "Confirmation That Sarah Palin's 'Servant's Heart' Comes with a $100,000.00 Price Tag," malialitman.wordpress.com, April 9, 2011.

40. Michael Carey, "The Beginning of Sarah Palin's End," *Los Angeles Times*, July 5, 2009.

41. Jeanne Devon, "Why the 'Tragedy' of Sarah Palin Isn't Really a Tragedy," *Huffington Post*, May 17, 2011.

42. Tom Kizzia, "Palin Foresees Positive Changes in Politics," *Anchorage Daily News*, September 2, 2007.

Chapter 18. Legacy and Prospects: A Republican Geraldine Ferraro or a Modern-Day Aimee Semple McPherson?

1. Douglas Martin, "Geraldine A. Ferraro, 1935–2011: She Ended the Men's Club of Politics," *New York Times*, March 26, 2011.

2. JoNel Aleccia, "Women's Support Proves Key in Battlegrounds; Female Voters Heavily Favor Obama, Helping Propel Historic Victory," msnbc.com, updated November 5, 2008, accessed November 17, 2011.

3. Martin, "Geraldine A. Ferraro."

4. Michael Carey, "Quitting Cost Palin Hope for High Office," *Anchorage Daily News*, July 8, 2009.

5. "The Kidnapping of Aimee Semple McPherson," University of Southern California library archives, www.usc.edu/libraries/archives/la/scandals/aimee.html.

6. "The History of the Foursquare Church: Aimee Semple McPherson," http://www .foursquare.org/about/aimee_semple_mcpherson.

7. *The Daily Show*, October 6, 2011, thedailyshow.com, accessed November 13, 2011. The episode includes excerpts from the text of the SarahPAC letter and from Bristol Palin's appearance on Fox, June 28, 2011.

8. David Ferguson, "Jon Stewart: Palin Swindle of Donor Money in 'Nigerian Prince Territory,'" rawstory.com, October 7, 2011, accessed November 13, 2011.

9. Draper, "The Palin Network."

10. Joshua Green, "The Tragedy of Sarah Palin," *The Atlantic*, June 2011.

11. Jeanne Devon, "The Real Tragedy of Sarah Palin," The Mudflats blog, May 20, 2011.

12. Interview with author and others, *KRUA*, University of Alaska, Anchorage, September 15, 2009.

13. Elspeth Reeve, "Bill Kristol Says Sarah Palin Shouldn't Be the GOP Nominee," *National Journal*, March 23, 2001, updated March 30, 2011.

14. Interview with the author.

15. David Brooks, "Why Experience Matters," *New York Times*, September 15, 2008.

16. Bailey, Morris, and Devon, *Blind Allegiance*, Prologue.

Source Notes

This book is based first and foremost on my experience as a journalist, following Sarah Palin's work after she ran for statewide office in 2002. Unlike some who have written about her Alaska record after she ran for vice president, I did not have to come to the state and start from scratch in learning about the issues and political players she dealt with. I closely followed the Palin administration's work on oil taxes and the natural gas pipeline project and attended portions of the special sessions held on both issues. I had many conversations with Palin's oil and gas team, her legislative allies, and those who criticized her handling of that issue.

Newspapers

The newspaper I worked for, the *Anchorage Daily News*, covered many aspects of Palin's work, and its electronic archive is an essential resource. The archive is online at http://www.adnsearch.com/. *Daily News* stories, editorials, and commentaries cited in this work can be found there. Searching is free but the paper charges for access to the full text. Much of the paper's coverage of Palin can also be found for free elsewhere on the paper's website. Dates cited in the notes section often refer to the date of web publication, which may be one day earlier than the date on the article as preserved in the *Daily News* archive. (Many of the web versions were published late on the day preceding their publication in the print edition.)

The *Juneau Empire*'s archive is another valuable source on Palin's record as Alaska governor. It was the only paper with a full-time, year-round correspondent in the state capital covering state government. Coverage from 2008 is here: http://www.juneauempire.com/legislature/archives/2008index.shtml.

Alaska Websites/Sources

Some primary sources from Palin's time as governor are available on the Internet. State of Alaska web pages, as of the day Palin left office, are preserved at this site: http://archive-it.org/public/collection.html?id=1200. I reviewed all her press releases and newsletters that relate to the topics covered in this book. Not all the hyperlinks were preserved in the web-archiving process, so at times it may be necessary to scroll manually through the available links, as with her news releases.

This link has the home page of Alaska governor's official site as of the day Palin left office: http://wayback.archive-it.org/1200/20090726070023/http://www.gov.state.ak.us/.

Her press releases are archived here: http://wayback.archive-it.org/1200 /20090726070203/http://www.gov.state.ak.us/archive.php.

The Alaska legislature's archive, known as BASIS, thoroughly documents the step-by-step progress on Palin's legislative proposals, accessible at www.legis .state.ak.us/basis. The main page includes links to past legislative sessions, including those when Palin was governor. She took office in December 2006 and resigned in July 2009.

For information on her budget vetoes, check the "Partial vetoes" link from 2007, 2008, and 2009. The site has her veto messages and detailed information on the line items she cut.

Her ethics legislation, passed in 2007, was HB109. Other ethics reform bills that passed can be found there as well. The legislation authorizing competitive bidding for the state's natural gas pipeline incentives was HB177, also passed in 2007. Later that same year, in a special session, the legislature passed HB2001, Palin's oil tax reform. The site allows the interested reader to follow the history of how those bills changed as they moved through the legislative process.

The Palin administration's voluminous research on the natural gas pipeline issue, including the justification for awarding the bid to TransCanada, can be found here: http://gasline.alaska.gov. The legislation authorizing that bid award was HB3001, and the legislative history on it can be found in the legislature's archive at www.legis.state.ak.us/basis.

Two important original source documents for the Troopergate scandal are:

> The Alaska Legislature's investigation, known as the Branchflower Report, submitted to the Alaska Legislature's Legislative Council October 10, 2008, by Stephen Branchflower, and
>
> The State of Alaska Personnel Board report, known as the Petumenos Report, submitted by Timothy J. Petumenos October 15, 2008, "In Re Ethics Complaint Dated August 6, 2008: Report of Findings and Recommendations."

The Alaska Personnel Board has other public reports on some ethics complaints filed against Palin at this site: http://doa.alaska.gov/dop/personnelboard/reports/.

The Alaska Division of Elections website has vote totals for state elections, including Palin's two races for statewide office, the 2002 voter initiative to promote an all-Alaska natural gas pipeline and other elections mentioned in this book: http://www.elections.alaska.gov/ei_return.php.

Blogs

Two Alaska bloggers closely followed Palin's work as governor, from a highly critical perspective. The Mudflats, by Anchorage resident Jeanne Devon, often had information that had not yet drawn attention in traditional media (it is currently posted at themudflats.net). Devon broke the story about the Palins' failure to notify local taxing authorities after building cabins on recreational property in the Matanuska-Susitna Borough. She would eventually collaborate with Frank Bailey on his critical book about working for Palin, with their third coauthor, Ken Morris.

Former Republican legislator Andrew Halcro ran as an independent for governor against Palin. His blog, andrewhalcro.com, broke the Troopergate scandal open by airing trooper Mike Wooten's allegations against Palin and her family. Halcro also closely followed Palin's failed effort to rescue the state-owned Matanuska Maid dairy. He took the oil industry's side in its battles with Palin over oil taxes and gas pipeline development incentives.

Internet (General)

Palin's Twitter messages from her time as governor can be found here: http://www.scribd.com/doc/22691806/AKGovSarahPalin-Tweet-Archive.

Her Facebook site has some comments about her work as governor: facebook.com/sarahpalin. Her postings are under the "Notes" link.

Politifact.com has fact-checked numerous claims Palin has made since being nominated for vice president. Its summaries were particularly useful.

E-mails

In June 2011, the state finally complied with several media organizations' request for e-mails from her time as governor, covering the period through September 2008. Several media organizations have searchable databases of those e-mails. The *Washington Post*'s site, http://www.washingtonpost.com/palinemails, was relatively easy to use.

Before that document release, MSNBC obtained a partial archive of Palin's e-mail records from the state. A less-than-ideal searchable database of those e-mails is at: http://palinemail.crivellawest.net/.

In late February 2012, the state released a second and final batch of Governor Palin's e-mails, covering the last ten months of her term. Various media organizations have assembled them into a searchable database.

The state redacted many passages of the e-mails and withheld others entirely. In withholding information, the state appears to have used a generous interpretation of the "deliberative process" exemption in Alaska's public records law—an exemption is intended to ensure the governor gets candid advice from her staff. Among the redacted or withheld e-mails are those in which Palin and her staff are drafting op-eds and other commentaries for media publications. The state has also asserted the right to withhold e-mails she sent to her husband, Todd, even if they deal with official state business, on the theory he was a "trusted adviser," even though he was a private citizen.

Palin maintained several private e-mail accounts and used them to discuss many subjects with her state-paid staff. Some of those e-mails were copied or sent to official state e-mail addresses and were included in the e-mail archive released by the state. E-mails that were exchanged exclusively on nonstate accounts were not disclosed to the public.

Books

Frank Bailey's book, *Blind Allegiance to Sarah Palin: A Memoir of Our Tumultuous Years* (Brentwood, TN: Howard Books, 2011), provides a candid, behind-the-scenes look at Palin's campaign for governor and her work after she was elected, from the perspective of a dedicated, socially conservative staffer who became disillusioned with her. He draws heavily on e-mails that he saved from working for her, including those on the private e-mail networks she and her staff used. I received a copy of Bailey's manuscript before it was published. The published version is different in some key passages. Where the two differ, I relied on the published version unless otherwise noted.

A useful one-volume resource on Palin's work on oil and gas issues is *Sarah Takes on Big Oil: The Compelling Story of Governor Sarah Palin's Battle with Alaska's "Big 3" Oil Companies*, by Kay Cashman and Kristen Nelson (Anchorage: PNA, 2008). It was compiled in a hurry after Palin was nominated for vice president, so it is a patchwork quilt of stories, rather than an integrated, comprehensive look at her work. It includes some helpful stories that may not appear in the archives of the *Anchorage Daily News* or the *Juneau Empire.*

Going Rogue (New York: HarperCollins, 2009) is Palin's own memoir, ghost-written with Lynn Vincent. It is a hodge-podge of autobiography and self-promotional material. It fails to deal in any comprehensive way with her record in Alaska, and of course, it offers no critical perspective on her performance.

Sarah from Alaska: The Sudden Rise and Brutal Education of a New Conservative Superstar by Shushannah Walshe and Scott Conroy (New York: Public Affairs, 2009) has some good perspective about Palin's time as governor, but the authors had no familiarity with her work as governor before she became a candidate for national office. They covered her run for vice president and focus on that phase of her career.

The Lies of Sarah Palin by Geoffrey Dunn (New York: St. Martin's, 2011) gives readers a she-could-do-no-right look at her career in politics and especially her personal life.

Trailblazer by Lorenzo Benet (New York: Simon and Schuster, 2009) is a brief biography by a reputable journalist. While he did manage to interview Palin for it, and does include some mildly critical perspective, he doesn't go into great detail about her time as governor.

Sarah: How a Hockey Mom Turned the Political Establishment Upside Down by Kaylene Johnson (Kenmore, WA: Epicenter Press, 2008) was published just before Palin burst onto the national scene in 2008. The brief volume has a useful summary of her rise to prominence in Alaska, including her run for governor, but is light on material about her time in office.

Index

About the Author

Matthew Zencey spent twenty-one years with the *Anchorage Daily News*, first as an editorial writer then as editorial page editor, and wrote frequently about Sarah Palin's performance as governor of Alaska. A five-time winner of the Best Editorial Writing award from the Alaska Press Club, Zencey edited and helped write a series of editorials about Palin's run for vice president, a project that was co-winner of the Alaska Press Club Prize for Public Service in 2009.

Zencey was a Nieman Fellow in Journalism at Harvard University, 1992–93. After relocating to Pennsylvania in 2010, he worked at the *Philadelphia Inquirer* as assistant editorial page editor and as an editor on the health and science desk. He now lives with his wife, Cindy, in West Chester, Pennsylvania, where he is thawing out from Alaska winters, getting up to speed on Pennsylvania affairs, and rooting for the Philadelphia Phillies to win another World Series.